Contents

PART 3 Beyond: Online TV and Web Drama

PART 4 Below: Worker- and User-Generated Content

EPHEMERAL MEDIA

Transitory Screen Culture from Television to YouTube

Edited by Paul Grainge

A BFI book published by Palgrave Macmillan

First published in 2011 by
PALGRAVE MACMILLAN

on behalf of the

BRITISH FILM INSTITUTE
21 Stephen Street, London W1T 1LN
www.bfi.org.uk

There's more to discover about film and television through the BFI.
Our world-renowned archive, cinemas, festivals, films, publications and learning
resources are here to inspire you.

Palgrave Macmillan in the UK is an imprint of Macmillan Publishers Limited,
registered in England, company number 785998, of Houndmills, Basingstoke,
Hampshire RG21 6XS. Palgrave Macmillan in the US is a division of St Martin's Press
LLC, 175 Fifth Avenue, New York, NY 10010. Palgrave Macmillan is the global
academic imprint of the above companies and has companies and representatives
throughout the world. Palgrave® and Macmillan® are registered trademarks in the
United States, the United Kingdom, Europe and other countries.

Cover design: Toby Cornish/Jutojo
Text design: couch

Images on pp. 77–81, 83 – © BBC; pp. 92, 95, 97 – courtesy of Red Bee Media; p. 92 –
courtesy of UKTV/Red Bee Media; pp. 163, 166 – © EQAL; p. 214 – © Rosamund Davies.

Set by Cambrian Typesetters, Camberley, Surrey
Printed in China

This book is printed on paper suitable for recycling and made from fully managed
and sustained forest sources. Logging, pulping and manufacturing processes are
expected to conform to the environmental regulations of the country of origin.

British Library Cataloguing-in-Publication Data
A catalogue record for this book is available from the British Library
A catalog record for this book is available from the Library of Congress
10 9 8 7 6 5 4 3 2 1
20 19 18 17 16 15 14 13 12 11

ISBN 978–1–84457–434–6 (pb)
ISBN 978–1–84457–435–3 (hb)

Acknowledgments

This book has grown out of two specially convened workshops on 'ephemeral media' held at the University of Nottingham in 2009, funded by the 'Beyond Text' programme of the Arts and Humanities Research Council (<http://www.beyondtext.ac.uk/>). I am especially grateful to the AHRC for their support and to Evelyn Welch and Ruth Hogarth for steering so energetically the wider Beyond Text community. The ephemeral media workshops brought together academics and media practitioners from a range of disciplines, and I would like to thank all the participants for making the events so enjoyable and rewarding, in particular the plenary speakers Barbara Klinger, Jon Dovey, Hugh Hancock, Rik Lander, William Uricchio, John Caldwell, Victoria Jaye and Charlie Mawer, who took part with terrific spirit. I could not have organised the ephemeral media workshops without the assistance of Helen Taylor, J. P. Kelly and Alessandro Catania. Their help was crucial at a number of key stages. Typically, colleagues within the Department of Culture, Film and Media at the University of Nottingham provided humour and support throughout, and I am especially grateful to Roberta Pearson, Liz Evans and Jake Smith for helping on the organising committee.

In bringing this book to fruition, I owe much to Rebecca Barden at the BFI whose professionalism and encouragement I deeply appreciate. As ever, I would like to thank David Grainge for his unfailing interest, enthusiasm and keen proofreading eye. Most importantly, I owe a great deal of thanks to my wife Claire, who, I am fairly sure, would be thrilled never to hear the word 'ephemeral' again. In the not so fleeting time of this project, she has put up with the most. For the fun they have brought 'between', 'beyond' and 'below' academic work, I wish to dedicate this book to my children, Daniel and Joseph, and to my nephews, Thomas, Adam and George.

Notes on Contributors

MARK BROWNRIGG was a Lecturer in the Department of Film, Media & Journalism at the University of Stirling, but sadly passed away during the preparation of this book. He published widely on the relationship between music and film and television, including articles on music in *Lord of the Rings*, in Luc Besson films and on the music director Muir Mathieson's contribution to British cinema in the 1930s and 1940s. His work on television idents appears in *Popular Music* and *Media Education Journal*.

JOHN THORNTON CALDWELL is Professor of Cinema and Media Studies in the Department of Film, Television and Digital Media at UCLA. His books include *Production Culture: Industrial Reflexivity and Critical Practice in Film and Television* (2008), *Televisuality: Style, Crisis, and Authority in American Television* (1995), *Electronic Media and Technoculture* (editor, 2000), *New Media* (co-edited with Anna Everett, 2003) and *Production Studies: Cultural Studies of Media Industries* (co-edited with Vicki Mayer and Miranda Banks, 2009). He has also published numerous articles and is the producer/director of the award-winning films *Rancho California (por favor)* (2002) and *Freak Street to Goa: Immigrants on the Rajpath* (1989).

ROSAMUND DAVIES has a background of professional practice in the film and television industries. As Script and Story Editor for Film London, she oversaw the development and production of over fifty short feature films. Her specialist area of practice is screen narrative and, as Senior Lecturer in Media Writing and Creative Industries, she lectures in screenwriting and visual narrative at the University of Greenwich. Her recent visual media work explores the intersection between narrative and archive as cultural forms.

MAX DAWSON is an Assistant Professor in Northwestern University's Department of Radio, Television and Film. His research examines television's fraught relationships with new media technologies, exploring the ways in which innovations ranging from the remote control to the mobile phone have unsettled long-standing notions of television's uses and cultural meanings. He has published articles in the journals *Technology and Culture*, *Convergence* and the *Journal of Popular Film and Television*, and has contributed chapters to the edited volumes *American Thought and Culture in the Twenty-First Century* (2008) and *Television as Digital Media* (2011).

JON DOVEY is Professor of Screen Media in the new Faculty of Creative Arts at the University of the West of England. He spent the first fifteen years of his working life in video production, progressing through the early years of Channel 4 as a researcher, editor and eventually as producer. He co-founded original scratch artists Gorilla Tapes in 1984, and his video projects have taken their place in the documented histories of UK Video Art. His authored and co-authored books include *Game Cultures* (2006), *New Media: A Critical Introduction* (2003), *Freakshows: First Person Media and Factual TV* (2000) and *Fractal Dreams, New Media in Social Context* (1996).

JOHN ELLIS is Professor of Media Arts at Royal Holloway University of London and Chair of the British Universities Film and Video Council. His books include *Documentary: Witness and Self-Revelation* (2011), *TV FAQ* (2007), *Seeing Things* (2000) and *Visible Fictions* (2000). Having been a TV documentary producer for nineteen years, he has written extensively about topics in the history of television.

ELIZABETH EVANS is a Lecturer in Film and Television Studies at the University of Nottingham. Her research interests include television audiences, transmedia storytelling and the impact of emergent media technologies on traditional forms of media engagement. Her research has been published in *Media, Culture & Society* and *Participations*. She is the author of *Transmedia Television: Audiences, New Media and Daily Life* (2011).

PAUL GRAINGE is Associate Professor of Film and Television Studies at the University of Nottingham. His books include *Brand Hollywood: Selling Entertainment in a Global Media Age* (2008), *Monochrome Memories: Nostalgia and Style in Retro America* (2002), *Film Histories: An Introduction and Reader* (co-author, 2007) and *Memory and Popular Film* (editor, 2003). He has published articles in journals including *Screen*, *Cultural Studies*, *Media, Culture & Society*, *The Journal of American Studies* and *The International Journal of Cultural Studies*.

VICTORIA JAYE is Head of Multiplatform Commissioning, Fiction and Entertainment at BBC Vision. She is responsible for overseeing the commissioning of comedy, drama and entertainment content and products across interactive and on-demand TV, the web and mobile media. Previously, she was multiplatform channel editor for BBC One and BBC Three responsible for driving both channels' multiplatform brand and content development.

J. P. KELLY is a doctoral student in the Department of Culture, Film and Media at the University of Nottingham. His thesis, 'Prime Times: Technology, Temporality and Narrative Form in Contemporary US Drama', examines the relationship between industry, technology and time in series such as *24* and *Lost*.

BARBARA KLINGER is Professor of Film and Media Studies in the Department of Communication and Culture at Indiana University in Bloomington, Indiana. Her research focuses on reception studies, fan studies, and cinema's historical and contemporary relationship to new media. She is author of *Melodrama and Meaning: History, Culture, and the Films of Douglas Sirk* (1994) and *Beyond the Multiplex: Cinema, New Technologies, and the Home* (2006). She has published articles in such journals as *Screen*, *Cinema Journal* and *Participations* and is currently working on a book, *Son of Casablanca: Classic Hollywood Cinema, the Aftermarket, and Immortality*.

CHARLIE MAWER is Executive Creative Director of Red Bee Media, a leading digital media company specialising in branding and broadcast design. He has led numerous branding projects for Red Bee, including the channel branding of BBC One, BBC Three, Discovery International, Orange IPTV, Bibigon and Star News India, and the complete network rebranding of UKTV, including the IPA gold-winning creation of Dave. He has won countless creative awards including over thirty Promax BDA, Creative Circle, Sharks and a Bafta nomination. In 2006, he chaired Promax UK's conference and awards, and has spoken at conferences across the globe about the creation of media brands.

PETER MEECH was a Senior Lecturer (now retired) in the Department of Film, Media & Journalism at the University of Stirling, and a member of the Stirling Media Research Institute. Since the mid-1990s, he has published articles on TV idents, promos and corporate visual identity in journals including *Screen*, *Popular Music*, *International Journal of Advertising* and *Media Education Journal*.

WILLIAM URICCHIO is Professor and Director of the MIT Comparative Media Studies Program and Professor of Comparative Media History at Utrecht University in the Netherlands. He has held visiting professorships at Stockholm University, the Freie Universität Berlin, the University of Science and Technology of China, and Philips Universität Marburg. His most recent books include *Media Cultures* (2006), on responses to media in post 9/11 Germany and the US, and *We Europeans? Media, Representations, Identity* (2009). He is currently completing a manuscript on the concept of the televisual from the seventeenth century to the present.

Introduction: Ephemeral Media

Paul Grainge

In 2009, Thinkbox, the marketing body for commercial television broadcasters in the UK, produced a commercial in response to growing ambivalence in the marketing industry about the effectiveness of the three-minute ad break. The commercial was staged, appropriately enough, as a therapy session. A bearded thirty-something man hypnotised in a chair is gently urged by a therapist to use 'your powerful subconscious mind and imagine that you are in a very happy place'. Asked what he can see, the man channels a series of quotes and jingles from memorable ads of the past three decades, performing them emphatically while reclined in his chair. The regression takes him to such a happy place that the therapist cannot bring him round. The ad ends with two straplines: 'Funny how thirty seconds can last a lifetime' and 'Television: where brands get their breaks'.

This commercial has much to say about marketing industry concerns about the viability of television advertising in the late 2000s. However, it also provides a starting point for thinking about the presence of transitory screen forms within audiovisual culture. In its therapeutic and nostalgic form of address, the ad makes a deliberate point of the short or otherwise fleeting texts which exist in the space around primary media and entertainment content. According to Thinkbox, happiness is the place in between television programmes. With an obvious trade agenda, its commercial tapped broadcast nostalgia for the promotional screen content that occupies the breaks and junctions of the television schedule. Quickly assuming a viral life, the Thinkbox commercial became a catalyst on YouTube for the circulation of clips from television's interstitial past, complementing amateur web archives such as TV Ark in its dedication to 'idents, programme promotions, opening title sequences, public information films, commercials, daily start-ups and closedowns, break bumpers and station clocks' (TV Ark, 2010). The Thinkbox commercial reaffirmed the value of the thirty-second spot against claims of its imminent demise. However, it also served to reflect more widely on *the ephemeral* in media life.

As a concept, the ephemeral connotes the evanescent, transient and brief; in definitional terms, it describes anything short-lived. While renowned collectors of printed ephemera such as John Johnson used the term in the 1940s to describe 'everything which would ordinarily go into the waste paper basket after use' ('Eavesdropping on the Past', 2010), its application to the study of screen media has been similarly concerned with the peripheral and throwaway, and to questions of cultural value. Within media criticism, the ephemeral is often used to describe screen forms and physical artifacts that are in some way remnants. For moving image historians, and within major screen collections such as the Prelinger archive, the term is most frequently associated with 'orphan' works no longer protected by copyright, or with non-theatrical genres such as ads, industrial films, training videos, home movies, educational pictures, religious shorts and medical hygiene films that have become critically marginalised despite their often significant relation to histories of the ordinary and the everyday (see Frick, 2008; Wilson, 2009). More broadly, the ephemeral has been used to signify moving image detritus. As Amelie Hastie suggests, this can be reflected in various textual and sensorial forms:

> Detritus can be seen and held in the souvenirs we have of viewing: ticket stubs, out-dated television sets and computers, even memories we trace through a sense of place, smell, image; it can be embodied in discarded or temporary forms and sites such as screen tests and out-takes, television ads, and installation spaces; and it can be recognized in the trash around the movie theater, television set, and archival spaces: popcorn and candy boxes, outmoded television schedules, decayed videos, and decomposed film stock. (Hastie, 2007, p. 172)

In grappling with the 'ephemeral nature of visual media experience, as well as the ephemeral experience of moving-image culture', Hastie is one of a number of critics to highlight the importance of maintaining or restoring 'a sense of materiality' in relation to screen culture. This brings into focus a diversity of media objects and practices, from fan collecting to matters of waste. Responding to media impermanence of varying kinds, interest in the ephemeral can be seen to extend from the video trading that takes place between TV collectors who record and exchange fleeting broadcast moments, to the buying and selling of film and television artifacts on eBay, to the electronic salvaging of old hardware in the 'contemporary junkyards, thrift shops and garages [that] have become shrines to structured obsolescence' (see, respectively, Bjarkman, 2004; Desjardins, 2006; Parks, 2007, p. 35). If, as Hastie suggests, examining the overlooked and thrown-away presents media studies 'with new objects to consider and the opportunity to expand what "counts" in media culture and in the very discipline of our study' (Hastie, 2007, p. 171), the ephemeral has become a site for examining the cultural life of media artifacts as they operate within cycles of time and circuits of value.

Whether television texts, traces of Hollywood's past or defunct technologies, the ephemeral has an important material and 'residual' dimension (Acland, 2007). However, the significance of the term cannot be contained within definitions of detritus or discussions of lost or leftover media. In a period where electronic communication has vastly increased the rate and delivery of mediated experience, the concept of the ephemeral, with its connotations of brevity and evanescence, can also provide a different way of expanding what counts in media culture, and of exploring contemporary media specificities. Put simply, it points to the burgeoning number of short-form texts that populate the audiovisual terrain, and throws into relief the durational and circulatory temporalities of media within the digital environment. For social theorists such as John Tomlinson, we live in a communicational culture of 'rapid delivery' and 'ubiquitous availability' where media is defined through, and in relation to, the instant speed and storage capacities of electronic technology (Tomlinson, 2007, p. 74). On the one hand, with the exponential growth of digital channels and platforms, contemporary audiovisual culture has seen a proliferation of short-form media geared towards mobile audiences whose attentions are more fleeting and dispersed. On the other hand, with the rise of media archives like YouTube and Google, images can live on and be shared indefinitely by viewing communities. In this dual movement towards speed and storage, immediacy and archiving, the ephemeral has assumed a particular cultural and textual significance. The Thinkbox ad was a product of its time in these two respects. As an instance of trade theorising, a figurative 'deep text' to use John Caldwell's term (2008), the commercial dramatised the pleasures of the ephemeral on behalf of TV advertising, re-enacting the transitory but retrievable content stored within media memory.

Within the terms of this book, 'ephemeral media' invokes screen forms defined by their briefness; it describes a range of temporally compressed media that can be viewed or consumed in seconds or minutes, from the promotional texts that function in television's interstitial space to the explosion of online short-forms enabled by web platforms such as YouTube. Equally, however, the term points to the circulation of media. Not only has contemporary screen culture become more ephemeral in the durative shortness of many of its key audiovisual forms (idents, promos, abridgements, mobisodes, web dramas, user-generated content), it has become so in the voluminous plurality of clips and snippets that abound within moving image culture: the internet provides a platform where texts that might previously have been considered fleeting become more permanent and accessible by vastly increasing the opportunities for their distribution and remediation. By examining ephemeral texts and relations as connected to case-specific developments in television and web entertainment, this book provides groundwork for analysing the transitory, and transitional, nature of screen culture in the early twenty-first century.

The ephemeral in media criticism: film, television, web

Before mapping these concerns further, it is worth situating how the idea of the ephemeral underlies critical understandings of particular media technologies and practices. The relationship between the ephemeral and audiovisual culture has been conceived in different ways around different mediums, often as a means of discussing media ontologies and epistemologies within specific historical eras. This finds early expression in connections made between the ephemeral, media technology and the history of modernity. According to Mary Ann Doane, developing observations made famous by Charles Baudelaire, the late nineteenth and early twentieth century was 'strongly associated with epistemologies that valorize the contingent, the ephemeral, chance' (Doane, 2002, p. 10). These epistemologies were clarified in relation to emergent technologies of representation, notably photography and cinema. As various critics have shown, these helped facilitate a new perception of time. While photography was 'consistently allied with contingency and the ability to seize the ephemeral', manifest in its indexical representation of things and moments, the *actualités* of early cinema 'produced continual evidence of the drive to fix and make repeatable the ephemeral' (Doane, 2002, p. 22). If photography's promise was the isolation and restoration of moments in time, film offered powerful ways to behold duration and movement. Ranging from slow-motion techniques applied to natural occurrences, such as the blossoming of flowers, to brief spectacles where everyday scenes and current events were made thrilling by their momentary capture and viewing, *actualités* delivered 'the cinematic smack of the instant' (Gunning, 2004, p. 49). Doane argues that photographic media, but especially cinema, 'directly confronts the problematic question of the *representability* of the ephemeral, of the archivability of presence' (Doane, 2002, p. 25; author's italics).

This presents a series of issues about the ability of media within capitalist modernity to capture and structure time. For Doane, modernity posed, and continues to pose, a number of representational and epistemic questions about temporality and 'the structuring of contingency'. Developing a strand of analysis that relates aesthetic and narrative expressivities to historical constructions of time and space, she suggests that technologies of representation like photography and cinema embodied 'a tension between a desire for instantaneity and an archival aspiration' (Doane, 2002, p. 29). In a different historical juncture, a similar tension may be observed within YouTube's dual function as video streaming platform and archival interface. In representational terms, it is perhaps no surprise that the spectacle of online video has drawn frequent comparison with film *actualités* (Broeren, 2009). Turning everyday scenes into short-form 'attractions', early cinema and online video are both characterised by an 'attractional' mode of display marked in different eras by their relation to emergent visual and temporal regimes. Whether growing from the shock of machine speed at the beginning of the twentieth century or the immediacy of information technology at the beginning of the twenty-first, the ephemeral has been associated in transitional periods of media development with particular textual forms such as early cinema and online video which, in their temporal immediacy and quotidian spectacle, have come to embody changes in the social and technological bases of modern cultural life.

Early cinema has been discussed in terms of the representation of the ephemeral, but conditions of film exhibition and reception draw attention equally to the ephemeral nature of screen performance. During the early cinema and nickel period, the length of cinema reels meant that films were brief, produced for quick consumption, and would often be exhibited for less than a week before being exchanged. Most urban storefront theatres in the US in the nickel era changed their programmes on a daily rather than a weekly basis, and did not advertise individual films, because they were not exhibited for long enough to make this worthwhile. The material fragility and low cultural status of film also meant that moving pictures were only sporadically preserved in the first decades of the twentieth century, accentuating their ephemeral life as screen artifacts. While the development of the Hollywood studio system would see motion pictures achieve greater solidity in their length, circulation and status as material property, film remained a time-specific and place-bound encounter, subject to contingencies of programming and local performance. The typical classical Hollywood movie, for example, played in second-run movie theatres on a double bill for three or four days and never returned. In these ways, film can be seen as a highly transient medium. In the postwar period, Hollywood movies would increasingly appear on network television and would surface as remastered works and in other kinds of specialist screening. However, before the domestication of video and DVD, both of which realised the value of archival film assets and greatly increased the availability of motion pictures for general audiences, the experience of film was largely based on occasional cinematic and broadcast screenings rather than, as now, via the precise time-shifting enabled by home viewing technologies.

Within film studies, the ephemeral has come to the fore in discussion of cinema's relationship with epistemologies of time, as it relates to the presentation and cultural status of film (in particular, the relegated categories of non-theatrical and orphaned film), and as it denotes objects and epiphenomena of moviegoing such as posters, pressbooks, lobby placards and photo cards. In critical terms, the ephemeral has been used as a heuristic device to think about particular questions of cinematic representation, film circulation, and the stuff of movie consumption and fan collecting.

The ephemeral has not generally been understood as a quality specific to the medium itself, however. This distinguishes it from television and the web, both of which have been conceptually defined *in terms* of their ephemeral properties.

That broadcast television is a fleeting and ethereal medium has become something of a critical truism. Writing in 1969, the British television critic T. C. Worsley published a collection of TV reviews called *The Ephemeral Art*. He ruminated: 'except for the occasional repeats, a television programme, however brilliant, disappears the moment it is finished, and almost before one has taken it in, something else has taken its place' (Worsley, 1970, p. 11). For Worsley, the 'ephemeral art' was a moniker that captured television's ebb and flow, and the challenge this posed to critical appreciations of the medium. The concept of flow would of course be theorised several years later by Raymond Williams (1974), providing one of the foundational metaphors for the emerging discipline of television studies. It is not my intention to rehearse the theoretical legacies of this concept. Suffice it to say, it is generally understood that network-era television is defined by the continuous flow of programmes and segments and by norms of synchronous linear viewing. The ephemeral nature of broadcast television stems from these medium-specific traits; it is the result of television's ontology of liveness and what Amanda Lotz, citing the industrial writings of Bernard Miége, calls 'the instant obsolescence of content' distinguishing broadcast television as a 'flow industry' (Lotz, 2007, p. 34).

The fleetingness of the broadcast moment is a cornerstone of critical understandings of network television. Urging audiences to 'stay tuned' for as long as possible, a sense of the ephemeral is built into television's structures of scheduling, forms of address and attempt never to be the same twice. While Derek Kompare (2005) usefully demonstrates the importance of repetition and reruns in the TV industry, television is nevertheless ephemeral in its moment of broadcast transmission. Kim Bjarkman reflects on the paradox of television as a 'medium that is at once pervasive and scarce' (Bjarkman, 2004, p. 230). For audiences, losing the broadcast moment has been, and in some sense remains, an endemic form of television scarcity. At the same time, television's impermanence has been qualified. While the development of VCR technologies in the 1980s enabled audiences to record, replay and possess TV broadcasts, the diffusion of DVR, DVD, video-on-demand and interactive downloading devices in the 2000s increased the ease and convenience of this storage process. Such developments have led TV scholars to discuss the impact of digital technologies on television's current ontology and business model (see Kompare, 2006; Lotz, 2007; Bennett, 2008; Gripsrud, 2010). By turning programmes into files (accessed via the internet) and physical commodities (such as DVD box sets), the post-network era has provided an expanded range of opportunities for audiences to control and capture television beyond the ephemeral broadcast moment.

According to James Bennett (2008), the ontology of television is in the process of being remediated from linear broadcasting flow to that of navigational database. As online television services and digital platforms increasingly dis-embed television content from the logic of the broadcast schedule, TV content has become more ubiquitous and available. This does not mean to say that television has ceased to be an ephemeral medium. Both J. P. Kelly and Elizabeth Evans observe in this volume that online content aggregators such as Hulu and proprietary catch-up services such as the BBC iPlayer offer programmes for a limited window of time before they disappear from view. The industry rhetoric of television's permanent availability – of TV 'whenever, wherever you want' – is qualified by the lingering suspicion of losing control of content property, and giving away things for free. Nevertheless, the basis of television ephemerality has changed in the post-network era. As broadcast transmissions have become subject to replay and remediation through a range of digital media platforms, television content has become more textually dispersed. Within the era of convergence television, programmes can be 'bundled' across multiplatform channels, but also simultaneously 'unbundled' into itemised episodes, scenes, snippets and segments (Dawson, 2007). In a burgeoning 'clip culture' where moving images are consumed swiftly and on the move, television has been adapted and abridged to fit the temporal and aesthetic specificities of mobile and internet-based platforms. This is witnessed in the production of mobisodes and webisodes as well as in the posting of short TV clips, trailers and ancillary materials onto video sharing sites and online portals. In accounting for the digital turn, one might say that television is now less ephemeral in the *evanescence* of programme content but much more ephemeral in the *brevity* of the promotional and paratextual forms that surround, mobilise and give meaning to that content.

If any platform captures the growing significance of short-form content in the last decade it is YouTube. The site has become, in the words of Pelle Snickars and Patrick Vonderau, 'the very epitome of digital culture not only by promising endless opportunities for viral marketing or format development but also by allowing "you" to post a video which might incidentally change the course of history (Snickars and Vonderau, 2009, p. 11). As Snickars goes on to say, since its launch in 2005, 'YouTube has been and remains the default website for a clip culture that is increasingly defining both web entertainment and online information' (Snickars, 2009, p. 293). Whether one understands YouTube as an archive or a medium in its own right, video length has become a key characteristic of the site, a high proportion of videos currently lasting between one and three minutes. Increasingly used as a vehicle for marketing entertainment culture, YouTube has become the platform *du jour* for what *Wired* labelled in 2007 'entertainment snacking'. Offering a 'Minifesto for a New Age', Nancy Miller wrote approvingly of the tasty 'morsels that fill those whenever minutes … a 30-second game on your Nintendo DS, a 60-second webisode on your cell, a three-minute podcast on your MP3 player' (Miller, 2007, p. 17). Rather than associate contemporary culture with deficits of attention and concentration – a lament ranging from Michael Ignatieff's (1989) postulations about 'three-minute culture' to Nicholas Carr's (2010) diagnosis of the digital 'shallows' – Miller framed the transient and brief as a component of new media life. Although *Wired*'s techno-populist embrace of the fleeting and fast would view snack culture as a satisfying but largely passive distraction rather than as a potential site of user engagement, its 'minifesto' highlighted the growing importance of short-form content within contemporary audiovisual culture. Platforms such as YouTube are indicative of this and bring into focus the ephemeral dimensions of the web.

In one sense, the web is ephemeral in its sheer abundance of content and communication; it has become a vast accumulator of data-stored texts, sounds and images. From the unceasing legion of emails, blogs, tweets and SMS messages to the many thousands of web videos posted every day, the web is defined by its array of 'small pieces, loosely joined' (Naughton, 2010, p. 11). Any cursory glance of YouTube, Google, Blogger, Flickr, Twitter, Amazon, eBay or one's own inbox would be enough to experience the web's incredible traffic of ephemeral media, a torrent of textual fragments, commodities and relations of exchange that can, at any time, be consumed, clicked through or deleted. In terms of the moving image, the web has become a boundless repository and auction house of ephemeral media history. On YouTube, the durative shortness of video clips has become part of the site's dynamic architecture. YouTube is ephemeral in the brevity of its clips but also in the way it can seemingly provide 'longitudinal slices of every kind of moving image material ever produced' (Prelinger, 2007, p. 116). Jean Burgess and Joshua Green suggest that the value of 'accidental archives' like YouTube is 'a direct result of its unfiltered, disordered, vernacular and extremely heterogeneous characteristics' (Burgess and Green, 2009, p. 89). Here, the concept of the ephemeral underlies the incredible profusion of media images made available by the internet as a high-capacity storage mechanism. An indicative Web 2.0 site, YouTube has become a hugely successful aggregator of ephemeral media; it is a platform for retrieving, remediating and ultimately sharing fleeting media images drawn kaleidoscopically from the audiovisual present and past.

YouTube is fundamentally a database. In this capacity, it demonstrates the potential of the web to offer a permanent archive of digital material. However, in terms of viewer and user experience, YouTube, like the web more generally, is defined by the constant threat of materials disappearing as specific links 'rot' and pages are taken down. It is in these terms that Steven Schneider and Kirsten Foot call the web 'a unique mixture of the ephemeral and permanent' (Schneider and Foot, 2004, p. 115). Here, the ephemeral refers to the transient construction of web content rather than to any particular web genre, subject, representation or performance. They suggest:

> Unlike theater, or live television or radio, web content must exist in a permanent form in order to be transmitted. The web shares this characteristic with other forms of media such as film, print, and sound recordings. However, the permanence of the web is somewhat fleeting. Unlike any other permanent media, a website may destroy its predecessor regularly and procedurally each time it is updated by its producer; that is, absent specific arrangements to the contrary, each previous edition of a website may be erased as a new version is produced. (Schneider and Foot, 2004, p. 115)

The ephemerality of web content presents challenges for those wishing to study or archive online material. For the individual, it can lead to the feverish hoarding of clips and information lest a website suddenly vanish. From a curatorial perspective, the practical difficulties of reconstructing websites in the form in which they are presented has become a pressing issue of digital policy and archival practice. In 2009, the chief executive of the British Library, Lynn Brindley, expressed her concern that despite the stockpiling of material on hard drives, the scale and unpredictability of websites and electronic files put at risk the ability to store an electronic legacy that could serve the national memory (Brindley, 2009, p. 31). Although the internet is able to construct vast archives, a number of techno-cultural instabilities in the electronic era create conditions for losing material. This ranges from the deterioration of technological hardware that enables downgraded formats to be played (old tapes, videos, laserdiscs, floppies) to the wilful discarding of content by website controllers. Within digital culture, ephemeral texts and images are constantly being captured, stored, retrieved and ordered on a range of electronic devices, from computers to cellular phones. However, because of the degradation of signals and obsolescence of formats, digital machines can also have a short and transitory shelf-life. These issues have generated discussion about how to 'future-proof' digital content such as websites, emails, blogs, and also how to make personal and institutional choices about *what* to save. While it remains the case that all digital inscriptions leave a nanotechnological trace and can therefore never be lost entirely, the web is distinguished by its fast, fleeting and upgradable nature. As a media environment, the web is ephemeral in its volume and variety of content, but also in its temporal structures of viewing and interaction.

Time and attention: the ephemeral in contemporary media culture

As a category of media analysis, the ephemeral has different conceptual registers; it signifies the relation of media forms to *regimes of time* (duration, shortness, speed) and *regimes of transmission* (circulation, storage, value). The 'ephemeral nature of visual media experience [and] the ephemeral experience of moving-image culture'

(Hastie, 2007, p. 172) can be figured around these two axes. Whether signifying the short-form, the short-lived, or both, the ephemeral has been used to consider and theorise particular media histories, ontologies and forms of screen encounter.

The ephemeral is, of course, a relative concept and can be applied to a variety of media artifacts and textual relationships. This book does not seek to provide an exhaustive account of the potential applications of the term 'ephemeral media'. It is possible to imagine entirely different anthologies that deal exclusively with the ephemerality (and material ephemera) of cinema or radio as historically constituted forms, or that explore instead the informal fragments, texts and utterances stemming from digital technologies such as personal computers, cellular phones, camcorders, email, websites, search engines, MP3 players and social networking sites. In a different vein, the term can be used to think about the cultural status and visibility of media texts, including those rendered unintentionally ephemeral because of their historical/ archival marginalisation or because they happened to be produced or consumed by groups with little social power. The concept of the ephemeral can be drawn in different directions. In this collection, it is used to examine the production of media which surround the output of networks and studios. The term is used to examine screen forms and relations that exist *between*, *beyond* and *below* the primary texts of contemporary entertainment culture. 'Ephemeral media' is deployed in this way as a critical rubric to explore, and claim as significant, moving image forms which exist in relation to the more solid and substantial film and television content traditionally privileged within screen studies.

Foregrounding screen texts that are short in length, fleeting in the way they circulate or that tend to be overlooked in academic study, the chapters in this book use the ephemeral as a platform to explore media at the edges, within the junctions, or that sit askance to longer, bulkier entertainment content. As an approach, this has affinities with what Jonathan Gray has called 'off-screen studies'. Examining the variety of paratextual materials that surround contemporary film and television shows, including trailers, intros, spoilers, mash-ups, promos, podcasts, bonus material and merchandising, Gray suggests that 'we need an "off-screen studies" to make sense of the wealth of other entities that saturate the media, and that construct film and television' (Gray, 2010, p. 4). Calling for the study of 'invisible', 'peripheral' and 'ancillary' screen forms, Gray is concerned with the meaning-making function of paratexts, and the way these constitute specific film and television texts. This contributes to a growing body of work considering how promotional and user-generated content circulate, in prolific yet disposable ways, within the contemporary audiovisual field. While John Caldwell (2008) suggests the value of analysing industry screen texts such as electronic press kits, studio previews, broadcast interstitials, 'making-ofs' and branding tapes, especially for what they reveal of the film and television industry's own theorising practices, Barbara

Klinger and Chuck Tryon both consider the remixing of Hollywood film and television in web parodies, mash-ups, fake trailers and online video shorts made and viewed in the home (Klinger, 2006, pp. 191–238; Tryon, 2010). Although different in focus, these approaches are joined by their concern with secondary screen artifacts that churn around and exist in conversation with studio and network content.

Several essays in this volume develop explicit forms of paratextual analysis, from Max Dawson's examination of television abridgements to John Caldwell's consideration of 'worker blowback'. However, the essays in this book are not principally driven by the exploration of the 'DNA' of discrete film and television shows, as in Gray's account. Rather, they are joined by a concern with the durational and circulatory temporalities of media that shape, structure and express something of our mobile and increasingly fractionalised encounter with screen entertainment. In a period where a minute-long performance on YouTube can outstrip the viewing figures of the biggest studio and network hit, the web in particular has served to reshape expectations about the mobility of textual forms, as well as the possibilities of media production, participation and use. This was aptly demonstrated in 2008 when a grainy amateur performance of the history of popular dance styles (Judson Laipply's 'The Evolution of Dance') jockeyed on YouTube with a glossy corporate music video (Avril Lavigne's 'Girlfriend') to become the first online video to be watched 100 million times. As with subsequent YouTube phenomena with massive hit rates, the fugitive nature of media viewing has given new visibility and impetus to short-form content, whether linked to the genetics of film and television shows or existing quite apart.

Teasing out the social context of short-form media, Barbara Klinger suggests that miniaturised entertainment is ideally suited to the rhythms of contemporary work, media and information cultures, 'fitting seamlessly into both the surfing mentality that defines media experience and the multitasking sensibility that pervades computer culture' (Klinger, 2006, p. 200). The proliferation of ephemeral texts can be seen, in this way, as a response to changes in the 'economics of attention' driven by new media technologies. In a digital media environment awash with information and content choice, attention has become, to use economic parlance, a scarce resource. This has produced a number of business and cultural theories about the importance of 'managing attention' in a world of information glut – of devising corporate, promotional and design strategies to overcome the limits of attention in an information-rich but time-compressed world (see Goldhaber, 1997; Davenport and Beck, 2001; Lanham, 2006). While capturing and counting 'eyeballs' has become the coin of the web, the challenge of getting attention has intensified within traditional media industries. Whether or not attention spans have become shorter in recent decades, there is a sense that media life has become more accelerated, driven by what John Tomlinson calls 'a world of increasing technology-driven velocity' (Tomlinson, 2007, p. 72). In a period in which digital channels and platforms continue to proliferate, and where media viewing has become decidedly mobile, attention itself has arguably become more ephemeral. This supposition is expressed in a repertoire of colourful industry terms for texts and techniques designed to arrest the wandering attention of consumers. While the multichannel environment has witnessed the growth of promotional 'stings' and 'teasers' in television's interstitial space, websites were in their early years measured by 'stickiness'. This described the ability to hold consumers to one site, and was a prevalent metaphor until platforms such as YouTube showed the value of spreading and embedding content across multiple sites. Whatever the overtones of consumers being stung and stuck, such terms suggest an anxiety about audience impermanence. In a digital media environment characterised by mobilities, compressions and fluidities in the circulation of moving image content, the ephemeral implies a relation *to* screen images as much as it describes any particular form *of* screen image.

In critical terms, *Ephemeral Media* has two objectives. Broadly, it seeks to illuminate particular media phenomena that are simultaneously fleeting and increasingly ubiquitous in contemporary screen life; it considers ephemeral forms ranging from TV idents, video abridgements, hypercast advertising and unbundled network content, to emergent forms of web drama, online fan re-enactment and user-generated video. By reflecting on the functions of such media and the economic and technological environments in which they exist, the ensuing essays consider how media producers have sought to capture and manage viewing attention in the between, beyond and below space of traditional media entertainment. More specifically, the book is concerned with transformations being wrought in relation to television as one aspect of a far bigger and broader set of developments within media. The early twenty-first century was a period in which television found itself struggling, in the words of William Uricchio in this book, 'to redefine itself and its relationship to the people once called its audience'. As has been widely theorised, the digital media environment recast the ephemerality of broadcast television in the 2000s, heralding a post-network era distinguished by non-linear, multiplatform logics (Lotz, 2007). *Ephemeral Media* is especially concerned with this period of transition within the television industry. The book analyses the opportunities and challenges faced by the TV industry in its attempt to structure viewers' mobile and often brief engagement with network schedules and TV shows. However, it also, necessarily, places these developments in relation to wider tendencies in the media sphere, examining the proliferation and circulation of ephemeral texts that, in different contexts and with different registers, have sought to address and engage contemporary viewing communities.

In his essay on the 'circulatory turn' within cultural studies and media theory, Will Straw suggests that while we must not presume that life is more mobile, fleeting or fragile in the world of new media technologies, we should be attentive to the 'ways in which media forms work to produce particular tensions between stasis or mobility' (Straw, 2010, p. 28). These tensions, in many ways, underlie the study of ephemeral media. The relation between stability and impermanence, the substantial and the evanescent, the monumental and the momentary, connects in different ways this book's critical concern with the short and fleeting texts that function within visual digital culture and that participate in a competitive 'attention economy'.

Ephemeral Media is organised in four parts and includes essays by renowned and emerging figures in television and new media studies, as well as interviews with key industry practitioners. Part 1 explores the ephemeral in relation to transitions within media history and practice. Specifically, it establishes vantage points on television's strategic and inadvertent deployment of ephemeral texts, as historical forms, as responses to television's changing status, and as signs of things to come. William Uricchio's essay directly addresses the meaning of the term 'ephemeral' and considers the various ways in which it can be seen as endemic to media. These definitional reflections provide a context for teasing out the distinctive role of ephemeral texts in existing commercial television regimes, and within new participatory television forms like YouTube. Foregrounding the critical significance of the fleeting and repeated texts that have long been central to television's programming flow, Uricchio goes on to consider the new centrality of 'short-form time-based media' in a moment where television, and ideas of flow, enter 'a phase of displacement and disaggregation'. This phase provides the main context for Max Dawson's essay. Extending perspectives on the transitions mapped by Uricchio, notably television's engagement with digital media platforms, Dawson explores the proliferation of abridged versions of TV shows that in the 1990s and 2000s became mainstays of commercial internet video sites and mobile media services. Considering the paratextual significance of video abridgements, Dawson's chapter underscores the importance of short-form content within the political and cultural economies of the convergence media environment. Precisely, he considers the industrial and textual utility of video abridgements and the relation these supremely ephemeral texts have to 'monumental' television serials such as *The Sopranos* (1999–2007), *Lost* (2004–10) and *Mad Men* (2007–present). The essays in Part 1 are paired to locate and exemplify the book's critical exploration of the circulatory and durational temporalities of screen culture. Addressing dimensions of change in the contemporary mediaspace, they provide perspectives on television time and scale, textual systems and short-form output.

The remaining parts of the book explore different forms of ephemeral media in case studies which move from broadcast and online television to web drama and worker- and user-generated content. Part 2 concentrates specifically on television interstitials and idents; it analyses the attempt by broadcasters to capture attention in the *between* space of television. While the digital environment enables viewers to download individual programmes and circumvent scheduling constraints through DVRs, broadcast television remains the principal experience of watching television for many. In the context of daily viewing and live television, the broadcast junction remains central; it is a strategic threshold used to brand networks, advertise programmes and transition audiences from one kind of content to another. Within this space, interstitials and idents present themselves as indicative ephemeral texts, fleeting and repeated, ubiquitous yet critically overlooked.

John Ellis begins Part 2 by considering the function of interstitials as 'a class of television output'. Making a case for the aesthetic and archival importance of interstitials, Ellis suggests that broadcast television's repeated idents, links, promos and commercials distil programmes and viewing habits; he argues that interstitials provide 'instruction manuals' on how to view and understand TV. Citing their allusive and synoptic beauty, Ellis proposes that interstitials are shaped by certain aesthetic criteria, production values and patterns of repetition, and that, as a result, they have the potential to define periods of broadcasting more clearly than programming itself. The opening chapter of Part 2 provides a framing argument for the cultural function and critical value of broadcast ephemera. The next two chapters explore specific examples of contemporary interstitial media, using idents and promos made for the BBC to draw out the audiovisual and brand strategies used to capture attention in a competitive broadcast environment. Mark Brownrigg and Peter Meech consider the aesthetics of channel idents with a detailed textual analysis of a sequence of idents made for BBC Two in the late 2000s. Their chapter explores the richness and diversity of channel idents as audiovisual forms, using music and sound to highlight the textual and sensory moods and pleasures they afford. My own interview with Charlie Mawer, who has overseen some of the most recognisable channel idents on British screens in the last fifteen years (including those of BBC One, BBC Three and Dave), provides a vantage on the creative work involved in short-form broadcast design. As Executive Creative Director of Red Bee Media, Mawer reflects on a media world where TV promotion had become subject in the 2000s to what he calls the law of the 'quick and the dead'. Focusing on the transient items that appear briefly but routinely between television programmes, Part 2 considers the textual significance and industrial function of the most ephemeral materials of broadcast content.

Part 3 provides a different perspective on the ephemeral within and beyond the TV industry. Connecting issues of duration to those of circulation, it examines how the digital media 'ecosystem' at the turn of the twenty-first century offered new opportunities and challenges for producers of television and web entertainment. In significant ways, the internet has made the ephemeral more *and* less important; the web provides transitory 'in the moment' engagement with media content while purporting to offer 'anytime, anywhere' access to that content. The essays in Part 3 examine some of the choices made by professional media producers around this balance, from the multiplatform initiatives of public service broadcasters (the BBC) and content aggregators (Hulu) to the creation of emergent forms of web drama. Considering what Jon Dovey calls the 'new rhythms of online attention flow' that were impacting the design and distribution of television in the 2000s – an especially pregnant period in which institutional practices and narrative conventions surrounding online TV and 'web native' media had not fully crystallised – the chapters reflect on attempts to manage and monetise attention *beyond* traditional broadcasting regimes (Meikle and Young, 2008).

Elizabeth Evans' interview with Victoria Jaye, Head of Multiplatform Commissions, Drama, Comedy and Entertainment at the BBC, provides a bridge from Part 2; the interviews with Mawer and Jaye illustrate the way that leading industry practitioners were navigating (and reflecting upon) changes in the broadcast and digital media environment in the 2000s. Specifically, Jaye helps capture a moment of transition in the way that the television industry, specifically here public service broadcasting, sought to adapt to a multiplatform environment in its emergent phase. Providing an illuminating account of how the rise of multiple, 24/7 platforms has enabled the once passing screen moment to live on and be shared indefinitely by audiences, Jaye reflects on how the development of an 'open, permanent architecture' for BBC content has allowed the Corporation to stretch the form of its programmes and to connect audiences with ephemeral materials drawn from its archive. J. P. Kelly is also concerned with the nascent world of online television. In this case, however, he uses Hulu, the major commercial aggregator of US film and TV content, to consider the economic strategies and distributional logics of the online environment. Developing distinctions made between television as 'flow' and 'file', Kelly uses Hulu to explore the flexible temporalities of online media and the various tensions between permanence and transience, contraction and extension, inherent within digital distribution.

The two chapters following Kelly's move the discussion of the digital media ecology on to emergent forms of web drama, exemplified by popular narratives such as *lonelygirl15* (2006–8) and *KateModern* (2007–8). According to Jon Dovey, web drama provides a fruitful site for investigating how TV mutates in the digital terrain. His chapter is especially concerned with 'web native' entertainment fiction; he considers how the temporalities of the attention economy are producing new transmedial cultural forms. Dovey explores the narrative and political economy of web drama and the challenges faced by professional media producers seeking to monetise the 'demotic creativity of the web'. Meanwhile, Elizabeth Evans uses the specific example of *KateModern* to assess forms of audience engagement with online drama. Reflecting on the way that modern technological developments have created a tension between the permanence of the media object and the ephemerality of the viewing experience, she examines how web drama exploits particular notions of ephemerality for new kinds of storytelling. Together, the chapters in Part 3 use online television and web drama to explore dynamics of temporality, availability and experience 'beyond' mainstream television, considering how digital and internet technologies impact on the form and circulation of (new) media content.

Rounding off the book, Part 4 considers the attempt by workers and users to arrest the attention of discrete audience constituencies; it examines ephemeral textual exchanges that take place *below* the visible texts of the film and television industries. This ranges from online 'worker-generated content' that circulates off-screen within professional film and TV production communities to particular subgenres of user-generated video that bring to the fore issues of performance, identity and the 'amateur aesthetic'. John Caldwell's chapter is concerned with paratexts that circulate within professional production cultures. These paratexts involve 'top-down' corporate ephemera such as DVD bonus tracks, marketing tapes, legal downloads and ancillary merchandise, but they also encompass a flipside of 'ground-up' worker ephemera such as demo tapes, comp reels, worker websites and below-the-line blogging. By relating industrial paratexts to particular socio-professional cultures in the film and TV industry, Caldwell demonstrates the way that corporate and worker ephemera have been used to respond to, negotiate, discipline and make sense of destabilising changes in work, technology and audience activity. He is especially concerned, in this context, with the proliferating forms of 'textual blowback' produced by worker and craft communities.

While Caldwell examines paratextual exchange in the worlds of professional media practitioners, Barbara Klinger considers the 'heavily trafficked networks of intertextuality that define cinema's contemporary existence'. Specifically, she examines the relationship between fan-produced ephemera and iconic Hollywood films. Focusing on a subgenre of internet shorts based upon movie re-enactment, Klinger uses the online production (and sharing) of restaged movie scenes to consider the relation of ephemera to the canon. While different in approach, both Caldwell and Klinger move the discussion of the ephemeral to the unauthorised and informal textual content that surrounds, influences, leaks into and maintains 'primary' film and TV content. They use indicative types of worker- and user-generated content to explore hierarchies, and relations of exchange, between 'substantial' and 'ephemeral' texts within production and reception contexts. The final chapter by Rosamund Davies moves away from the territory of film and TV altogether. Using an auto-ethnographic method to reflect on the aesthetic features and temporal properties of user-generated video, she takes as a reference point one of the vast number of home-produced clips that appear on the web and which offer themselves as ephemeral attractions. Examining the fleeting but time-looped representation of ordinary, everyday experience, Davies considers how values of immediacy and intimacy are performed in contemporary online video texts and in the way they are circulated. Fittingly, she turns not to paratexts or intertexts, but to the discussion of a pet video featured on a website with its own transitory principle – 'Today's Big Thing'.

By looking between, beyond and below the output of networks and studios, the four parts of *Ephemeral Media* explore a tangible set of organising practices, strategies and textual forms helping producers and publics alike to negotiate an increasingly fragmented and fleeting mediascape. Central to the book are questions about the dynamics of brevity and evanescence in the television and new media environment. Specifically, how have particular kinds of short-form text been stimulated by changes in the contemporary media ecology? To what extent do new digital distribution and exhibition technologies affect or enact ephemeral logics in the delivery and experience of media content? What creative, commercial or political challenges are faced by those who make the momentary, but arresting, media that surround mainstream entertainment content? How do short, secondary and seemingly insubstantial texts operate within media's circulatory systems? Focusing on screen forms that are defined by transient temporalities of duration and display, this collection of essays uses the ephemeral to reveal new perspectives on transformations and developments in the TV industry, and within screen culture more broadly. Centrally, the book considers textual and distributional methods used to get attention in a fast-paced media environment, and develops thinking about the kinds of attention that should be given to ephemeral texts in a critical and analytic sense.

Bibliography

Acland, Charles R. (ed.) (2007) *Residual Media* (Minnesota: University of Minneapolis Press).

Bennett, James. (2008) 'Television Studies Goes Digital', *Cinema Journal*, 47 (3), pp. 158–66.

Bjarkman, Kim. (2004) 'To Have and to Hold: The Video Collector's Relationship to an Ethereal Medium', *Television & New Media*, 5 (3), pp. 217–46.

Brindley, Lynne. (2009) 'We're in Danger of Losing our Memories', *The Observer*, 25 January, p. 31.

Broeren, Joost. (2009) 'Digital Attractions: Reloading Early Cinema in Online Video Collections', in Pelle Snickars and Patrick Vonderau (eds), *The YouTube Reader* (Stockholm: National Library of Sweden), pp. 154–65.

Burgess, Jean and Joshua Green. (2009) *YouTube: Online Video and Participatory Culture* (Cambridge: Polity Press).

Caldwell, John Thornton. (2008) *Production Culture: Industrial Reflexivity and Critical Practice in Film and Television* (Durham, NC: Duke University Press).

Carr, Nicholas. (2010) *The Shallows: How the Internet Is Changing the Way We Think, Read and Remember* (New York: Atlantic).

Davenport, Thomas H. and John C. Beck. (2001) *The Attention Economy: Understanding the New Currency of Business* (Boston, MA: Harvard Business School Press).

Dawson, Max. (2007) 'Little Players, Big Shows: Format, Narration, and Style on Television's Smaller Screens', *Convergence*, 13 (3), pp. 231–50.

Desjardins, Mary. (2006) 'Ephemeral Culture/eBay Culture: Film Collectibles and Fan Investments', in Ken Hillis, Michael Petit and Nathan Scott Epley (eds), *Everyday eBay: Culture, Collecting and Desire* (New York: Routledge), pp. 31–43.

Doane, Mary Ann. (2002) *The Emergence of Cinematic Time: Modernity, Contingency, the Archive* (Cambridge, MA: Harvard University Press).

'Eavesdropping on the Past – The John Johnson Collection: An Archive of Printed Ephemera' (2010) <http://www.jisc.ac.uk/news/stories/2010/06/ephemera.aspx> accessed 30 June 2010.

Frick, Caroline. (2008) 'Beyond Hollywood: Enhancing Heritage with the "Orphan" Film', *International Journal of Heritage Studies*, 14 (4), pp. 319–31.

Goldhaber, Michael. (1997) 'The Attention Economy and the Net', *First Monday*, 2 (4), <http://www.firstmonday.org/issues/issue2_4/goldhaber/> accessed 9 May 2011.

Gray, Jonathan. (2010) *Show Sold Separately: Promos, Spoilers and Other Media Paratexts* (New York: New York University Press).

Gripsrud, Jostein (ed.). (2010) *Relocating Television: Television in the Digital Context* (London: Routledge).

Gunning, Tom. (2004) 'Now You See It, Now You Don't: The Temporality of the Cinema of Attractions', in Lee Grieveson and Peter Krämer (eds), *The Silent Cinema Reader* (London: Routledge), pp. 41–50.

Hastie, Amelie. (2007) 'Detritus and the Moving Image: Ephemera, Materiality, History', *Journal of Visual Culture*, 6 (2), pp. 171–4.

Ignatieff, Michael. (1989) 'Cleverness Is All', *The Independent* (Weekend), 7 January, p. 25.

Klinger, Barbara. (2006) *Beyond the Multiplex: Cinema, New Technologies and the Home* (Berkeley: University of California Press).

Kompare, Derek. (2005) *Rerun Nation: How Repeats Invented American Television* (New York: Routledge).

——. (2006) 'Publishing Flow: DVD Box Sets and the Reconceptualization of Television', *Television & New Media*, 7 (4), pp. 335–60.

Lanham, Richard A. (2006) *The Economics of Attention: Style and Substance in the Age of Information* (Chicago: University of Chicago Press).

Lotz, Amanda. (2007) *The Television Will Be Revolutionized* (New York: New York University Press).

Meikle, Graham and Sherman Young. (2008) 'Beyond Broadcasting? TV for the Twenty-First Century', *Media International Australia*, 126, February, pp. 67–70.

Miller, Nancy. (2007) 'Minifesto for a New Age', *Wired*, 15 (3), pp. 16–28.

Naughton, John. (2010) 'Everything You Need to Know about the Internet', *The Observer* (New Review), 20 June, pp. 8–11.

Parks, Lisa. (2007) 'Falling Apart: Electronic Salvaging and the Global Media Economy', in Acland (ed.), *Residual Media*, pp. 32–47.

Prelinger, Rick. (2007) 'Archives and Access in the 21st Century', *Cinema Journal*, 46 (3), pp. 114–18.

Schneider, Steven M. and Kirsten A. Foot. (2004) 'The Web as an Object of Study', *New Media & Society*, 6 (1), pp. 114–22.

Snickars, Pelle. (2009) 'The Archival Cloud', in Pelle Snickars and Patrick Vonderau (eds), *The YouTube Reader* (Stockholm: National Library of Sweden), pp. 292–313.

—— and Patrick Vonderau. (eds) (2009) 'Introduction', *The YouTube Reader* (Stockholm: National Library of Sweden), pp. 9–21.

Straw, Will. (2010) 'The Circulatory Turn', in Barbara Crow, Michael Longford, Kim Sawchuk (eds), *The Wireless Spectrum: The Politics, Practices and Poetics of Mobile Media* (Toronto: University of Toronto Press), pp. 17–28.

Tomlinson, John. (2007) *The Culture of Speed: The Coming of Immediacy* (London: Sage).

Tryon, Chuck. (2010) *Reinventing Cinema: Movies in the Age of Media Convergence* (New Brunswick, NJ: Rutgers University Press).

TV Ark. (2010) <www.tv-ark.org.uk/> accessed 12 January 2010.

Williams, Raymond. (1974) *Television: Technology and Cultural Form* (London: Fontana).

Wilson, Pamela. (2009) 'Stalking the Wild Evidence: Capturing Media History through Elusive and Ephemeral Archives', in Janet Staiger and Sabine Hake (eds), *Convergence Media History* (New York: Routledge), pp. 182–91.

Worsley, T. C. (1970) *Television: The Ephemeral Art* (London: Alan Ross).

PART1 MEDIA TRANSITION AND TRANSITORY MEDIA

1 The Recurrent, the Recombinatory and the Ephemeral

William Uricchio

Although America's film critics had mixed reviews of Oliver Stone's *Natural Born Killers* (1994), many agreed in their assessment of the film's editing, singling out the rapid cutting pace and using terms such as 'frenetic', 'radical', even 'hallucinatory'. Some argued that the film stood as proof of the corrosive impact of television advertising and video-clip culture, evidence that their formal strategies were leaching into the cinematic mainstream. It sounded very promising indeed! At the time of the film's American premiere, I was in the Netherlands, carefully tracking the reviews and counting the weeks until the Dutch release of the film. The big day arrived, and I vividly recall sitting through the usual block of product advertisements, previews and instructional messages, only to find the opening salvo of Stone's film a bit, well … plodding. In fact, with a few glorious exceptions, the pace of the entire film failed to evoke the descriptions issuing forth from American reviewers. The reason for the discrepancy was clear: most reviewers saw their films in special press screenings, free from the distractions of the popcorn-eating crowd, and cut loose from the larger enveloping context of previews and ancillary material (pre-film advertisements were in any case not yet common in US cinemas). By contrast, my viewing of the film in Utrecht was preceded by fifteen minutes of visual material (including some ads also run on television) dominated by bursts of shots lasting one and two seconds. Stone's film was certainly more quickly paced than those of his Hollywood contemporaries, but compared to the ads and previews that prefaced my viewing, it felt much closer to standard cinematic fare.

Cinema advertisements, previews and instructionals certainly deserve more serious critical attention than they have received. As cinematic texts, they are, after all, viewed significantly more often than the features they accompany. The same short-form films often accompany multiple features; and while we tend towards a single viewing of feature films, we might view the same ads or instructionals every time we go to the cinema over a three-month period. One form of ephemeral cinema, these texts deserve scrutiny as such. But my interest is less with the textual specificities of these short and frequently re-viewed films than with their contextual potentials. Rather, I am interested in the ephemeral as a textual condition, and specifically in the metatextual implications of ephemeral texts. In time-based media such as film, radio and television, where the flow of texts both ephemeral and privileged is constructed by its exhibitors and experienced by its audiences, how might we account for the frisson produced by placing one text next to another, and by the excess of meaning that might be generated? Gérard Genette (2001) has explored this space more thoroughly than most, focusing on the domain of the literary (the book) rather than on time-based media. This has yielded many sharp insights regarding the role of textual positioning (paratexts, for example) in shaping the meaning and import of the central text, but it has also left certain issues hanging precariously on the margins. Sergei Eisenstein also considered the role of textual positioning primarily through his theories of montage. His contributions (and those of the generation of film-makers who studied with Lev Kuleshov) focused on the micro-level of shot-to-shot relations and their implications for the decentring of the shot as a unit of meaning, shifting attention instead to the interaction of shots, the shot sequence, as the site of meaning. His insights, like Genette's, bear on the discussion to follow. This essay will attempt to situate and briefly develop some of these insights as they relate in particular to the role of ephemeral texts in existing commercial television regimes, and in the emerging practices within participatory television forms such as YouTube.

The ephemeral

The word 'ephemeral' carries with it a curious tale. Among the clusters of available definitions, the *Oxford English Dictionary* Second Edition (Simpson and Weiner, 1989) offers the following:

> **Ephemera, n. 1.** An insect that (in its imago or winged form) lives only for a day. In mod. entomology the name of a genus of pseudo-neuropterous insects belonging to the group *Ephemeridæ* (Day-flies, May-flies).
> **2.** *transf.* and *fig.* One who or something which has a transitory existence.

The mayfly literalised the ancients' understanding of the transitory, granting it an iridescent form and fleeting yet pristine beauty that lingers on as an object lesson in our language. But to our contemporary ears, this definition of the ephemeral-as-transitory generally skews differently, evoking Baudelaire's notion of modernity as the 'transient, the fleeting, the contingent' (Baudelaire, 1964 [1864], p. 13). An affect or stance that speaks to the myriad sensations that constitute our present, to impressions more evocative than substantive, this sense of the transitory and ephemeral arises from such late-nineteenth-century conditions as overstimulation, from mechanically enhanced tempos, and from new cacophonies anything but natural in their order. And they are manifest in time-based media in at least three ways.

First, both recorded and transmitted image and sound – the telephone, television, radio, gramophone and film – are experienced in a perpetual present. We engage in an always fleeting but nevertheless persistent embrace of the images and sounds in the fullness of their 'nowness'. The images (or sounds) that we have already seen (or heard) function as a just-witnessed (and now remembered) past, fundamental to our experience and sense-making, but fundamentally different in possibility, their potentials always-already realised. As viewers, we are poised on the cusp of the known and the unknown, and witness there the unfolding actualisation of near-infinite possibility into concrete images and sounds … and meanings. This present, in which we 'watch' a film or television programme or 'listen' to radio, is at odds with our notion of media as a physical product (a reel of tape), or as a referenced or advertised text or programe entity, or as a copyrighted legal entity. These conceptions are outside of time's flow; but not the experience of listening or viewing, which are very much part of it.

A second sense of the ephemeral that seems intrinsic to media draws upon the melancholia lurking in Baudelaire's notion of modernity, and concerns the vulnerable state of its materiality. Although celluloid, magnetic tape and vinyl disks have not yet been put to the test of time that stone, paper and the pigments of antiquity have survived, it seems clear from archival authorities that contemporary media are transitory. Far fewer than one hundred years have been sufficient to demonstrate the instability of celluloid nitrate; fewer than fifty for the pink colour in Eastman Color; and fewer than twenty for the oxidation of magnetic tape. The 'ideal' lifespans suggested by archivists for the supporting media for digital information are nearly as short as the life of the ever-changing formats into which that data is encoded. Our media, as physical objects subject to wear, tear, reformatting and ultimately decay, are fleeting in ways that we are only now beginning to realise.

A third sense in which the ephemeral is endemic to media can be found in the ways that we study it. Historically, before the era of consumer-grade tape recorders, film and television scholars had to rely on what was broadcast or screened (or could be found at the archive). The very contours of a culture's productivity were subject to shape-shifting and change thanks to the happenstance of preservation, the legal and market opportunities of distribution, the state of the larger media environment and, of course, one's location within it. Beyond the aleatory (or, alternatively, canonical) availability of texts, their very mode of survival and storage also revealed limits. Consider, for example, the nature of what is deemed worth saving. Every medium has

its challenges, but the archive's radical decontextualisation of television, in which programmes are plucked from their local setting and textual mix, from the flow that
Raymond Williams did so much to excavate, stands as an example of the medium's
ephemeral status. We only have access to certain aspects of programming, the larger
textual logics of programme flow, of advertising, programme idents and bumpers
having long since vanished without a trace. And this has shaped the ways that we
study, for example, television, attending to the feature texts that survive and are accessible, and removing them from their flow.

The *OED* reminds us that the fleeting temporal qualities of the term ephemeral
have, over time, taken on other meanings as well. The Additions Series (Simpson and
Weiner, 1993) offers this definition:

> **ephemeron**, *n. pl.* **ephemera**. Printed matter of no lasting value except to collectors, as
> tickets, posters, greetings cards, etc. **1938** *Proc. Special Libraries Assoc.* I. 55 (*heading*)
> Pamphlets and ephemera. **1943** *Gloss. Libr. Terms* (Amer. Libr. Assoc.) 53 *Ephemera*.
> 1. Current material, usually pamphlets and clippings, of temporary interest and value.
> 2. Similar material of the past which has acquired literary or historical significance.
> **1956** *Library* Sept. 8 (Advt.), Catalogues offering rare and interesting books, pamphlets and
> ephemera post free. **1973** M. Amis *Rachel Papers* 126 Faddy ephemera covered its walls:
> posters of Jimi Hendrix, Auden and Isherwood, Rasputin ...

A reminder of why the *OED* is such an interesting read, the undulating and accreting
definitions and uses of the term reveal evidence of its cultural dynamics (Hendrix,
Isherwood, Rasputin?). The combination of 'material of the past which has acquired
literary or historical significance' with 'printed matter of no lasting value' to describe
the same term speaks to its uneasy dynamics, at once both valuable and valueless, and
very much dependent on the eye of the beholder. The category of objects enumerated
– tickets, greeting cards – also suggests that the temporary value of the ephemeral is
related to multiplicity. Objects of this sort are created in such abundance that they are
rarely valued beyond their initial use; they are among the first bits of material culture
to find their way to the dustbin of history. Not surprisingly, this sense is more recent
(as the *OED* quotes demonstrate), reflecting the modern as a moment of mass reproduction. In a sense, it is one of the unspoken critiques behind the lament for the
auratic taken on by Benjamin. The point here is that the notion of abundance through
multiplicity renders the status of any one particular instance insignificant – at least until
such time as scarcity restores its importance.

The lurking implication of multiplicity's relationship to the ephemeral plays out
in a particular way with time-based media, namely as repetition. The more frequently repeated, the more multiple, the more the value of any one instance might

be considered fleeting, ephemeral. This is the domain excavated by Williams in his meso- and micro-level analyses of televisual flow, a domain absent from the newspaper listings of the evening's programming, absent in the archiving of the primary programme text … but perhaps not completely absent from our experience.

The recombinatory

VI [Channel 7 news desk] (Announcer 2)
A mayor in Alameda County is working for a proposition to ban further apartment construction in his city. But his wife and six daughters are working for the other side. Reporter (film of street in city; cars and houses): The proposition is being voted on tomorrow. The issue is legal and environmental. Further development, it is said, will reduce open spaces and lead to extra traffic pollution.
VII Woman (film: hand-spraying from can; table dusted): Liquid Gold furniture polish; brings new sparkle to your furniture; it's like meeting an old friend again.
VIII Man (film clip): The 6:30 movie is *Annie Get Your Gun*. Betty Hutton as the sharpest-shooting gal the Wild West ever saw. (Williams, 1992, p. 95)

This excerpt from Raymond Williams' 'medium range' analysis of a broadcast sequence from San Francisco's Channel 7 on 12 March 1973 (5:42 p.m.) traces a series of shifts in time, space, voice and mode of address.[1] From a live news desk, to a presumably recently filmed location report, to an 'evergreen' studio-shot advertisement, to a clip from George Sidney's 1950 film with a recent voice overlay, a few seconds of television time yields quite an experiential range. While read as 'disruptive' to a cultural outsider like Williams, the sequence flows along quite well for native viewers. Williams' close-range analysis goes a step further, demonstrating the art of segue so important in the broadcast era. While not discussed by Williams, who was more interested in perceived temporal continuities, the repetition and recycling of these elements further complicates the story. Texts, as cultural artifacts, carry associations, so how might we think about the repositioning of those elements (texts and their associations) into new contexts? The 1973 broadcast of a 1950 film might come inscribed with particular meanings for a viewer who first saw it at the cinema twenty-three years earlier; or, repositioned in a broadcast environment where the promo for *Annie Get Your Gun* follows a report of a shooting by a woman, it might take on a whole new meaning. The advertisement for Liquid Gold might normalise domestic divisions of labour in 1973, or, shown in a different era, might be appreciated for documenting early 1970s lifestyles or critiqued as an instrument for maintaining gender inequality. While hypothetical examples, they point to the role of sequence, context and association in the construction of meaning, and the tensions inherent in ordering and reordering the bits of time, space and event that they constitute.

This recombinatory practice, built on an ever-changing sequence of programme units many of which are ephemeral in the sense of being both fleeting and repeated, is difficult to recover from newspaper listings or television archives. And yet, it reflects the logics of most western television systems, while also relating to the idea of montage. The durational assemblage of divergent materials, montage relies upon sequence and ever-changing context for its effect. In cinematic terms, the principles of montage found early articulation through Lev Kuleshov, briefly the teacher of Eisenstein and a great influence on Pudovkin, Vertov and other Soviet film-makers. Just after the Russian Revolution, at a time of minimal film imports and poor production resources, Kuleshov experimented with the recombinatory effect of film editing, recutting found footage to construct new meanings. By intercutting footage of an actor's face with a bowl of soup, a coffin and a girl, he was able to construct a nuanced performance for audiences, who read identical images of the actor's face as expressing hunger, loss and quiet joy. The 'Kuleshov effect', as the results of this and other experiments became known, demonstrated that shot sequence and context were far more determining than expected, and that the meaning of a particular shot, long considered self-evident and relatively stable within the painterly and photographic tradition, was in fact highly malleable and context dependent.

Kuleshov's insights gave voice to a temporal recombinatory practice that is older than the film medium, evident for example in nineteenth-century programming of magic-lantern exhibitions, where showmen learned to build – and to rework – stories from the slides that they happened to have. But these early practices, particularly as they appeared through film's first decade or so, actually made use of recombinatory logic in a double sense. First, in the hands of film-makers such as Edwin S. Porter and D. W. Griffith, the sequence of shots was manipulated to construct overall textual meaning (just as Kuleshov would later theorise and experimentally demonstrate). Second, the positioning of the films of Porter, Griffiths and others into full programmes (complete with lantern slides, *actualités* and other narratives) could itself radically transform the meanings of individual films. Here, the programmer (usually the projectionist) could, through simple manipulation of film sequence, comment upon or build different frameworks of coherence for a particular film. This metalevel of recombination was not discussed by Kuleshov and, indeed, largely took residual form in exhibition practice. But it *was* seized upon by television (and radio), where programmatic recombination would emerge as the economic lifeblood of the industry in the form of the rerun. And it provides one of the keys to television's distinctive deployment of ephemeral programme elements.

Television's programming logics turn on a triad of organisational principles when it comes to texts, ephemeral and not: sequence, interpenetration and repetition.

- *Sequence* pertains to the careful orchestration of programme units particularly relevant during the broadcast era programming (but residually present as well in its successor regimes), in which the programme day addressed a changing constituency of viewers, and in which the programme 'line-up' was designed to enhance the chances of continuous viewing. Sequence, as well, speaks to the notion of temporal contiguity and thus contextualisation that is the driving force of both the Kuleshov effect and programmatic historical framing (and in this, it remains highly relevant, even for the self-programmer of YouTube segments).
- *Interpenetration* can be found in the practice of parsing out particular texts over time and over the broadcast schedule (e.g. weekly or daily series, where the programme day and our lives are interpenetrated), and of fragmenting individual programmes with advertisements and announcements of various sorts, effectively constructing a metatext beyond the control of the individual text's author. Far more egregious in commercial television settings, interpenetration also refers to the practice of using programme 'bumpers' and 'hooks' (displaced micro-programme elements) to keep viewers watching. The effect, paradoxically, is both to rupture engagement in a particular programme and to interconnect programme elements into a larger whole. But the punctuation of programme sequence is not always subtle: a well-timed advertisement for aspirin during the evening news can undercut the most serious economic reports, as can an unfortunately timed advertisement for gasoline following news of the latest evidence of global warming.
- *Repetition* refers to the recycling of footage, programmes and programme units, whether in a single channel environment or across channels. Examples range from heavily circulated iconic footage (the collapse of the World Trade Center), to advertisements (where frequency of repetition is part of their persuasive logic), to programme segments (CNN Headline News' repetition of news stories and sequences on a thirty-minute rotation), to entire programme reruns (whether repeated or syndicated).[2]

While interpenetration and repetition may seem at odds with an ideal viewing experience, they are central to the notion of television as a larger textual system (as opposed to 'television as the provider of individual programme texts'). Moreover, they bear heavily on the re-construction of textual meaning and reflect the current state of television's economy. Interpenetration brings textual elements of a different temporality and intent into the primary textual domain. They can be assimilated as part of a larger text (an aspirin ad can be read as inadvertently commenting upon the latest bad news from Afghanistan), or bracketed out as a minor annoyance (and ignored), but in either case they redefine the temporality of the primary text and thus the viewing experience and meanings. Repetition, in turn, invariably takes place in a new cultural present, and can reactivate the past of the primary text (recalling original impressions upon first seeing the programme or, through the text, its fuller cultural moment), or recast it through the knowledge that has since been acquired.

The already alluded to notion of flow, one of the most developed discursive strands in television studies, touches directly upon this point. Closely associated with Raymond Williams' path-breaking contribution to the study of television, the concept has gone on to support very different arguments and, in the process, has helped both to chart shifts in the identity of television as a cultural practice and to map various undulations in the terrain of television studies (Williams, 1992 [1974]; Gripsrud, 1998; Uricchio, 2004). It has been deployed perhaps most consistently in the service of defining a televisual 'essence', adhering to Williams' description of flow as 'perhaps the defining characteristic of broadcasting, simultaneously as technology and as a cultural form' (Williams, 1992 [1974], p. 80). It has been used to describe the structure of textuality and programming on macro, meso and micro levels. And it has given form to the viewing experience, serving as a framework within which reception can be understood (variously activated in terms of larger household regimes and the logics of meaning-making).

The disjunctions, discontinuities and endless recombinatory possibilities of flow lead to a medium-specific dimension of television's (meta-)textual production, and thus its particular manner of encouraging meaning-making. This process works in tandem with the textual units, both ephemeral and not, constructed by programme-makers – documentaries, dramatic fictions, advertisements, news, programme bumpers, promos, idents – effectively transforming any particular text's original meaning and epistemological status. My point is relatively straightforward: although something like the associational logic captured by 'the Kuleshov effect' is axiomatic when we think about the grammar of time-based texts and the manner in which individual shots accrete into meaningful utterances, our approaches to the study of television have usually failed to extend these insights into the relationship of programme elements to one another. Instead, we (and our archives) tend to focus on individual texts, plucked from their environment, stripped of their framing context, freed from notions of repetition or interpenetration or larger programme sequence, and exempted from any consideration of the particular heterochronic regime of which they are a part. As a result, television texts are analysed very much like film texts; and while for the better part of the post-World War Two era, we have abandoned the notion of stable meanings, we have for too long assumed the existence of the stable and unitised television text somehow plucked from its programme flow. This approach has of course yielded a wide range of insights; and yet, particularly when we are considering how texts help to situate meanings, the larger heterochronic dimension is also vitally important. It helps to account for the variable status of a particular shot or programme, and for the embedding of ever-shifting bits of recorded time into new contexts. Television's complex temporality renders it into a generator of endlessly reworked meanings. And central to this complexity are the most frequently repeated programme units – those texts that we call ephemeral.

The recurrent

Television's configurations of technology and cultural form have morphed over time. The situation today is indeed quite different from that of the broadcasting era that formed the basis for Williams' notion of flow, and the medium's broad definitional contours remain very much in a state of contention. Yet television – even when distributed through the internet – has maintained its roots in the twin definitional logics of a particular representational and temporal order ('live' in the sense of potentially immediate, continuous and coexistent). And more than simply changing, these tele-visual configurations have accreted, and exist side by side: for example, it is still possible to view programmer-dominated, broadcast-like television over the internet, still possible to experience 'old' cable, and at the same time, experience new DVR- or IPTV-enhanced television flow. Yet, particularly if we listen to supporters of the traditional television industry, these new affordances seem to be eroding the very essence of the medium by enabling viewers to 'cherry-pick', jumping from text to text in precisely the sequence that they desire, and allowing them with the push of a button to circumvent the ephemeral in the form of advertisements, idents and promos. The essence of the medium for these critics is often economic, and the erosion is one that affects the logics of television advertising and audience metrics. Yet ever since the popularisation of the remote control – and its coeval, the VCR – audiences have been able to renegotiate the sequence of programme flow and flummox the audience metrics bean-counters. Leaving aside these economic concerns, what about the metatextual implications of these new affordances? What about flow and the place of ephemeral texts?

Contemporary viewers enjoy several affordances unavailable to earlier generations. *Access* to content continues to expand greatly, with global television increasingly coming online and massive archival digitisation projects increasing access to the tele-visual (and filmic) past. *Agency* is also shifting, and to more than one model: we are becoming much more dependent on programme metadata and on search engines, and can see increasing signs that social recommendation systems will play an important role in how we imagine navigating the medium. At the same time, the blurring of producers and users, and the active distribution of the results, promises even greater variation of content. Most importantly, users can control the flow of programme elements, constructing contexts and playing with the ensuing meanings. Together, these affordances in the areas of access and agency enable viewers to look beyond their regions or nations, accessing the world from outside a viewing position long controlled by national institutions and transnational industries. Audiences can find new compilers of texts, new sites of accretion, new pathways, as they navigate a rich mix of programme possibilities, either refashioning their own texts or recombining contexts and causal sequences of texts to express new meanings. The shift under way is from the art of selection (the broadcast and cable eras) to the art of aggregation, and the far more active reassembly of sequence. And if we complicate this by factoring in the increasing importance of cross-platform prowling, the possibilities are daunting.

As television – a medium with a long history of entanglements with other media, from the telephone to film to the radio – continues its latest pas de deux with the networked computer, the direction of flow is changing. In our online world, we read *and* write; we download *and* uplink; we consume *and* 'cut and paste' *and* produce. YouTube emblematises this participatory turn (and television's increasingly close relationship with the internet), and its implications for the ephemeral in television go far beyond the simple 'evacuation' and evasion feared by the industry.[3] Although mainstream television is flirting ever more intently with user-generated content (*America's Funniest Home Videos*, 1989–present; BBC's *Video Diaries*, 1991–2; and citizen journalism forms such as *CNN: I-Reports*, 2006–present), much YouTube content is predicated upon the viewer/user's reappropriation and recontextualisation of existing televisual and film material. Feature programmes, advertisements, idents, bumpers and so on are disassembled, recycled, remixed with materials of other provenance and recast as new texts – some funny, some absurd, some biting in their commentary. In many cases, the ephemeral has come all the way around to emerge centre stage. And sites such as YouTube provide outlets for their distribution, for further recycling and for commentary. As we consider the accretion of videos around new topics, and the pace of user remixing and sequence intervention, we are witnessing nothing less than the emergence of a new production system generated within communities of interest, not nation states or corporations. And as often as not, the textual forms considered ephemeral in a commercial setting are the building blocks of these new textual systems.

The internet has enabled this process to a large extent, as YouTube's centrality and the new affordances offered to communities of interest suggest. But the major American broadcasting and cable television networks have also played their parts, thanks to their own online operations, in many cases positioned under the umbrella of their trans-media parent companies. CBS Interactive, FOX Interactive Media, Turner (CNN, TNT, TBS, Cartoon Network) and Viacom Digital (MTV, BET, Paramount), plus industry-backed portals such as Hulu (NBC Universal and News Corp.), offer a spectrum of services from providing scheduling information, to channelling fan activities, to providing various levels of access to television shows, films and music. Other portals such as Joost provide an international assortment of television, film and music, and sites such as Mysoju take a more nation- and genre-specific approach, offering access to unlicensed Japanese, Korean and Taiwanese soaps. Although the interfaces and services provided by these various sites differ widely, several things stand out. First, the online presence of disaggregated television content has been normalised and is growing steadily; second, virtually all mainstream American television programmes have been spoken for by their parent companies, and at a moment of aggressive intellectual property protection, this leaves very little for outside players such as YouTube and Joost; third, ephemeral texts are alive and well, both stimulated by these developments and deployed in very different ways.

If the networks are largely monopolising their own television content, then what kind of television is left over for YouTube? YouTube, of course, has licensing deals with CBS, BBC and many others, but deals do not necessarily mean feature television programmes. CBS, for example, allows access to a range of promotional and ephemeral material (interviews, previews, programme headers, logos, advertisements), and some historical shows, news and local affiliate coverage – but not its current features. YouTube has responded to these constraints by launching what it calls 'short-form content': clips of popular primetime shows like *Lost* (2004–10), *Desperate Housewives* (2004–present) and *Grey's Anatomy* (2005–present) in which the feature programme is rendered into something that looks ephemeral, as well as behind-the-scenes footage, celebrity interviews, online-only specials. Considering these constraints, YouTube is not a destination for the viewer seeking standard television fare or formats. But for the trans-brand or trans-network fan, the synoptic viewer, the lover of ephemera and the growing cohort of young cellphone viewers, it is fast providing an array of alternatives, from new textual forms to community-building strategies, all consistent with its user-driven profile. In an ironic twist, the networks have effectively encouraged a new prominence and value for the ephemeral thanks to their constraint of feature programming.

A telling instance of this 'twist' may be found in YouTube's embrace of another medium: film. From the echoes of cinema-style theatrical release, to format-specific appeals to the amateur movement, to film festivals, the development teams at YouTube work through familiar categories while in fact offering far more than simply the main event – the film artifact itself. In many cases, they offer everything *but* the artifact itself. Consider YouTube's promotional blurb for the Sundance Film Festival:

> The Sundance Film Festival recently launched a YouTube channel that allows all of you
> movie enthusiasts to get a glimpse of what took place during the 25th anniversary year of
> the influential festival. For those of you interested in the filmmakers behind the films,
> there's the 'Meet the Artists' playlist, featuring interviews with filmmakers from around the

world and clips of the films that brought them to Sundance. If you're looking for coverage on the ground – from premieres to parties and more – you can check out the Live@Sundance segments. And to hear what some of the film industry's leading thinkers had to say about the state of the business today. (YouTube, 2009)

Although in most cases we are only given access to 'clips of the films that brought them to Sundance', the trappings, the ephemera, of the festival constitute the main YouTube event and are covered in their full glory. Just as in the example of its 'short-form' approach to mainstream television, YouTube has seized the periphery, providing access to the 'scene' far more effectively than to the films (or television shows) themselves. YouTube's game channels operate in similar fashion. Games, by definition interactive, are watchable rather than playable in the YouTube context. The various channels provide walkthroughs, commentaries, trailers, previews, sneak peeks, cheats, play highlights and event coverage across the various gaming platforms. These elements are the topic of much commentary, effectively reinforcing the community-building strategies that seem to lurk behind the event coverage 'peripheral' to television shows and films.

Conclusion

Intellectual property constraints have led to a new centrality for the ephemeral, at once driven by the evacuation of the primary text in settings like YouTube and by a participatory turn, which remixes and recirculates the texts to which it has easy access. Moreover, current trends suggest that feature programming itself is subject to a process of *ephemeralisation*, as programmes are cut down to teaser-size for the small screen with the blessings of their network producers (and protectors). As viewing platforms continue to decentre the traditional television-set-in-the-living-room, shifting instead towards smaller, more mobile and interactive screens, one can imagine that this trend will continue to intensify.

This chapter has argued that the ephemeral and media are inexorably intertwined, certainly if we step back and consider the nature of our experiential encounters with time-based media, and their archival lives and afterlives as objects of study. In a more particular sense, we have seen that in traditional television regimes, ephemeral texts are an essential part of programming flow, and as such offer a determining if far too often overlooked framework for the interpretive act. The frisson of text against text offers a site of contextualisation and potential meaning production and as such offers a metatextual process worthy of closer critical attention.

As television enters a phase of displacement and disaggregation, with its texts unbundled from the flow that has defined the medium for the greater part of its last seventy-five years, the ephemeral has found a new place. At least during this transitional moment, several factors are at play. Television's traditional industries, panicked by rapid changes in technology, audience behaviours and the underlying economic logics of their sector, are holding tight to their intellectual property rights as they struggle to reinvent their business model. A new generation of digitally enabled collectors and archivists have opened access to vast collections of ephemeral material and extra-national television texts. And new participatory communities have discovered the pleasures of producing and sharing their own texts, and in an era where a cut-and-mix aesthetic enjoys widespread support, this has encouraged the recycling and recirculating of existing – often ephemeral – textual elements.

The ephemeral has found new life as television struggles to redefine itself and its relationship to the people once called its audience. At a moment when the capacities, sizes and locations of our screens continue to change, certainties are elusive. But it seems clear that textual formats and viewing habits are responding to this new environment and that short-form time-based media are on the rise. Whether or not we will continue to call these forms 'television' is anyone's guess, but they suggest both a continued slippage between the clearly defined textual forms that we today take for granted, and an increased value for the forms that we take as ephemeral.

Notes

1. This section 'recombines' elements developed for a related argument about television's relationship with history first published in Uricchio (2010).
2. Derek Kompare (2005) offers an excellent overview of this practice.
3. True, most of the actions that I will describe circumvent the existing system for profit production based on viewing advertisements, but that says more about the accounting system than the logics of textual engagement. This section draws from arguments developed in Uricchio (2009).

Bibliography

Baudelaire, Charles. (1964 [1864]) *The Painter of Modern Life and Other Essays*. Translated and edited by Jonathan Mayne (New York: De Capo).

Genette, Gérard. (2001) *Paratexts: Thresholds of Interpretation* (New York: Cambridge University Press).

Gripsrud, Jostein. (1998) 'Television, Broadcasting, Flow: Key Metaphors in TV
Theory', in Christine Geraghty and David Lusted (eds), *The Television Studies Book* (London: Arnold, 1998), pp. 17–32.

Kompare, Derek. (2005) *Rerun Nation: How Repeats Invented American Television* (New York: Routledge).

Simpson, John and Edmund Weiner (eds). (1989) *Oxford English Dictionary*, Second Edition
    (Oxford: Oxford University Press).
——. (1993) *Oxford English Dictionary*, Additions Series (Oxford: Oxford University Press).
Uricchio, William. (2004) 'Television's Next Generation: Technology/Interface Culture/Flow',
    in Lynn Spigel and Jan Olsson (eds), *Television After TV: Essays on a Medium in Transition*
    (Durham, NC: Duke University Press), pp. 232–61.
——. (2009) 'The Future of a Medium Once Known as Television', in Pelle Snickars and Patrick
    Vonderau (eds), *The YouTube Reader* (Stockholm: National Library of Sweden), pp. 24–37.
——. (2010) 'TV as Time Machine: Television's Changing Heterochronic Regimes and the
    Production of History', in Jostein Gripsrud (ed.), *Relocating Television: Television in the
    Digital Context* (London: Routledge), pp. 27–40.
Williams, Raymond. (1992 [1974]) *Television: Technology and Cultural Form* (Hanover, NH:
    Wesleyan University Press).
YouTube. (2009) 'Blog', <www.*YouTube*.com/blog> accessed 23 January 2009.

2 Television Abridged: Ephemeral Texts, Monumental Seriality and TV-Digital Media Convergence

Max Dawson

The late 1990s and early 2000s were for US television networks a period of opportunity and introspection. Confronted with the possibilities and challenges presented by new digital distribution and exhibition technologies and the nation's recently re-regulated media marketplaces, networks re-evaluated many of the axiomatic assumptions and sedimented practices of television's broadcast era. Though responses to changing technologies and market conditions varied greatly, a number of networks took the upheavals of this period as an opportunity to adopt more flexible business models characterised on the one hand by their emphasis on synergy and vertical integration, and on the other hand by their deviation from the comparatively rigid temporalities of broadcasting. The most adventurous networks exploited the affordances of convergence and conglomeration to tinker with television's nightly and weekly timetables; with the timing of development cycles and the scheduling of new programme debuts; with the windows separating programmes' initial airings, reruns and releases into ancillary markets; and with the durations of seasons and individual episodes. As a result of these experiments, by the turn of the millennium the customary clockings and calendars of the US television industry had begun to give way to a heterochronic mix more compatible with the abbreviated textual forms, erratic production schedules and idiosyncratic consumption styles associated with digital media platforms.

As television networks gradually adopted these flexible business models, some also experimented with heterochronic multiplatform programming and promotional strategies. Take, for instance, FOX's handling of 24's (2001–10) various web and mobile video iterations. Like many of the most lucrative television franchises launched in this period, FOX's espionage thriller was a *scalable* 'transmedia' property (Jenkins, 2006), made available to viewers in multiple versions tailored to television's increasingly diverse technologies and contexts of reception.[1] In presenting 24 on digital platforms, FOX broke with the US television industry's long-standing tradition of exclusively offering scripted programming in fifteen-, thirty- and sixty-minute intervals, creating and commissioning versions of *24* of varying durations. *24* thus appeared on television (on both the FOX network and the affiliated cable network FX), on mobile phones (in the form of a spin-off series of one-minute 'mobisodes' shot specifically to be legible on the screens of handheld devices) and on the web (in various forms, including three-minute excerpts viewable at Hulu.com, a series of five-minute 'webisodes' sponsored by a deodorant company and full-episode downloads and streams) (Dawson, 2007). These multiple versions of *24* provided an inexpensive source of branded content for the proliferating array of platforms operated by News Corp. (FOX's parent conglomerate). They also afforded FOX opportunities to access the audience marketplaces then coalescing around television's new distribution platforms, including the marketplace for short-form web and mobile video content.

Of the many forms of heterochronic versioning practised by US television networks during this period, perhaps the most common involved the creation of fast-cut web videos that abridged serialised television narratives for more efficient online viewing. By the mid-2000s, these abridgements were ubiquitous on networks' homepages and at video aggregation sites such as YouTube.com. At NBC.com, 'Two-Minute Replays' summed up the major developments of weekly instalments of *Friday Night Lights* (2006–11) and *Heroes* (2006–10). Basic cable channel FX followed a similar template, producing 'Three-Minute Replays' of *Damages* (2007–present) and *Sons of Anarchy* (2008–present). More comprehensive video abridgements condensed entire seasons of primetime serials: since 2005, ABC has released five-minute videos that review past seasons of its dramas under the label 'ABC Starter Kits' on an annual basis, while the boutique cable network AMC has produced a *Breaking Bad* (2008–present) 'Six-Minute Catch-Up' video to introduce the series to a wider audience (AMC, 2010). *The Sopranos* (1999–2007), *The Wire* (2002–8), *Lost* (2004–10) and *Battlestar Gallactica* (2004–9), four of the decade's most critically acclaimed dramas, were all during their runs the subjects of video abridgements that condensed multiple seasons of these programmes into impressively comprehensive synopses.

Video abridgements such as these are supremely ephemeral texts. The brevity and evanescence of, for instance, an NBC Two-Minute Replay stands in stark contrast to the monumentality of the primetime serials that are these videos' most frequent subjects. For while programmes of all genres and vintages appear in abridged forms online, contemporary primetime serial dramas are surely the most frequent subjects of these ephemeral videos. This is by no means coincidental: in the same period that US television networks began experimenting with heterochronic multiplatform versioning strategies, they also introduced a spate of serial dramas distinguished by the intricacy of their multithreaded narratives and the scope of their sweeping season- and medium-spanning story arcs.[2] Video abridgements condense and groom the intricate, expansive and in many instances *fragile* narratives that television's monumental serials construct. Thus, while video abridgements are supremely ephemeral, they are by no means insubstantial. Quite the contrary, they erect around television's most elaborate (and delicate) narrative constructions a form of paratextual scaffolding, and by extension help television networks and viewers contend with the considerable financial and epistemological pressures that such serials exert upon them.

This essay explores the relationship between some of contemporary television's most ephemeral and monumental texts, and in the process reflects on the flexible business models and heterochronic multiplatform programming strategies adopted by these television networks during the 1990s and 2000s. As I have argued elsewhere, television's multiplatform programming strategies are overdetermined, having been shaped to varying degrees by technological determinants, workaday theories of medium specificity, unchallenged assumptions about the tastes and tolerances of multiplatform viewers, and the US television industry's own inherent aversions to change and risk (Dawson, 2007, 2011). To this inventory of influences this essay adds another factor: the monumental serial's emergence and subsequent flourishing in the 1990s and 2000s. Monumental serials earned television, its storytellers, and their network and studio patrons unprecedented levels of prestige, and in some instances significant profits as well. But on account of the unconventional storytelling techniques many of them employed, these programmes also exposed various sectors within the industry to heightened economic risks. Television networks have in many instances sought to manage these risks *textually*, employing a variety of supplemental texts to protect their growing economic and ideological investments in monumental seriality. Apart from enabling television networks to establish presences in emerging media markets, then, video abridgements also have factored as one of the means by which networks have attempted to solidify their positions within television's established, and yet increasingly unstable, audience marketplace.

Though my focus in the sections that follow is on texts and practices that have gained prominence only since the 1990s, this essay draws insights into the relationship between television's monumental serials and their video abridgements from historical studies of literary abridgements. Within literary contexts, the term 'abridgement' is used as a designation for a derivative text that 'shortens and simplifies' another text on the behalf of a population of readers who publishers presume would find the original difficult, offensive, boring or otherwise unpalatable (Hansen, 2010, p. 21; Leonard, 1958, p. 211). Perhaps the most well-known examples of literary abridgement (and a fitting point of reference for television's video abridgements) are *Reader's Digest*'s condensed books. Launched in the 1950s as a direct-mail venture, the Reader's Digest Condensed Book Club distributed four times a year a roughly 500-page volume containing abridged versions of at least two original works of fiction as well as a non-fiction title. These abridgements were immensely popular, so much so that for many years the club's editions routinely outsold the full, unabridged versions of the works that were their subjects (Volkersz, 1995). The series' success spawned numerous imitators, fostering a quite competitive mid-century market for abridged middlebrow literature.

Reviewing a number of critical discussions of the practice of abridgement, William G. Hansen proposes that literary abridgements are characterised by their 'intention to assist the reader' (Hansen, 2010, p. 23). Abridgers act on this intention by transforming their parent texts in accordance with their (or more likely a publisher's) suppositions about a specific population of readers' competencies, tastes, expectations or priorities. In the case of *Reader's Digest*'s condensed books, this population was comprised of aspiring readers – 'busy people, people who don't have time to do all the reading they would like to do' (or, in one less generous writer's account, readers who wished to be spared 'the pain of unnecessary reading') (Leonard, 1958, p. 211; Levy, 1968, p. 221). The *Reader's Digest*'s selections and editorial techniques (which condensed, clarified and expurgated source texts) were devised specifically to transform notable works of middlebrow fiction into versions that would be more appealing to members of this 'aspirational' population. At other moments in history, abridgers have targeted different populations, including children, remedial students, women, people overseas and working-class readers. Across all of these examples, abridgements remain *reader-focused* texts that manipulate their source materials in order to more efficiently satisfy desires their publishers ascribe to their intended audiences. Ultimately, however, the desires that abridgements most directly serve are those of the publishing industry. Abridgement reconfigures a book into a version tailored for members of a market segment that otherwise might not read it, and therefore expands the size of its potential audience. More than just an act of textual manipulation, then, abridgement is also a process by which the distributors of narrative media reach out to new audiences, and educate consumers about the appropriate ways to consume texts.

Appropriating this literary definition of 'abridgement' to describe Two- and Three-Minute Replays, Starter Kits and other web videos allows me to speak with greater precision about the common functions of an otherwise diverse category of television ephemera. Video abridgements may take many forms, ranging from two-minute condensations of single episodes to five-minute didactic summaries to nine-minute megamontages of entire series. What connects these videos is not the editorial strategies they employ. Rather, it is the pragmatism that they so self-consciously display as they go about 'assisting' members of the specific audience segments to which they are addressed (Hansen, 2010, p. 37). Video abridgements acknowledge, describe, comment upon and even parody (all in more or less explicit ways) their own status as *useful* texts expressly created to 'help' viewers efficiently satisfy their desires for pleasure, knowledge and cultural capital. They advertise their utility to viewers via their texts (particularly via the pacing of their montages), but even more so via their packaging – in other words, via the titles, captions, links, images and comments that surround them online.

Video abridgements are, like their literary counterparts, engineered to stimulate, channel and ultimately reconcile the desires of members of specific audience segments with the aspirations of the distributors of cultural goods. While television networks' economic aspirations would appear self-evident, a closer examination of these texts and the paths of their circulation reveals tensions inherent to the US television industry's flexible business models and heterochronic multiplatform programming strategies. Furthermore, the identities of these videos' audiences are by no means clear. Who are the intended viewers? How do they endeavour to assist these viewers? And of what nature are the desires that they promise to fulfil on these viewers' behalves? To address these questions, the sections that follow examine both the content and the packaging of a selection of video abridgements, considering both their texts and the broader political-economic, cultural and technological contexts in which these ephemeral videos are produced and consumed.

Serial television's synoptic paratexts

My designation of these videos as 'abridgements' is intended to align them with their literary counterparts, but also to distinguish them from the 'previously on …' recaps that precede television programmes with continuing storylines. Both abridgements and 'previously on …' recaps are, to appropriate the terminology of Gérard Genette (2001, p. 2), *paratexts*, or components of the 'threshold' of prefatory, derivative and supplemental texts through which viewers pass en route to their encounters with television programmes. Though Genette originally introduced the concept of paratextuality to describe the thresholds that surround literary texts – for instance, book jackets, prefaces, advertisements, reviews, etc. – recent work by film and television studies scholars has demonstrated its applicability to screen media (Gray, 2010; Kernan, 2004). As is the case with literary works, screen media are surrounded by dense accumulations of paratexts, which in the case of television programmes may include promos, opening credit sequences, websites and vast quantities of user-generated media.[3] Television's myriad paratexts open entryways into their parent programmes, fostering encounters between audiences and texts. As they do, they also prepare viewers for these encounters, providing them with both subtle and explicit cues about the 'correct way' to watch (Gray, 2010).

Video abridgements are in many respects similar to television's 'previously on …' recaps, so much so that networks, journalists and viewers often use the term 'recap' to identify examples of both of these categories. Video abridgements and 'previously on …' recaps employ a common repertoire of editorial techniques to shorten and simplify the narratives of their parent texts. Only, they do so in different contexts, and to different ends. 'Previously on …' recaps are 'inexorably bound to the episodes they precede' (Johnson, 2007). To borrow another of Genette's (2001, p. 5) terms, they are *peritexts*, or paratexts that are directly attached to texts. 'Previously on …' recaps are positioned immediately prior to specific television episodes in both space and time, and are created with the explicit understanding that they will be viewed immediately prior to these episodes. And so while the content of their montages is drawn exclusively from series' pasts, the summaries they provide are primarily intended to establish frameworks for interpreting future narrative developments (Gray, 2010, p. 72).

By contrast, video abridgements are *epitexts*, or paratexts that are detached from their texts (Genette, 2001, p. 3). Temporally speaking, video abridgements *succeed*, as opposed to *precede*, their parent texts, appearing online in the interim between programmes' weekly instalments, or during their hiatuses.[4] Video abridgements' separation in space and time from their parent texts exempts them from the durational limits placed on recaps, allowing them to provide longer, more comprehensive summaries of entire episodes, seasons or even series. Even more importantly, abridgements' autonomy exempts them from recaps' obligation of preparing viewers for the specific episodes that immediately follow them. Cleared of the onus of setting up imminent narrative developments, the abridgements that appear online may redirect their energies toward other tasks, including annotating and analysing series' pasts. They also may address broader audiences than recaps, including viewers with little or no background knowledge about the programmes that are their subjects.

Abridgements and 'previously on …' recaps both belong to a larger category of *synoptic paratexts* that summarise the narratives of television programmes, and which also includes written summaries, clip shows and various varieties of viewer-created videos. While the majority of these examples are web texts, the existence of synoptic paratexts predates the advent of the web – to give one example, soap opera plot summaries have appeared in print for nearly as long as serial melodramas have been a part of US networks' daytime schedules (Luckett, 2006). In the 2000s, industry programming trends and technological developments created an environment within which synoptic paratexts have proliferated and grown in importance for television networks and their audiences. Two factors in particular were instrumental in elevating the status of these paratexts. These were the marked increase in the number of hour-long serial dramas airing in primetime, and the emergence of the web as a viable video distribution platform.

Hour-long serial dramas have long been a part of US television networks' prime-time schedules, but historically have been far outnumbered by sitcoms, procedural dramas and other programmes whose narratives resolve themselves within thirty- or sixty-minute episodes.[5] Starting in the late 1990s, however, this gap began to narrow (Ryan, 2003, p. 1; Steinberg, 2006; Brass, 2005, pp. 1–2). Following the successes of such programmes as *The Sopranos*, *The O.C.* (2003–7), *24*, *Desperate Housewives* (2004–present) and *Lost*, in the 2000s US networks embarked on an unprecedented serial television binge, and by 2006, broadcast and cable networks were dedicating greater portions of their primetime schedules to serial dramas than ever before in the medium's history.

A handful of the serials that debuted in this period were certifiable hits. Others attracted smaller audiences composed of disproportionate numbers of coveted 'upscale' viewers. For example, in 2003 FOX's *24* finished forty-second overall in the year-end Nielsen ratings, but was the nation's top-rated programme among viewers with household incomes over $150,000 (Ross, 2003, p. 14). Serials were particularly valued by networks and their advertisers for their ability to attract members of desirable demographics. But even the most commercially successful of these serials proved risky investments for networks and studios. For starters, serials are considerably more expensive than episodic programming – in 2006, at the pinnacle of the serial television boom, an hour-long serial cost on average more than $3 million to produce, versus $2.3 million for an hour-long episodic drama (Benson, 2006). Serials also generate smaller revenues in domestic syndication. *Lost*, one of the few true hit serials to emerge from this period, earned only $500,000 per episode in the US syndication market, less than a quarter of the going rate for episodic dramas (Guthrie, 2010).

Serials' weekly ratings presented networks and studios with even more pressing dilemmas. Generally speaking, serials require viewers to tune in consistently, or else risk missing out on events or information that will be instrumental to their understanding and enjoyment of future episodes. This was true of the monumental serials that came into vogue in this period. These large-scale serials taxed viewers' memories and patience, and required them to commit substantial amounts of time and energy to tracking their storylines (Mittell, 2009). Compounding the demands their expanded storylines placed on viewers, a number of the serials introduced in this period featured high-concept storytelling gimmicks, or what Jason Mittell (2004, p. 35) calls 'narrative special effects'. Seasons of *24*, for instance, spanned twenty-four hour-long episodes, each corresponding to an hour in a day in the life of a counterterrorism agent. *Lost* employed flashbacks, flashforwards, time travel and parallel universes to allow its mysteries to unfold across multiple temporal axes. *Day Break* (2006), another ABC serial, concerned a detective condemned to endlessly repeat the same day of his life until he could solve the mystery of who had framed him for murder.

On account of the monumentality of their storylines and their (at times gratuitous) employment of narrative special effects, many of these serials earned reputations for being impenetrable and confusing. These reputations were not entirely unwarranted – the narratives of many of television's monumental serials were decidedly fragile constructions, easily upset by missing so little as a single episode. By skipping an episode of *Lost*, for instance, viewers risked missing out on developments in the relationships between the members of its large ensemble cast, the revelation of clues related to the programme's enigmatic mythology or storytelling gambits that could radically transform its narrative structure, as when at the end of its third season, the serial traded its signature flashbacks for flash*forwards*. First-time viewers faced even more daunting challenges when tuning in to a programme such as *Lost*. In an interview with *The New York Times*, one ABC executive conceded that inviting new viewers to join *Lost* during its third season was like ' "ask[ing] people to pick up Chapter 13 [of a book] and start reading" ' (Carter, 2008).

The literary analogy employed here is telling – by comparing *watching Lost* to the act of *reading* literature, the executive acknowledges the difficulty of picking up its plot *in media res*. But this analogy also implies an aesthetic parity between serial television and a far more respected narrative medium – the novel. 'Novelistic television' is a term of distinction frequently applied to television's monumental serials, many of which have drawn favourable comparisons with revered works of literature, including most notably Charles Dickens' serially published fiction (McGrath, 1995; Miller, 2007; Kois and Sternbergh, 2008; Lavery, 2009). But the very qualities that earned television's monumental serials critical approbation and comparisons with canonical literature also compromised their commercial viability. Many of the serials introduced in this period struggled to grow their audiences, and a number were cancelled during or immediately following their first seasons (rendering the issue of syndication revenues moot). Even the most successful of these programmes experienced significant declines in their viewership over the course of their runs. *Lost*, for instance, finished its first season ranked fifteenth in the year-end Nielsen ratings, but by its sixth and final season had lost nearly a third of its audience, slipping to thirty-first place (Gorman, 2010). In the end, *Lost*'s literary associations (and aspirations) were both an asset and a liability, especially in light of literary culture's tacit prohibitions against starting works of fiction anywhere other than on their first pages.

Confronted with the challenge of maintaining (let alone building) the audiences for their primetime serials, US television networks have made innovative uses of the expanding range of digital platforms available to them to shore up these programmes' fragile narrative constructions. In particular, networks have used digital platforms to distribute synoptic paratexts geared toward supplying lapsed viewers of serial dramas with efficient ways of catching up on episodes they have missed, and new viewers with opportunities to quickly familiarise themselves with serials' premises, histories and narrative special effects.[6] Network homepages have become repositories of synoptic paratexts, including essays, inter-

AMC's *Breaking Bad* website offers video abridgements and other synoptic paratexts for new or lapsed viewers interested in quickly catching up on past seasons

views, episode guides, clips from recent episodes, recycled 'previously on …' recaps and, from 2005 onward, video abridgements.

Exemplifying the lengths to which networks go to combat attrition and qualify their serials' reputations for impenetrable complexity is the *Breaking Bad* mini-site that AMC launched in late 2009 prior to the debut of the critically acclaimed, yet low-rated series' third season. 'New to the show?' asks a banner on the site's front page. 'Here's all you need to catch up.' Drilling down deeper into the site, visitors encounter character biographies, essays, an in-depth episode guide, five-minute recap videos, fan forums, a highlight reel showcasing the series' 'Ten Baddest Moments' and a 'Six-Minute Catch-Up' video that summarises the series' narrative through its first twenty episodes. Though the synoptic paratexts collected at this mini-site take on a variety of forms, their message remains consistent: specifically, they assure new and lapsed viewers that, contrary to what they might have heard, and contrary to the impression they might receive from watching an episode of the series, it is never too late to catch up on *Breaking Bad*'s first two seasons.

As US networks increased their commitments to monumental serials, they ramped up their production of video abridgements and other synoptic paratexts capable of functioning as 'narrative CliffsNotes' for uninitiated viewers of serial narratives (Kantor, 2005). These paratexts both underscore and qualify monumental serials' reputation for inscrutable complexity, and encourage uninitiated viewers to feel comfortable about joining serials' audiences in the middle of their runs. The question of whether or not these paratexts have been effective at overcoming audiences' apprehensions about monumental serials is beyond the scope of this essay. Suffice it to say that regardless of their efficacy, by 2007 video abridgements were an established component of the paratextual scaffolding that US television networks erected around their more narratively and economically precarious programmes.

Catching up and cutting to the chase

Having established video abridgements' economic utility for the networks that create and commission them, we may turn our attention to the functions they carry out on (and on the behalf of) their intended viewers. Demographic data about the viewers of specific online videos is a closely guarded industry secret, making it difficult to speak with certainty about who actually watches video abridgements. That said, we may deduce a great deal about these videos' intended addressees from the packaging that surrounds them and from the ways they manipulate their parent texts. Video abridgements (and all synoptic paratexts, for that matter) use various strategies to segment their audiences into two populations of viewers: those with a desire to repeat and remember the narratives of serial dramas, and those with a desire to fill gaps in their knowledge, so as to gain entry into a serial's diegesis and/or one of the interpretive communities that surround it.

The first of these audiences is comprised of regular viewers of the series being abridged, whom networks invite to use abridgements to re-watch (or, in FX's and NBC's terms, *replay*) episodes or seasons that they have already seen. In many instances, the packaging that surrounds video abridgements identifies them to regular viewers as *mnemonic* devices that facilitate pleasurable forms of repetition and remembering. For example, the caption accompanying an abridged version of the first season of the HBO series *Hung* (2009–present) on YouTube encourages viewers who have already seen the first season to 'Relive all the exciting moments of the last season before the new season premieres on Sunday, June 27 only on HBO'. But in addition to facilitating repetition and remembering, abridgements also inform regular viewers about how these activities should take place. Their content – specifically their inclusions and exclusions – supply knowledgeable viewers with fairly unambiguous instructions about the 'proper way' to relive serial television narratives.

Repetition has long factored prominently in the social rituals of television spectatorship in the US, thanks in no small part to the US television industry's habit of recycling previously aired programmes as reruns, in syndication and more recently on digital platforms (Kompare, 2005). Abridgements streamline and automate television's rituals of repetition by pre-selecting and compiling on viewers' behalves exemplary moments that, in their creators' estimation, are worth reliving (Dawson, 2011). The logic underlying video abridgements' selections and exclusions is not unlike that which informs the production of sports highlight reels. In both cases, editors isolate and compile spectacular moments. In the case of video abridgements, these 'highlights' are typically dominated by narrative climaxes – for instance, a shot of a character walking in on his wife and best friend on the verge of kissing, as appears in FX's Three-Minute Replay of the *Rescue Me* (2004–11) episode 'Breakout', or a tearful reunion between a runaway teenager and her mother, as is featured in an NBC Two-Minute Replay of the first season finale of *Parenthood* (2010–present). Narrative high-lights may also include moments of light comic relief, scenes that succinctly illustrate breakthrough character developments, or even standout performances. A Two-Minute Replay of the *Friday Night Lights* episode 'The Son' thus centres around two dramatic 'highlights', both of which showcase performances by actor Zach Gilford (portraying Matt Saracen, the episode's titular son). In the first of these highlights, Gilford's char-acter delivers an extended monologue on the eve of a memorial service for his estranged father. The video concludes with another lengthy sequence featuring an equally powerful, yet entirely wordless, performance by Gilford, in which Matt fights through tears as he angrily shovels dirt onto his father's grave.

Through their omissions and inclusions and the emphasis they place on certain arcs, characters or themes, abridgements like this one reinterpret their parent texts in response to a number of different pressures. For instance, Two-Minute Replays may be cut so as to showcase the performance of a character who has demon-strated promise of becoming a breakout star, or, alternatively, to minimise the sig-nificance of a narrative arc featuring a new character to whom viewers have responded negatively. Apart from designating an episode's, season's or series' most memorable highlights, then, abridgements can also identify, via their exclusions, those scenes or storylines which viewers may comfortably forget – or, put another way, scenes or storylines which producers might *wish* their regular viewers would forget. The use of abridgements as mnemonic devices is matched by their utility as tools for transforming or even suppressing viewers' memories, so as to bring view-ers' desires to repeat and remember into line with producers' or networks' preferred interpretations of programmes.

Though typically it is video abridgements' packaging that acknowledges the presence of regular viewers within their audiences, some abridgements embed within their syn-opses visual or verbal references that only committed viewers could possibly recognise. Such is the case with respect to '*Lost* in 8:15', an ABC promo that rapidly summarises *Lost*'s first three seasons. '*Lost* in 8:15' abounds in insider jokes and obscure allusions, including, for instance, a reference to the fact that one of the series' characters, whom the narrator refers to as 'Mr Friendly', 'throws like a girl'. 'Mr Friendly' is the nickname that *Lost*'s writers and members of its internet fan community used to identify a recur-ring supporting character before that character's name was revealed as 'Tom' during the show's second season finale.[7] The narrator's deadpan declaration that this character 'throws like a girl' adds a snarky commentary on top of a shot of Tom awkwardly toss-ing a football. It also alludes to the rampant online fan speculation that took place about Tom's sexual orientation after a throwaway line in which he assured a woman that it was fine for her to change clothes in front of him, as she wasn't his 'type'.

'*Lost* in 8:15' belongs to a subcategory of parodic abridgements that reserve special rewards for regular viewers who use them to remember and relive monumental
serials. Examples of this subcategory, which include 'Seven-Minute *Sopranos*', '*The
Wire*: Four Seasons in Four Minutes' and 'What the Frak Is Going on with *Battlestar
Gallactica*?', are characterised by their juxtaposition of frenetically edited synopses with
deadpan voiceover narration, and by their incorporation of arcane references comprehensible only to a programme's most committed viewers.[8] As Mittell has noted,
these videos 'affectionate[ly] parody' their parent texts – for instance, through the
repeated use of iconic shots as a kind of shorthand for recurrent story tropes (Mittell,
2009). They also flatter their parent texts' fans, addressing them as insiders in posses-
sion of exclusive knowledge about these programmes' narratives and production histories. Parodic recaps implicitly endorse a particular way of consuming television's
monumental serials, one predicated on the conscientious consumption of television
programmes and their paratexts, but also on participation in the internet fan communities that surround these programmes. In fact, '*Lost* in 8:15' is so densely packed with
references to unofficial character nicknames, message-board snark and wiki speculation as to be as much about the reception practices of *Lost*'s global fan community as
it is about *Lost* itself. And so while the video is only of marginal utility to uninitiated
viewers seeking a 'straight' synopsis of *Lost*'s first three seasons, it rewards the series'
most committed fans by offering them multiple opportunities to see themselves in
Lost's text.

For viewers who have missed one or more episodes of a television serial and wish
to catch up, video abridgements are not mnemonic devices, but rather function as
remedial texts that fill in defined gaps within their knowledge of programmes' pasts,
allowing them to enter (or, in the case of lapsed viewers, re-enter) serial television narratives. All abridgements make allowances of one form or another in the interest of
transforming non-viewers into viewers. Some, such as HBO's '*Hung*: Catch up on
Season One', weave expository dialogue from their pilots into and out of their synoptic montages to locate their parent texts within specific interpretive frameworks and
textual frames of reference. Others take a much more overtly didactic approach.
ABC's Starter Kits, for instance, explicitly pledge to satisfy new viewers' epistephilia.
Like reference books, Starter Kits are broken up into sections with headings that
include 'Three Things You Gotta Know', 'Starting Line-up' (an introduction of the principal cast members), 'Glossary', 'Starter Map' and 'Footnotes'. Networks promote
video abridgements to lapsed and prospective viewers by stressing their information
density and efficiency. Frequently, this entails highlighting the time viewers stand to
save by watching abridgements as opposed to entire episodes or seasons. ABC's
Starter Kits are prefaced by an opening segment in which a narrator tells viewers that
the videos will fill them in on 'everything you need to know' in order to be prepared

for programmes' season premieres 'in less than five minutes'. Along similar lines, AMC's 'Six-Minute Catch-Up' of *Breaking Bad* announces its function, and, equally notably, its duration, in its title, while NBC and FX promote their Two- and Three-Minute Replays through references to their short running times.

Abridgements such as these brandish their efficiency as a marker of their usefulness and appeal, encouraging audiences to make duration the basis of decisions about what – and how – to watch television (Chamberlain, 2007). As I have discussed elsewhere, web video's prevailing aesthetic through the 2000s has been an 'aesthetic of efficiency' that places the highest priority on expositive economy and information density (Dawson, 2011). Video abridgements translate television's monumental serials into forms compatible with this contemporary fetish for brevity in the interest of quickly bringing new or lapsed viewers up to speed, but also with the intent of appealing to those who are unable or unwilling to invest hours of their lives in tracking serials' narratives. A caption accompanying a 'Video Recap' of the second season of *Mad Men* (2007–present) on AMC's homepage, for instance, invites viewers who cannot or are unwilling to spare the hours required to watch all thirteen episodes in 'real time' to catch up instead with a four-minute abridgement featuring all of the season's highlights: 'Maybe you weren't able to spend thirteen hours watching the marathon on Monday. (Hey, we're not judging.) But surely you can spare four minutes to check out this recap of Season 2. You'll find all the major milestones from last season' (AMC, 2009). As this copy suggests, television networks may promote their abridgements to lapsed or prospective viewers as suitable substitutes for episodes or even entire seasons of serial dramas. In this example, AMC actually encourages viewers to feel no reservations about substituting this four-minute video for *Mad Men*'s thirteen-hour second season, assuring them that they will not be 'judged' for taking advantage of this shortcut to quickly catch up. In contrast to '*Lost* in 8:15', which salutes that series' most dedicated fans for committing hours upon hours of their lives to parsing its mysteries, AMC's *Mad Men* video commends non-viewers of the period drama for being too busy to watch it.

To take AMC up on its offer of substituting this abridgement for *Mad Men*'s second season would entail forgoing the temporal pleasures that the serial delivers to those willing to submit themselves to the patient pacing of its thirteen-episode seasons. *Mad Men* is a distinctively *uneventful* drama, renowned for its luxuriant visuals and elevation of theme and mood over plot. Within its storyworld, emotions are suppressed and action is deferred, until neither can be put off any longer. AMC's '*Mad Men* Season 2 Recap', by contrast, is purely proairetic. It isolates the series' highlights (referred to here as its 'major milestones') and arranges them alongside one another in a tightly edited montage that readily yields information about the season's primary narrative arcs, but that subordinates the series' temporal pleasures to the baldly utilitarian objective of rapidly supplying viewers with the knowledge they will require to catch up in time for *Mad Men*'s third season debut. In this edit, *Mad Men* is reduced to a sequence of confrontations, revelations and consummations, arranged so as to suggest a linear chain of narrative causality – in other words, *Mad Men* becomes exactly the sort of plot-heavy melodrama that Matthew Weiner, the series' creator, has sought to distinguish it from.

On the surface, the example of AMC's '*Mad Men* Season 2 Recap' would seem to suggest a conflict between the aesthetic aspirations of a recognised television auteur and the commercial aspirations of his network patron. After all, *Mad Men* has hardly been a ratings success; despite earning critical accolades and three consecutive Emmy awards for best dramatic series, through its first four seasons its weekly audience has rarely exceeded three million viewers. By highlighting its own brevity, by presenting itself as a suitable substitute for its parent text, and by fabricating eventfulness and causality, AMC's *Mad Men* abridgement makes efficiency a higher priority than maintaining fidelity to the vision of its creator. However, rather than undercutting *Mad Men*'s reputation as challenging and rewarding 'novelistic television', the video corroborates it. Much in the same way as the selection of a work of fiction for abridgement at the hands of the *Reader's Digest* editorial board singled out that particular title as a noteworthy book, the sheer existence of AMC's '*Mad Men* Season 2 Recap' nominates the series as a television programme worth knowing about, if not watching in its entirety.

As Hansen notes, 'All abridgements appeal, at one level or another, to the desire for "cultural capital", or the status that goes along with having read a respected work' (Hansen, 2010, p. 31). This is as true of abridgements of contemporary television serials as it is of canonical novels. In both literary and televisual contexts, abridgements traffic in *useful knowledge* about texts of some distinction. Specifically, they help members of their audiences rapidly acquire knowledge about texts that they may easily convert into cultural capital in any of the number of contexts where everyday talk about narrative media takes place – for instance, around water coolers, at dinner parties or in online forums. As television serials have ascended to a cultural strata previously occupied by novels, video abridgements have come to perform functions similar to those previously carried out by *Reader's Digest* and other literary abridgements – namely, to supply viewers with means of rapidly acquainting themselves with approved texts that are likely to be subjects of discussions among their friends or co-workers, or within the publications, websites or television programmes that they read or watch. Video abridgements offer aspiring viewers the means of entering into the narratives and diegeses of television's monumental serials. But they also tantalise viewers with the possibility of gaining instantaneous entry into the interpretive communities that often surround such programmes (Gray, 2010, p. 36). In this respect, video abridgements shape viewers' understandings of television's serial texts, but also of what it means to be a television viewer.

Conclusion

On account of their forthcomingness about their own utility, video abridgements reveal a great deal about the relationship between television's two extremes of scale, and also about the changing ways that US television networks have incorporated the web and other digital platforms into their multiplatform programming and promotional initiatives. When US television networks first ventured online in the mid-1990s, they did so cautiously, wary of upsetting time-honoured arrangements governing their industry's customary divisions of risks and profits. For much of the following decade, networks employed the web more as a promotional tool than as a viable narrative medium. Early web video content thus was dominated by network promos, many of which chided viewers to turn off their computers and turn on their television sets. As the 2000s progressed, however, networks became bolder in their use of web video, first developing original web series and commissioning web-only spin-offs of primetime series (Dawson, 2011). Networks also explored the use of web videos as a paratextual scaffolding for the increasingly elaborate, expansive and fragile narratives that populated their primetime line-ups. As the sections above have demonstrated, during the mid-2000s, networks came to rely on web videos to reinforce, redact, valorise and demystify serial narratives. Far from mere promos, these paratexts nourished and sustained the boom in monumental television serials that took place in the US between the late 1990s and 2010.

The year 2010 marks a fitting end point for this study, as it saw three of the standard-bearers of monumental seriality conclude their runs. A number of commentators have taken the conclusion of *Lost* and the cancellations of *24* and *Heroes* as an occasion to ponder whether television's (brief) era of monumental seriality had come to a close (Barker, 2010; Barnhart, 2010). But well before these programmes aired their final episodes, US networks had already begun taking measures to reduce the number of serials in their primetime line-ups, and to steer the showrunners of those serials that remained on the air toward producing more self-contained storylines (Guthrie, 2010). As early as October 2006, trade papers were reporting that US networks had 'overdosed' on a 'glut' of 'open-ended shows with season-long story arcs'. 'The current wisdom is that audiences simply don't have the wherewithal to commit their time and attention to so many new serialized shows', *Broadcasting & Cable* observed, 'no matter how well-crafted and engaging' (Benson, 2006). Following the disastrous performances and rapid cancellations of many of the expensive, high-profile serial dramas that debuted during the 2006–7 season, US networks beat a rapid retreat to more comfortable (and economically reliable) forms of episodic television.

What consequences these developments will hold for video abridgements and other web paratexts remains to be seen. Certainly, it is reasonable to suspect that an ebb in serial drama production will be accompanied by a commensurate decline in the production of video abridgements. Thus far, however, the opposite has occurred, and US television networks and studios have unleashed their abridgers on a more diverse array of programmes, including some highly unlikely candidates. In 2007, Sony partnered with News Corp. to launch the Minisode Network, a branded video channel on the social networking site MySpace.com dedicated to five-minute abridged versions of *Who's the Boss?* (1984–92), *T.J. Hooker* (1982–6), *Charlie's Angels* (1976–81) and other series from the Sony Pictures Television archive. To transform the archival surplus of Sony's television division into minisodes, editors strip programmes of establishing shots, transitions and subplots. A twenty-two-minute episode of the sitcom *Diff'rent Strokes* (1978–86), for instance, boils down to a five-minute minisode, leaving just enough time for a Honda commercial, a chorus of the show's catchy theme song, six compressed scenes and an obligatory recitation of star Gary Coleman's catchphrase, 'What you talkin' about, Willis?'

Though Sony's minisodes may appear to be cut so as to provoke the maximum amount of ridicule from MySpace's core base of snarky millennials, they perform far more complex operations on their sources. With only a few edits, Sony's editors transform passé programmes that long ago had exhausted their value in television's syndication marketplace into advertiser-supported video snacks that the studio and its partners market to members of the 'YouTube Generation' as a new form of ultra-efficient web text (Sherwin, 2007). Much like the ephemeral video abridgements discussed above, Sony's minisodes play a part in processes by which television networks and studios confer value – on programmes, on audience members and on particular ways of watching. These are both economic and aesthetic operations, involving transactions of financial and cultural capital. By examining these transactions, as I have in this essay, we stand to gain a more rich and detailed appreciation of the political and cultural economies of convergence television.

Notes

1. My use of the term 'scalable' to describe these texts is distinct from Lev Manovich's (2001) use of this same term to describe the variability of new media objects. For Manovich, scalability is an ontological distinction: new media objects are scalable because they are composed of digital code, and thus can be rendered at a multiplicity of different dimensions. By contrast, the forms of narrative scalability I discuss in this essay are an

outcome of reflexive industry practices – namely, the flexible programming strategies developed by US television networks and studios during the late 1990s and early 2000s.

2. For more on these programming trends, see Jenkins (2006), Lavery (2009), Mittell (2004), Sconce (2004).

3. As Jonathan Gray (2010), Henry Jenkins (2006) and others have convincingly argued, viewer-created paratexts represent a crucial component of television's paratextual surround. There are certainly examples of viewer-created paratexts whose reach and cultural impact have exceeded those of networks' official promos. That said, in the interest of maintaining focus on the ways that US television networks use abridgements to promote specific dispositions toward, and interpretations of, their primetime programming, the present study does not consider the forms and functions of these 'unofficial', viewer-created paratexts.

4. By my definition, video abridgements are more than simply recaps that have been unbundled from their source texts and placed online. They are paratexts that have been expressly created to stand alone as self-contained videos. This is not to suggest that recaps cannot stand alone, but only that they are not created for this purpose.

5. The historic dominance of episodic programming is a side effect of a regulatory system that prohibited networks from patronising studios owned by their parent companies, and an economic model in which networks licensed programming from studios for a fraction of production costs. These arrangements made American television studios dependent upon secondary markets, including domestic syndication, to recuperate the losses they incurred on production. This reliance on domestic syndication encouraged the production of open-ended programmes capable of surviving at least long enough to accumulate the eighty to one hundred episodes required for syndication. Furthermore, it compelled studios to produce programmes that would attract high prices on the syndication market. Serials earn their producers far less in syndication than programmes with self-contained storylines, with the result that for much of television's history studios have produced them only reluctantly, and at their own risks (Anderson, 2005, p. 83; Lotz, 2007, pp. 85–97; Mittell, 2009).

6. In addition to employing the web for these purposes, networks also created and commissioned synoptic paratexts that they aired on television. See Mittell (2009) for more on these paratexts.

7. See Lostpedia (n.d.) for more on the speculation over this character's name and identity.

8. 'Seven-Minute *Sopranos*' supplied the template that these other parodic abridgements followed. The video was created and uploaded to YouTube.com in 2007 by two fans of *The Sopranos*, one of whom happened to be employed by a subsidiary of HBO. While representatives of the network maintained that the video was not an 'official' promo for the series, they and David Chase, *The Sopranos*' creator, publicly endorsed it in interviews with the press (Heffernan, 2007).

Bibliography

AMC. (2009) 'Got 4 Minutes to Spare? Check Out This Video Recap of Season 2',
    <http://blogs.amctv.com/mad-men/2009/08/video-season-2-recap.php> accessed 27 July
    2010.

——. (2010) 'New to the Show', <www.amctv.com/originals/breakingbad/newtoshow/>
    accessed 27 July 2010.

Anderson, Christopher. (2005) 'Television Networks and the Uses of Drama', in Gary R.
    Edgerton and Brian G. Rose (eds), *Thinking Outside the Box: A Contemporary Television
    Genre Reader* (Lexington: University of Kentucky Press), pp. 65–90.

Barker, Cory. (2010) 'The Dead-End Serial Discussion: It's Not Happening',
    <http://tvpasttheaughts.blogspot.com/2010/02/dead-end-dead-serial-discussion-its-
    not.html> accessed 11 August 2010.

Barnhart, Aaron. (2010) 'Ratings Are the TV Serial Killers', <www.kansascity.com/
    2010/02/13/1742461/barnhart-ratings-are-the-tv-serials.html> accessed 19 March 2010.

Benson, Jim. (2006) 'Networks OD on Serial Dramas', <www.broadcastingcable.com/article/
    91642-Networks_OD_on_Serial_Dramas.php> accessed 17 August 2010.

Brass, Kevin. (2005) 'DVDs Surge as Back-End TV Market', *TelevisionWeek*, 31 October, pp. 1–2.

Carter, Bill. (2008) 'Tropical Teaser: "Lost" Clues Decoded', <www.nytimes.com/2008/
    01/30/arts/television/30lost.html> accessed 22 February 2008.

Chamberlain, Daniel. (2007) 'Watching Time on Television', <http://flowtv.org/?p=615>
    accessed 19 August 2010.

Dawson, Max. (2007) 'Little Players, Big Shows: Format, Narration, and Style on Television's
    New Smaller Screens', *Convergence*, 13 (3), pp. 231–50.

——. (2011) 'Television's Aesthetic of Efficiency: Convergence Television and the Digital Short',
    in James Bennett and Niki Strange (eds), *Television as Digital Media* (Durham, NC: Duke
    University Press), pp. 204–29.

Genette, Gérard. (2001) *Paratexts: Thresholds of Interpretation* (New York: Cambridge
    University Press).

Gorman, Bill. (2010) 'Final 2009–10 Broadcast Primetime Show Average Viewership',
    <http://tvbythenumbers.com/2010/06/16/final-2009-10-broadcast-primetime-show-
    average-viewership/54336> accessed 3 July 2010.

Gray, Jonathan. (2010) *Show Sold Separately: Promos, Spoilers, and Other Media Paratexts*
    (New York: New York University Press).

Guthrie, Melissa. (2010) 'An Entire Genre May Be *Lost*', <www.broadcastingcable.com/article/
    446730-An_Entire_Genre_May_Be_Lost_.php?rssid=20065> accessed 1 August 2010.

Hansen, William H. (2010) ' "So Far as What There May Be of a Narrative": Abridgement and
    Moby Dick', *Leviathan*, 12 (2), pp. 21–40.

Heffernan, Virginia. (2007) 'Gotta Minute? So, There's This Guy Tony …'
    <www.nytimes.com/2007/04/06/arts/television/06sopr.html> accessed 11 August 2010.

Jenkins, Henry. (2006) *Convergence Culture: Where Old and New Media Collide* (New York: New York University Press).

Johnson, Derek. (2007) 'The Essential Recap: Memory, Amnesia, and Anticipation in Serial Television', <http://mediacommons.futureofthebook.org/imr/2007/09/20/the-essential-recap-memory-amnesia-and-anticipation-in-serial-television> accessed 13 March 2009.

Kantor, Jodi. (2005) 'The Extra-Large, Ultra-Small Medium', <http://www.nytimes.com/2005/10/30/arts/television/30kant.html> accessed 13 March 2009.

Kernan, Lisa. (2004) *Coming Attractions: Reading American Movie Trailers* (Austin: University of Texas Press).

Kois, Dan and Adam Sternbergh. (2008) 'Debating the Legacy of *The Wire*: Did Season Five Tarnish the Show That Invented the Dickensian Aspect Ratio?', <http://nymag.com/daily/entertainment/2008/03/debating_the_end_of_the_wire_t.html> accessed 13 July 2010.

Kompare, Derek. (2005) *Rerun Nation: How Repeats Invented American Television* (New York: Routledge).

Lavery, David. (2009) '*Lost* and Long-Term Television Narrative', in Pat Harrigan and Noah Wardrip-Fruin (eds), *Third Person: Authoring and Exploring Vast Narratives* (Cambridge, MA: MIT Press), pp. 313–22.

Leonard, Frank G. (1958) 'Cozzens without Sex, Steinbeck without Sin', *The Antioch Review*, 18 (2), pp. 209–18.

Levy, Alan. (1968) *The Culture Vultures* (New York: G. P. Putnam's Sons).

Lotz, Amanda. (2007) *The Television Will Be Revolutionized* (New York: New York University Press).

Luckett, Moya. (2006) 'Recap Nation', <http://flowtv.org/2006/08/recap-nation-repetition-and-the-tv-program-as-commodity> accessed 19 October 2010.

McGrath, C. (1995) 'The Triumph of the Prime-Time Novel', <www.nytimes.com/1995/10/22/magazine/the-prime-time-novel-the-triumph-of-the-prime-time-novel.html> accessed 1 March 2003.

Manovich, Lev. (2001) *The Language of New Media* (Cambridge, MA: MIT Press).

Miller, Laura. (2007) 'The Best TV Show of All Time', <www.salon.com/entertainment/tv/feature/2007/09/15/best_show> accessed 19 July 2010.

Mittell, Jason. (2006) 'Narrative Complexity in Contemporary American Television', *The Velvet Light Trap*, 58, Fall, pp. 29–40.

——. (2009) 'Previously On: Primetime Serials and the Mechanics of Memory'. <http://justtv.wordpress.com/2009/07/03/previously-on-prime-time-serials-and-the-mechanics-of-memory> accessed 12 August 2009.

Ross, Chuck. (2003) 'Targeting Affluent Viewers: Special Study of High-Income Households Produces Some Surprises', *Television Week*, 7 April, p. 14.

Ryan, L. (2003) 'Networks, Studios Reintroduce Serials to Development Diet', *Television Week*, 1 December, p. 1.

Sconce, Jeffrey. (2004) 'What If? Charting Television's New Textual Boundaries', in L. Spigel and
     J. Olsson (eds), *Television after TV: Essays on a Medium in Transition* (Durham, NC: Duke
     University Press), pp. 93–112.

Sherwin, Adam. (2007) 'It's TV for the YouTube Generation: Get the Mission, Fight, Chase,
     Fall in Love, Catch the Baddie – The End', <http://technology.timesonline.co.uk/tol/news/
     tech_and_web/the_web/article1750004.ece> accessed 7 September 2009.

Steinberg, Jacques. (2006) 'Digital Media Brings Profits (and Tensions) to TV Studios',
     <www.nytimes.com/2006/05/14/business/yourmoney/14studio.html> accessed
     22 February 2007.

Volkersz, Evert. (1995) 'McBook: The Reader's Digest Condensed Book Franchise', *Publishing
     Research Quarterly*, 11 (2), pp. 52–62.

PART2 BETWEEN: INTERSTITIALS AND IDENTS

3 Interstitials: How the 'Bits in Between' Define the Programmes

John Ellis

At the end of 1994, I was producing a series of ten-minute dramas for BBC Two, *French Cooking in Ten Minutes*,[1] based on the classic cookery book by Edouard de Pomiane. On the first day of shooting, our BBC executive producer communicated the latest management edict: all programmes were to be reduced in length by one minute to allow for more promotional material. This, apparently, was to be applied no matter what the commissioned length of a programme, even a ten-minute one that specified its duration in its title. In retrospect, this was the moment when the BBC, a public service broadcaster, decided to participate in a decisive shift that was taking place in the nature of commercial broadcast TV. Interstitials were becoming more important, literally eating into programmes. The most extreme development of this trend is the erosion of slot length on the US commercial networks. A programme made for an hour slot now lasts less than three-quarters of an hour. The FOX series *House* (2004–present) ran for forty-four minutes in 2010. This makes for some odd effects when such programmes are shown on a BBC channel with no advert breaks, or indeed watched on DVD or online. The series *24* (2001–10) relies on the fiction that it unrolls in real time, yet, made for a channel with breaks, it runs between forty-three and forty-four minutes when watched on DVD. Perhaps it should have been retitled *18* for the DVD release. Even when shown on commercial channels outside the US, *24* usually fails to maintain its equivalence of broadcast time with dramatic time, since if it starts on the hour, it will finish two or three minutes before, leading into an advertising break. In the US, most network break patterns are now radically different to the practice in many other markets. The changeover moment at the top of the hour is too important for the broadcaster. To maintain viewer attention, the end of one show and the beginning of the next run up against each other. In other markets, the break at the top of the hour is still maintained.

These abbreviations of programming are not simply the result of erosion by commercials: interstitials take many forms. So what are interstitials, and why are they

important, not only to the commercial health of broadcasters but also to our experience of TV? Few dedicated studies exist on the topic, the most cogent being Catherine
Johnson's (2011) study of television branding practice (see, in particular, Chapter 5).
Interstitials are anything from broadcaster identifications (idents) to spot adverts, programme trailers, announcements, sponsorship 'bumpers', theme-night packaging: anything, in fact, that cannot be classified as a 'programme'.[2] An unreflecting view sees
them as an annoyance or an interruption, to be avoided especially if they have been
seen before. I argue that interstitials have a key role for current viewers. They show
how television regards itself (its brands); how it wants its programmes to be read (the
trailers); and how good it could be if only it had budget and time (the commercials as
aspirational production values). Interstitials, in short, are a series of distillations of television, and an internal metacommentary on ordinary TV. In a world of multiple media
opportunities, interstitials are little instruction manuals on how to read TV. In the
future, then, interstitials will be the material which enables future generations to
understand archival programmes as historical evidence. In the present moment, trailers and idents attract viewers; in the future, they will be the means of decoding the
programmes of the past.

What is an interstitial?

The growth of interstitials cannot be attributed simply to growth in airtime sold for
commercials, as the BBC example shows.[3] Spot advertisements and sponsor 'messages' are an established feature of most broadcasting markets, forming the largest
single blocks of interstitials. Some channels intersperse spot commercials with their
idents, a practice that, in the UK, goes back to the beginnings of commercial broadcasting in 1955 with an ident called 'sunburst' created by one of the first ITV companies to go on air, Associated Rediffusion. Spot commercials are free-standing and are
usually edited together in no particular order. Some advertisers jostle for attention by
buying particular positions in an ad-break; by inserting hyper-short reminders of their
main ad; and even by buying out the whole break and making a special short film to
fill it. The sponsor message is a relatively recent development in the UK but was present from the outset in the US. It frequently takes the form of 'bumpers' into and out
of the sponsored show, and so is often made as a linked series of fifteen-second
cameos that can develop a narrative progression of their own. For example, the sponsors of feature films on Film4 in the UK in 2010 developed a series of bumpers which
tell the story of Little Red Riding Hood.

Increasing competition between broadcast channels has prompted the growth of
other forms of interstitials: trails, announcements, promos and channel idents.

Early broadcasting, with its frequent technical problems, used a live studio announcer to ease viewers through the flow (and the hold-ups) of an evening's broadcasting, and these presenters often became major celebrities, the public faces of the otherwise faceless broadcaster. Live presenters can still be found, mainly stitching together programme 'zones' for the young (for example, children's broadcasting or such as Channel 4's T4 aimed at sixteen- to thirty-four-year-olds) or for high-profile special themed evenings. Mainly, however, their role has been relegated to that of voiceover announcements,[4] and their on-screen space has been taken up by promotional material of various kinds. Channels promote their upcoming programmes with trails (which reveal some of the content) and teasers (which do not). Channels promote themselves by showcasing their 'best' material – their most spectacular and familiar images in montages of plenty with feel-good music. Channel idents have developed into sophisticated, brief and often enigmatic commercials which somehow incarnate the channel's brand. Catherine Johnson (2011) points out the market-specific nature of these developments, with channel idents being far more important in the UK than the US.

Spot commercials and the various kinds of trails, announcements, promos and idents form the two major categories of interstitial material in television's 'between' space. A third category of interstitials are not strictly interstitial at all. These are the materials which invade programmes, and the elements *within* programmes that might be better considered as interstitials. Title sequences have all the hallmarks of interstitials. They are short, synoptic, often repeated and high budget. Programme credits also have some of the same hallmarks. There is a difficult borderline between the interstitial and the textual if the textual is understood as 'the programme'. Title and credit sequences gesture towards the fact that the individual programme has to be considered as part of a larger series whole, telling the viewer that the individual programme is not a totally self-contained identity, and has no particular finality to its meaning (see Gray, 2010, Chapter 2). However, the title sequence itself, along with the theme tune, is a disappearing entity except on premium channels in the US market, at least.[5] The title sequence is becoming the audiovisual equivalent of hardback binding on a book, denoting quality, seriousness of intent and the buyer's willingness to pay more. In the US, the new top-of-the-hour rush into the next programme has virtually extinguished the title sequence. The first stage of this process was the creation of pre-credit sequences, which gave a quick synopsis of previous episodes ('previously on …'), a creation of the multichannel environment in US broadcasting at the start of the 1980s. These were a new form of interstitial at the time: something that was part of the programme but also not part of the programme, a kind of metadata, bringing previous episodes back from the past into fleeting recall. Often they reach back several episodes or even into previous series. To reasonably regular viewers, they prefigure the week's plot developments and featured characters. For new viewers, they provide an initial orientation. Until recently in the US, and still elsewhere, these pre-credit montages lead into a title sequence, displaying the main selling points of the show (the stars and their names) and setting a tone. The title sequences of the 1980s series *Dallas* (1978–91) and *Dynasty* (1981–9) are canonical: both associate their stars with the *mise en scène* which is most closely identified with their roles.

Recently, the title sequence has begun to disappear, replaced with a simple sting. This has reached its apogee on US network television, where commercial breaks within the shows are crucial in providing structure to fictional series (apart from those on commercial-free premium channels like HBO and Showtime). A series like *Desperate Housewives* (2004–present) had a complex title sequence for its first few seasons starting in 2004. By 2009, this had become a single title sting, often some ten minutes into the programme, where it would be the lead back into the show from the first major break. Instead of a title sequence, extensive credits are superimposed over the opening scenes of the programme, detailing cast and major production personnel. The drama gains an extra minute or even more by this elimination; the show loses the important identifier of Danny Elfman's music and the cultural marker of the title sequence's animated transformations of old master paintings.

Something is happening in the textual borderlands: interstitials are increasingly 'invading' programmes themselves, through the erosion of clearly delineated title sequences and on-screen credit elements. The class of interstitials that was once 'internal' to programmes has changed in form, sharing their screen with added visual layers, stings and trails, and their aural space with announcements. Linear broadcast television requires that any metadata (e.g. details of cast, crew and copyright) is displayed as data within the programme. Displayed at the end of a programme, this metadata creates a problem for broadcasting organisations which would prefer to push the broadcast flow onwards, hoping to continue to engage the viewer of the broadcast stream so they do not switch channels. So when end credits roll, many broadcasters insert their own trailers or voiceover announcements. Channel 4's instructions to its suppliers specify exactly the format: 'Channel 4 will cover the right-hand side of the screen with an information panel' and 'Background audio will be dipped live on transmission' (note that title music has been demoted to 'background audio' here) (Channel 4, 2009). The maximum length of any credits is twenty-five seconds for an hour slot. End credits are a problem, because they refer to the past rather than the future, even if it is the very immediate past of the show just watched. Broadcast professionals and production companies insist on credits, as they advertise their roles. There is a history of tension between broadcasters, their suppliers and their creative teams over the erosion of end credits. In the UK, both PACT (representing production companies) and the Royal Television Society (representing professionals) have made complaints about the illegibility of end credits in the current broadcast regime of the UK.

Interstitials can therefore be found within programmes as well as around them. They constitute a class of television output rather than a genre. They consist of messages or declarations addressed to the viewer from outside the diegetic worlds of fiction or the discourses of news, documentary and factuality. They consist of metadata about both the programme of the moment and the future plans of the broadcaster. They bring together the past and future of broadcasting within its present moment. In addition to this metadata function, other forms of interstitial come from agencies beyond the world of broadcasting who are given conditional access to broadcasting: the advertisers, the sponsors and the government in the form of its public service announcements. This is a whole class of television output: heterogeneous, but occupying a distinct position in relation to the other class of television that comprises programmes of whatever genre. Sometimes interstitials overlap with or invade programmes. They make up a class that we have to learn to distinguish. One of the problems of arriving in a new television culture is learning how the interstitials work – what they are trying to tell you; how they interlace with the programmes; how they shape the spaces that the programmes occupy; and how they build anticipation and delay into the development of those programmes. It can take an appreciable amount of time to become a skilled viewer as a result.

Interstitials as a class of television output

The interstitial class is characterised above all by its ability to avoid the meaningful association between any of its units. We expect, desire and construct meaningful associations between the different scenes of fictional and factual programmes and even news broadcasts. Fiction depends on this practice for its emotional effect; factual material for its power to explain and to involve. But when it comes to the breaks, we abandon any such practice of viewing. One thirty-second commercial follows another with no interplay between them: commercials, in turn, for automobiles, accident cover, medical treatment and legal services can follow each other without generating a narrative or any effects of irony. No meanings are generated from accidental collisions in a sequence of interstitials, even of the same kind. Although each interstitial will use montage, often of an advanced kind, there seems to be no possibility of generating any montage effect between them, despite their brevity. As viewers, we hold interstitials apart from each other, aware of their separation, ignoring their potential to generate more meanings. We recognise them as objects whose existence is bound up with repetition not combination. We expect to see them again, but in a different order, and their repetition is tolerated far more than the repetition of television programmes.

Interstitials stand out from programmes because they are designed for multiple repetition in the same broadcast space. Programmes can be given multiple broadcasts in different channels; interstitials are designed for multiple repetition in the same channel space and in close temporal proximity to each other. They stand out from the flow of ordinary television for that reason. Commercials, in particular, also exhibit a textual density that would be impossible to achieve in the linear narratives of programmes. Designed to be seen again and again, they are able to yield their meanings slowly. Some can seem obscure on first viewing, requiring knowledge of how they end before their beginnings become even comprehensible. Some use a subtle and sly humour which 'grows on you', or can be appreciated after a while for the sheer panache of its delivery. This is a key aspect of the commercial whose repetition is intrinsic to its appeal; the details of its execution can be relished on repeated viewing (which also helps them to 'go viral' on YouTube).[6] Commercials for big ticket items like cars become exhibitions of visual pleasure which, perhaps, is meant to invoke driving pleasure. Much use is made of complex or evocative music, which seems to bear more repetition than visual material.

Commercials are allusive, synoptic and dense. They are often excessive in relation to norms set by programmes, norms both of production values and ability to generate meaning. Commercials for national and international brands incarnate the production values to which programmes merely aspire. They have been a feature of broadcasting since its early years, and seem to have functioned within the system as one of the drivers towards increased production values and visual complexity (Caldwell, 1995; Lury, 2005). Through the history of television, commercials have functioned just as much to sell lifestyles as any particular product. They educated their viewers in consumption, redefining needs in terms of products and desires in terms of consumption activities (for a classic exploration of this aspect of TV, see Spigel, 1992). In one sense, both the programmes and adverts of television in the era of scarcity were exploring ways of living with consumption. As many critics have noted, the history of TV advertising can be seen as the progressive development and refinement of desire, introducing ever greater levels of product differentiation (see Butler, 2007, pp. 388–444; Dunnett, 1990; Silverstone, 1994, p. 104). Early commercials strike the modern viewer as strange not only because of their modest production values but because the products advertised are so basic: generic soaps rather than the myriad of cleaning products we have today. Without television commercials, it is doubtful that we would have reached the stage where a different cleaner is required for each domestic eventuality, even if they are made from the same small range of ingredients plus perfumes.

This huge work of differentiation of product and desire for products implies two aspects of textual work. The first is an activity of explanation ('this is what this product can do') and the second is an activity of aestheticisation. Commercials, and indeed interstitials more generally, are deeply concerned with the generation of a sense of beauty. This is the reason why they stand out from the TV that surrounds them, and why they have greater production values. It also enables viewers to watch and enjoy the most stylish commercials even when they have no intention of buying the products. Interstitials often identify beauty in the mundane, from the impossible perfection of their domestic interiors to the sheen on the product label. Their repeatability depends on the attainment of a few seconds of textual perfection ('not a hair out of place'). Any faltering, and bloopers, will become glaringly obvious to even the most distracted viewer after a few exposures. So the vast majority of interstitials, channel idents and trailers, as well as commercials, have more resources per minute poured into their creation than the surrounding programmes. They can be said to set aspirational standards for programmes, in terms of the elegance and perfection of their images. Quality drama programming will seek to emulate the 'look' of advertising, but will often set a different, more contemplative, pace to its action in order to differentiate itself. The graphic visual language of idents similarly sets the standard for the graphics packages adopted by gameshows, variety and talk shows. Many interstitials are more spectacular in their displays of graphical virtuosity. Channel idents are often produced in sets around a theme, and their use on any one night will be varied to give a sense of difference with an overall unity. BBC One uses a series of spectacular circles produced from movements of people and animals; Channel 4 'discovers' its iconic 4 logo in the momentary assemblages of objects within a moving view (Fanthome, 2007). Bravo in the US has adopted an explicit ident system which selects keywords from a mini-lexicon to define the particular experiences on offer. In their search for beauty, interstitials often present a vision of television as it could be … if only it were even more costly than it already is.

Interstitials in themselves are synoptic, allusive, spectacular. Grouped together they do not generate any sense of sequence; they are merely a succession of different items. Yet groups of interstitials have an important structuring function. They provide the patterns of anticipation and fulfilment to the experience of watching TV. This is why their increased presence on most channels has brought about the atrophying of the title sequence. In fact, the placing of commercials has long since impacted on the construction of TV shows of all kinds. They provide the opportunity for in-episode cliffhangers and powerfully mark the passing of time within fictions, as *24* made explicit. Non-fiction formats have developed their own in-programme interstitial announcements: 'after the break', 'coming up', 'in a moment', 'next time'. The airwaves and cables are thick with promises of more to come, pacing the pleasures of entertainment and stimulating the curiosity of the factual. These lead-ins to commercial breaks are increasingly complemented by lead-ins to the programmes in some formats, especially now that the breaks consist not only of adverts but also of trailers for future programmes. It is often necessary to 'welcome back' viewers to the programme, to emphasise that the present moment of the broadcast stream has returned. The groups of interstitials within programme breaks tend to project the viewer into the future: the future of consumption both of advertised products and of television shows themselves. Time perspectives expand in the breaks, furthering the anticipation that is already implicit in the narrative of the programme. Often this involves an explicit pre-diction of what will happen 'after the break', especially in interview or talk-show for-mats where the presenter turns to camera to make such a prediction of upcoming content. The future-facing nature of the interstitials has the important effect of inten-sifying the present-moment currency of the programme. By contrast, the interstitials demonstrate that the programme itself belongs to the present moment. The pro-gramme is now and is current; the interstitials, by contrast, address a hypothetical future. Groups of interstitials have two important functions in relation to programmes: they provide a structure which allows for a viewing experience of anticipation and ful-filment, and they also frame the currency of the programme as the imagined 'live' presence of broadcasting.

Trails and other user guides

If one division of the interstitial class (the adverts) has historically specified how to act as a consumer, then another division (trailers and idents) is now specifying how to act as a consumer of television. Trailers pick out key moments from programmes, and in doing so they define a number of vectors of significance. They will identify who the leading stars or faces are, including any special appearances. They may inscribe indica-tors of the programme's generic status and the important or novel aspects of its format. So in their attempt to parade the most marketable aspects of the programme, they pro-vide condensed definitions of the market. Anything from the career status of a star to the state of a genre like reality TV can be judged from a study of trailers. They will also summarise programmes, pointing to the crucial plot developments that are currently taking place in a series, or giving highly explicit summaries of the state of play in series like *Britain's Got Talent* (2007–present) and *Strictly Come Dancing* (2004–present) ('will X survive this week?'). Finally, the trailers pitch the mood of their programme to poten-tial audiences. They excite emotions that often remain unrequited, provoking anger, fear or righteous indignation, and then direct the viewer to the programme for the development and fulfilment of these emotions. They stimulate curiosity, emphasising the enigmatic or mysterious qualities of both factual and fictional programming. Because they are interstitials, they also tend to emphasise the spectacular, high-budget aspects of any given series. In television markets that perceive themselves as crowded or highly competitive, trails are important in attracting attention to a series, and to making certain that it is placed before its key demographic segments. Trails also 'leak out' to (or, more likely, are deliberately placed on) sites like YouTube and more specialist venues, taking television's values and definitions beyond its own confines.

Trails distil programmes into their most appealing essentials, defined by the tastes of the market into which they are pitched. So they act as definers as well as marketing devices. Indeed, many channels now self-promote, offering super-trailers which define the whole channel experience, or promote the new season's most important attractions. ITV1 has experimented with a cross between the channel ident and the trailer, using their key contract stars to lend their faces and bodies to attempt to define what is specific about the channel. Despite their growing importance within the system, trailers have an ephemeral life within the TV industry, even more so than commercials. It is extremely difficult to get hold of old trails for shows, whereas there is now a thriving quasi-commercial circulation of commercials and idents. Yet trailers as definers of the specific experiences offered by television have a growing value. Their value is not purely historical: as television finds a new place among the growing range of moving image and sound media, it may well lose its taken-for-granted status. This status means that, currently, television's genres, its ways of structuring series and the nature of its viewing experiences are known by virtually everyone. Television has evolved, but it is still television. We still watch television on TV screens: bigger, flatter, with colour and superior sound reproduction, yes, but still TV screens. We have more channels, but we still have channels. We still watch TV predominantly in our everyday living spaces for entertainment and information. We still multitask while doing so. But this line of development is now being disrupted. Current advances offer us not so much better TV as different TV. In the future, potential viewers will increasingly need induction into the rules of genres like the sitcom, the nature of open-ended multistranded narratives, and even the specific ways of watching that attach to them.

New means of access, particularly the internet, are also providing access to archival TV. These new means of delivery, as well as historical distance, will increase the problems in understanding and appreciating television material. In future, it will be necessary to define not only what something meant, but how it was watched. Trailers can do this: where researchers are able to get access to historic trailers (through DVD extras in some cases), then their interpretive function can be important. Television material is beginning to present researchers with substantial problems of interpretation, and not only for students of TV. Increasing availability will mean that new users will appear who want to use archival TV material for purposes ranging from historical illustration to data-mining. They will have to understand the status of what they are dealing with, the purpose for which it was made. Old television is losing the transparency that it once had for its original viewers and anyone who had an 'insider's' intimate knowledge of its time. After almost seventy years of history, rising generations have little immediate empathy with much of the television material from the early period. Genres have mutated beyond recognition, or have almost disappeared from the canon. References to contemporary events, personalities and mores are now obscure. The pace is 'off'; the visual regimes seem simplistic; the conversation appears stilted and the accents are quaint. Patient contextualisation is often needed to develop a real enjoyment and understanding of these programmes. Trailers both condense and define programmes, providing both a snapshot of how they were regarded at the time, and a summary of their main features as texts. They are a metalanguage every bit as powerful as the written cataloguing data that accompanies archival TV material. And they can be more powerfully evocative.

Interstitials comprise a quarter of every hour of US network TV, 15 per cent of the hour on UK commercial channels. They constitute a class of television output which is treated differently to other classes of output. Groups of interstitials provide the pace and structure to broadcast TV, regulating its timings and providing a speculative, future-oriented time-out from the present moment of the programmes. They are regarded as more ephemeral than programmes, yet have substantially more production finance invested in them per minute of screen time. Their importance in everyday TV is increasing; their importance to scholarship has hardly begun to be acknowledged.

Notes

1. BBC Two, April–May 1995 (dir. David Giles, sc. Nick Cooper), 6 x 9 minutes,
    <http://www.youtube.com/watch?v=lzjyfqPe7ZE>.

2. Channel 4's delivery requirements for independent producers list sixteen different types
    that producers might supply as forms of presentation for its channels alone. The final
    category is 'Any other taped presentation TX material, which does not constitute a
    programme or commercial' (Channel 4, 2010).

3. When broadcasting in the UK, the BBC shows no commercials, as it is financed from a
    licence fee. BBC World and similar non-UK services designed for international markets do
    carry commercials.

4. This seemed a revolutionary gesture in 1982 when Channel 4 decided to launch with no
    on-screen announcers, just voices.

5. David Simon's *Treme* (2010–present) and Mark Olsen and Will Scheffer's *Big Love*
    (2006–11) on HBO have elaborate title sequences. AMC's *Mad Men* (2007–present) has a
    title sequence that evokes the movie credits of Saul Bass. Some cinema films have also
    dispensed with title sequences, but the tendency is not universal.

6. Honda's 'Cog' commercial made for the UK market is an example. By the beginning of
   2011, it had been viewed 1,311,127 times on YouTube, and has its own very detailed
   Wikipedia entry. The editorial discussion about this article includes interesting musings
   about the correct way to designate the title, through italics (implying that it is a short film)
   or with inverted commas (implying that it belongs to another class of audiovisual text).

Bibliography

Butler, Jeremy G. (2007) *Television, Critical Methods and Applications* (New York: Laurence
   Erlbaum), pp. 388–444.

Caldwell, John T. (1995) *Televisuality: Style, Crisis and Authority in American Television* (New
   Brunswick, NJ: Rutgers University Press).

Channel 4. (2009) 'End Credits Information Sheet Version', 23 March,
   <http://www.channel4.com/corporate/4producers/resources/resources-guidelines.html>
   accessed 22 October 2010.

——. (2010) 'Channel 4 Interstitials Specification', <http://www.channel4.com/corporate/
   4producers/resources/resources-guidelines.html> accessed 22 October 2010.

Dunnett, Peter J. S. (1990) *The World Television Industry: An Economic Analysis* (London:
   Routledge).

Fanthome, Christine. (2007) 'Creating an Iconic Brand: An Account of the History,
   Development, Context and Significance of Channel 4's Idents', *Journal of Media Practice*,
   8 (3), pp. 255–71.

Gray, Jonathan. (2010) *Show Sold Separately: Promos, Spoilers, and Other Media Paratexts*
   (New York: New York University Press).

Johnson, Catherine. (2011) *Branding Television* (London: Routledge).

Lury, Karen. (2005) *Interpreting Television* (London: Hodder Arnold).

Silverstone, Roger. (1994) *Television and Everyday Life* (London: Routledge).

Spigel, Lynn. (1992) *Make Room for TV: Television and the Family Ideal in Postwar America*
   (Chicago: University of Chicago Press).

4 'Music Is Half the Picture': The Soundworld of UK Television Idents

Mark Brownrigg and Peter Meech

As the previous chapter suggests, television idents are an intriguing class of ephemeral television output. These short texts have been a regular feature of television since the advent of the analogue era, but they now herald programmes on most of the UK's digital and online channels too. Idents are thus ubiquitous, recurring and virtually inescapable items, which we experience many times a day. As such they can be irritating, especially if badly produced or scheduled, while the best, the products of marketing acumen and creative flair, provide entertainment and inspire affection. Some have even attained cult status, with dedicated web archives created by amateur enthusiasts, and blogs discussing ident life and design. Other idents have had their popularity confirmed through parodied versions posted on YouTube. Despite this interest, channel idents have traditionally been overlooked in academic research. This chapter deepens this book's consideration of idents as a distinctive short-form in the 'between-space' of television. Specifically, it examines the importance of sound, both music and sound effects, as a key factor in the competition for attention in the cluttered junctions between programmes. Providing a detailed analysis of idents produced at the end of the 2000s for BBC Two, the Corporation's second terrestrial television channel, the chapter focuses on the interconnection between the aural and visual elements of TV idents, and considers how different moods are evoked for different audiences across a repertoire of branded channel iterations.

Sound has long been an important, although relatively neglected, component of TV channel idents. There are several reasons for both this importance and this neglect. First the importance. Music or sound effects combine with visual images to aid channel recognition. For audiences and television executives in today's multichannel environment, this has developed into a key role since the days of broadcast scarcity and restricted choice. As Collett and Lamb (1986) demonstrated a generation ago, many of those sitting at home in front of a television set may not actually be watching the screen for periods of time. In such cases, sound becomes the more important element of an ident, directing the attention to the screen during a junction between programmes for those who may be watching inattentively, who are visually impaired or who are outside the room where the TV is located. For this reason, early 1950s' channel idents typically took the form of a short fanfare, a single signature tune to represent a particular channel. In this chapter, we show the extent to which present-day idents have developed in form and function from their predecessors half a century or more ago.

For one thing, it has become a regular feature of TV channels in recent years to have more than one version of an ident. The end-logo comprising the all-important channel name remains a constant, but the process by which it is arrived at may vary considerably in terms of subject matter, style and tone from one version to another. Such a repertoire of idents can then be scheduled not simply to function, if necessary, as a tactical buffer between contrasting genres of programming but to help create an appropriate emotional mood by way of introducing the programme that follows. In so doing, idents cushion the impact of an abrupt change of mood, thereby enhancing television's 'flow' and the aesthetic pleasure it affords. More strategically, and in tandem with the visual component, the soundtrack of an ident attempts to associate audiences with a particular channel. Channel 5, for example, the UK's last terrestrial channel, claimed at its launch in 1997 to be 'brave, fast, irreverent' and commissioned idents to express these qualities in relation to its rivals. Such positioning is assisted by the repeat transmission of idents, which ensures that they linger in the mind as an aural mnemonic triggering familiarity and, it is hoped, positive emotional associations with a channel. But over and above this, they also function as a form of *corporate* 'sonic branding'. In doing so, they express what are hoped to be shared values between the larger entity, the broadcaster itself, and audiences, characterised as 'brandcasting' (Meech, 1999). However, no matter how creative or how strategically adroit idents are, they count for little – and may even prove counterproductive – should a channel's programming not live up to the expectations they engender, as was the case with Channel 5 (Fanthome, 2003, p. 153; see also Weissmann, 2010, pp. 73–5).

In previous publications, we explored the soundworld of UK TV idents, tracing their development from the 1950s with illustrations drawn from a variety of television channels (Brownrigg and Meech, 2002). Examining key examples of ident design for the BBC, ITV and Channel 4, we discussed the move in British channel branding from audiovisual approaches that adopt a singular 'fanfare' style to those which invest in more varied 'funfair' utterances; that rely, in other words, less on grand anthems and static logos than on a changing roster of visual images and audio styles. As part of this argument, we referred to the relative lack of critical attention paid to the audio characteristics of channel idents, arguing that if the 'promotional surround' is routinely overlooked in academic research into television, then the 'sound of the surround'

remains doubly neglected. And it's not just the academy that all but ignores the phenomenon. The BBC itself sometimes appears to regard the soundtrack as a mere after-
thought. In press releases announcing the launch of new BBC One and BBC Two idents
in 2007, for example, the focus was entirely on the look (the images, colours, typeface
and where the filming was done), together with quotes from executives extolling the
idents' simplicity, modernity and contribution to corporate branding. The sole reference to the music in the idents – a brief mention of the composers used – was buried
at the end of the publicity announcements (see BBC, 2007a, 2007b).

And yet sound is an essential part of any ident and consequently has to meet similarly exacting criteria of appropriateness and likely audience appeal as the visual element. This means that in contemporary practice it is not a late addition, as the
Corporation's press releases would suggest, but something that figures in the initial
gestation stage. Speaking of the sound design of the 2007 BBC One idents, for example, Red Bee Media's Charlie Mawer (who is interviewed in the next chapter) says:

> From very early on we wanted the sound and music design to play a crucial role.
> We wanted it to be flexible enough to match the range of moods and tones we were
> striking with the visuals, whilst retaining a signature tune that over the years would emerge
> as a strong and subtle branding device. (Cited in Bartholdy, 2007, p. 251)

Mawer is explicit about the importance of sound and describes the 'amazing choice of
composers and bands' that pitched for the job. This prompts the question as to why
this key communication channel should be accorded so much less attention than the
visual within critical and publicity discourse. We suggest there are three main reasons.
First, the jingles that were introduced to UK broadcasting in the 1950s, while highly
memorable (and thus of value in advertising terms), made no claim to musical sophistication or distinction. As a likely consequence, the soundtracks for idents have also
been regarded as too trivial for academic study. Second, we live in an environment in
which the eye is privileged over the ear, a 'primarily visual society', as the musician
Daniel Barenboim (2006) lamented in the second of his 2006 Reith Lectures, entitled
'The Neglected Sense'. And third, there has been an understandable reluctance to
engage with the subject because of the intrinsic difficulty of using words to describe
musical forms of any kind. By contrast, the verbal analysis of visual forms seemingly
presents far less of a problem for non-specialists.

It is clear that the process of ident production, including sound, has become a
good deal more professional since the growth of multichannel television in the mid-
1990s. Previously, it had tended to be managed in a competent though somewhat
amateurish way, as suggested by Martin Lambie-Nairn's account of the devising of
Channel 4's original musical motif:

We put a brief out to the music industry, but the tapes we got back in return all sounded alike. Predictably, there were lots of fanfares. Only one tape stood out as interesting; one which came from the composer David Dundas. I got together with Dundas and he played the four-note theme on the piano. It sounded okay, but a little dull. I found myself saying, 'At least make one of the notes shorter than the others', and that is pretty much how the final sequence came out. (Lambie-Nairn, 1997, p. 77)

Nowadays, idents, like promos, are regarded as important weapons in the strategic marketing armoury of TV companies. But it was not always so. The BBC in-house Promotions Department, for example, used to have responsibility for creating idents, and the Transmission Department for their selection and on-air play-out. With the dramatic increase of television channels during the 1980s and 1990s and the growing importance of ratings, however, a need for more specialist marketing expertise became apparent. To this end, staff appointments were increasingly made from the worlds of advertising and marketing, appointments who have since come to play a key role in ensuring that on-air idents are aligned with wider promotional and corporate strategies (Born, 2004). The value of brand expertise also spurred the growth of independent production companies specialising in broadcast design such as Red Bee Media. Created in 2005 as a result of the privatisation of BBC Broadcast, Red Bee, as Paul Grainge suggests, has sought 'to develop a visual and graphic language for the culture of media convergence, creating logos, promos and other forms of branded content that promise, as a function of design, to facilitate more emotional and interactive modes of audience engagement' (Grainge, 2010, p. 52). Sound has become a key component of this process, with specialist sound design companies such as Adelphoi Music and Beetroot used to provide soundtrack material for the range of title sequences, idents, trailers or trails (the BBC's preferred term) that are increasingly outsourced by media corporations, including the BBC.

If the creative production of trails and idents became more professionalised in the 1990s and 2000s, so too has their placement within the television schedule. Deciding which promotional item to transmit in a particular junction used to be done in a rather ad hoc way. Nowadays, BARB audience research data, long employed in the buying of TV advertising, also informs BBC media planners in making such decisions. Thus, trails are scheduled to achieve specific ratings (TVRs) among a particular audience segment. And, as Andrew Davies, the Corporation's Media Planning Group Head, says, 'We are able to use audience data from BARB to assess the wear-out factor of certain idents and their shelf-life' (Davies, 2010). In the late 2000s, the aligning of ident production and transmission with marketing was made explicit in a change to the BBC's management structure, Promotions reporting directly to Marketing, Communications and Audiences.

The people responsible for making idents, those working in TV promotions, have tended in the past to feel that their work was undervalued, not least by senior television executives. A survey of industry opinion conducted in 1998 indicated a sense that their skills were insufficiently recognised. As one promotions manager colourfully put it, describing his relationship with television executives, the problem was 'explaining myself to people with the creative thoughts of a pea' (Meech, 1998). In recent years there has been a shift in perceptions towards a greater understanding of the value of promotional work. Championing the cause of professional recognition for the sector since 1989 has been Promax UK, a subsidiary of the global Promax organisation. One of its initiatives has been to start its own training scheme, while another encourages students on relevant courses at higher education institutions through the award of annual prizes.

For many years, anyone interested in idents was frustrated by their ephemeral character: unless they made VHS recordings, the only possibility of experiencing them was when they were actually broadcast. But with the coming of the digital age, such enthusiasts can now access dedicated websites such as the ident gallery (<www.theidentgallery.com>), TV Ark (<www.tv-ark.org.uk>) and Andrew Wiseman's television room (<http://625.uk.com>) that offer a valuable historical archive. The internet has thus given a degree of permanence to these fleeting creations, extending their accessibility across borders while removing them from their original locations between programmes. Capitalising on audiences' fondness for certain idents and introducing an element of interactivity, the BBC has even directly appealed to enthusiasts of the BBC Two logo to create their own versions. They were encouraged to do this by downloading a template of the numeral in the correct font and using it as a window on scenes of their own choosing. The best of these so-called 'citizen idents', complete with soundtrack, were subsequently posted on the BBC website, providing a novel feedback loop and a valuable exercise in corporate public relations (BBC, 2007c).

The remainder of this chapter comprises a close reading of the soundworld of a selection of the 2007 BBC Two idents, designed by the advertising agency Abbott Mead Vickers BBDO and produced by Red Bee Media, with music composed by Vince Pope (Beetroot). These iconic, award-winning items are especially productive in allowing us to consider in detail the creative and aesthetic form of contemporary idents, and the diversity of ways in which they combine sound and vision to achieve different moods and effects.

BBC Two, launched in 1964, was the Corporation's second TV channel. In common with the other BBC domestic public services, it is funded by the licence fee and is thus free of commercial advertising. In contrast to the flagship service provided by BBC One, its programming may be characterised as less populist and mainstream, more discriminating and eclectic. As Simon Winchester, the then Creative Director of the channel, said in 1997: 'BBC One is like a supermarket, BBC Two more like a deli' (Winchester, 1997).

Initially, this positioning did not translate itself into the channel's idents. It was not until 1991 – as a belated response to Channel 4's 1982 launch and groundbreaking idents, as well as to the new satellite and cable channels – that BBC Two's own idents acquired their distinctively offbeat character. In one respect, these followed the Channel 4 innovation of appearing in different versions – in this case, all variations on the numeral 2 colour-coded in viridian green – but in another respect, they broke entirely new ground. The familiar 20th Century-Fox-style fanfare adopted from the cinema was ditched and replaced by a repertoire of softer, 'treated' sounds (Brownrigg and Meech, 2002, p. 347). Ten years later, a replacement set of idents introduced an eclectic mix of whirring or clicking noises and dance music to match a similarly diverse range of visuals. But whatever the differences of style, the intention remained the same: to brand the channel as intelligent and discriminating, but also as playful and capable of delivering surprises.

This essay considers the third generation of modern channel idents created for BBC Two since the early 1990s, and that was first broadcast in January/February 2007. Collectively known as 'Windows on the World', this sequence offers a range of musical accompaniments that differ widely in terms of instrumentation, melody, harmony and rhythm. Three groups of idents are considered here, many of which are available to be viewed online at <http://www.bbc.co.uk/bbctwo/idents/>:

- the 'Main' channel idents
- a further sequence of idents referred to as 'Tent' idents by the channel
- a series of idents referred to as 'Tagging' idents by the channel and often used before 'edgier' programming. These idents will not be analysed in the same depth, as they are used less frequently.

The idents vary widely in dramatic tone, ranging from the suspenseful to the beautiful, the comic to the restful, and also in their aesthetic construction, from the simple to the complex, the improvisational to the spectacular. The music used to underscore them varies considerably in turn, on a surface level at least. In addition, large sections of this music are designed to be talked over by a continuity announcer. Accordingly, the ident soundtracks tend to be structured with the most intense passage of music and sound events front-loaded, before what we hear then recedes not just in volume but in density of aural activity so as not to compete with the voiceover. This section of the soundtrack is termed the 'living hold', an extensive passage allowing the announcer an element of flexibility when fading the music unobtrusively out once the announcement is over.

The 'Main' idents are linked visually by being shot in one take and featuring the number 2, most often acting as a framing device through which action is viewed. For the most part, the idents are unique but two strands of the 'Main' idents constitute a series of instalments, one depicting a five-part chase sequence, another a two-part meditation on a cup of cappuccino. Each of these strands is given its own distinctive music and sound effects, as are each of the individual, stand-alone idents. The 'Tent' idents are scored with separate but linked music tracks which also incorporate ambient sound effects, while the 'Tagging' idents feature no music at all, favouring sound. By looking in detail at various iterations of the BBC Two idents, we can begin to understand the aesthetic sophistication of one of broadcast television's essential short-forms. The following analysis provides a close reading of each group of idents; it considers the rich audiovisual design of BBC Two idents at the end of the 2000s in ways that demonstrate the sheer creativity and inventiveness of these most transitory, but oft-repeated, items of television culture.

'Main' idents

Typifying the trend in contemporary broadcast design towards brand iteration, the 'Main' idents present us with a series of different situations, predominantly shot through the screening device of a figure 2. Formally, we have an image track pulling in two directions, one towards diversity (variation in what we see through the 2) and another pulling back towards unity (the 2 used as a screen device throughout). All are shot in one long take, offering a further, subliminal, sense of unity to the otherwise heterogeneous group.

As with the eclectic nature of the visuals, a wide variety of musical idioms is drawn on in the 'Main' sequence: dance music, orchestral music, percussive riffs, soft-rock and so on. There is no jingle-like recurrent motif to unite the soundtracks, unlike BBC One's reiterated, if reorchestrated, three-note mnemonic figure of 6th-5th-tonic (la-soh-doh). But if this echoes the visual impulse to diversity, we also find a series of recurring elements on the soundtrack that work in the direction of unification. As well as the front-loaded living-hold structure, we find a fairly static sense of harmonic progression; a reliance on motific repetition, unchanging bass pedal notes and/or chord progressions rather than organically evolving melodic development; a mixture of highly motivated sound effects and music; a link suggested between the music we hear and the dramatic space we see; and, finally, the electronic treatment of all musical elements whether digital in source or recorded digitally.

Chase: 'Grab 2', 'Through 2', 'Torches', 'Up Tree', 'Pit'

The Chase idents comprise a sequence of five visual scenarios that share an identical musical accompaniment. For the purpose of this chapter, we restrict ourselves to an analysis of the first in the series.

This begins *in media res* as a young man is pursued through a forest by men with dogs, the 2 appearing (behind occasional puffs of misty vapour), hewn through a rock panel that affords us a frame-within-a-frame perspective on much of the action: the unfolding drama is viewed through the 2. Shooting in one long take, the Steadicam, zoom-ing slowly out and in, is kept at a

BBC Two, Chase (2007)

distance (we are offered no close-ups of the man or of those chasing him) and the rock panel acts like a screen separating us from the heart of the action. On the other hand, the rock screen implicates us, placing us in either a voyeuristic position or suggesting that we, too, are in hiding – behind the rock in our case. The ident is remarkable for its enigmatic ambiguity: we do not know who is pursuing whom, for what reason or, effectively, what our viewing position is. The colour palette is limited to subdued, desaturated greens, greys, brown and black. The ident presumably takes its name from the moment in which, having fallen, the young man grabs onto the base of the 2 in order to pull himself back up again.

The music is predominantly percussive with occasional, abstract synth noises and the fleeting implication of a double bass line. Foregrounded are steel-drum-like sonori-ties playing a figure based around the three notes of a minor triad with an added second. The music does not occupy the soundtrack alone, as we also hear the sounds of the pursuit: the young man's footsteps, heavy breathing and exclamation as he falls; an ambient backing track of woodland insect noise and birdsong; the barking dogs, the shouts of those chasing and so forth. In addition, we might note also the momen-tary silence at the start of each ident. It is customary practice, during editing, to bring sound up before image, effecting a smooth opening to a sequence, but here we are presented with a subliminal beat of silence, subtly calling attention to a break in the flow of programming, drawing attention to the message to follow.

Sunroof

This ident offers an extreme low angle of the inside of a car ceiling, into which the number 2 is cut like a sunroof: the detail of the base of the figure we open up on indeed suggests a conventional sunroof. Smoothly, the tinted glass glides back and the camera rotates clockwise, the 2 shifting from a horizontal to a vertical position.

BBC Two, Sunroof (2007)

Through the 2 we see the green leaves of trees flash by and the blue sky and white clouds of a sunny day beyond. As with all of the Chase idents, this is filmed in one take and the colour palette, though not as desaturated as before, remains limited: grey, white, blue and green, recalling the similar colour scheme of many of the 2s from a different generation of idents, specifically a distinctive set of viridian-green animated idents featuring the numeral '2' that were broadcast between 1991 and 2001.

The ident opens with the sound of a car engine moving up through the gears, and, from the heart of this, music emerges that is different from that used in the Chase idents. A floaty, Sigur Ros-style guitar opening evolves into a driving, repeating riff constructed from just two chords. This plays in a fusion soft-rock/ambient electronica style, suggesting that it might be diegetic and emanating from the car radio or CD player. Over the start of the music, a female voice sings a heavily, dreamily echoed line in which the words are indistinct, then is never heard again, the music moving into its living hold. If the primal rhythms of Chase situated us in the natural world of the forest, this rocky music can also act as a signifier of space if we choose to hear it as diegetic sound issuing from the car stereo. Again, music and sound effects are mixed.

Seascape

Here we see a wild seascape with tempestuous waves throwing themselves against the black, jagged rocks of a cove, the distant sky coloured by the light of either a rosy-fingered dawn or shepherd's delight sunset. The camera tracks back to reveal that we have been looking through the screening device of yet another 2, this time constructed from smoothly weathered ship's timbers. The troubled waters of the foreground crash through the 2, again insisting on a link between what lies behind and in front of the figure. As usual, the ident is filmed in one take.

As with the car stereo rock of Sunroof, the symphonic cast of the music is unique to this ident. In keeping with the vastness of the scene, rhapsodic synth strings play an ecstatic, ascending three-note figure anchored by the undertow of the bassy, thundering waters. The use of full orchestra here suggests a sense of epic scale and works well with the slightly warmer colours used by this ident (pinks and blues brightening another otherwise monochromatic palette); it also evokes the orchestral tradition of sea music by Debussy, Ravel, Britten and others. If many of the idents in the sequence overall are remarkable for their shared sense of rhythmic propulsion, this particular one seems out of place: here the music drifts, rising and falling like the waves it underscores, freed from the overtly and insistently percussive, and offering a sense of freedom from containment as it does so.

BBC Two, Seascape (2007)

Cappuccino: 'Sugar Lumps', 'Scoop'

A chocolate powder 2 is dusted onto the froth of a cup of cappuccino through a stencil screen and, as the camera pulls back from the coffee cup, the stencil is lifted past and over it as two sugar lumps are dropped in, leaving the 2 largely intact. A hand appears and stirs the 2 into the froth in two clockwise stirrings of the spoon. Again, the colour palette is limited: all is monochrome save for the brown of the powder dusting.

If Seascape called upon the symphonic, Cappuccino offers a drum machine playing an upbeat rhythm suggesting a lively, youthful, contemporary, fashionable urban environment. An ascending phrase is heard on electric guitar above it, a driving, ascending synth bass line sounding below. The reverbed guitar continues with a rapid, descending sequence of notes that is repeated as the sounds of the café move up in the mix: the steam hiss of the coffee machine heating milk, cutlery sounds, the customers' chatter in the background.

In the second in this sequence, as with the Chase sequence of idents, the music is played without variation under the new visuals, offering continuity between the two instalments and giving a sense of unity to the Cappuccino ident-strand as a whole. Visually, the difference involves the two-stage scooping up of the chocolate powder 2 with the teaspoon,

BBC Two, Cappuccino (2007)

BBC Two, Mirror (2007)

punctuated by a suitable gap as it is relished by the off-screen mouth.

Mirror

We pull out from a raindrop on a 2-shaped wing mirror that is moving at speed through a city at night, shot from a fixed camera mounted on the side of the driver's door. The length of the exposure causes the roadside lights to trail and flare, while the fast-motion photography produces a mazy, hypnotic, crepuscular, protean cityscape.

The music here seems to be working according to a law of antithesis as, pulling against this sense of rapid motion and dizzying visual stimulation, we find its slow and calm serenity for once hard to link to the space constructed by the images it underscores. The bright lights and hypermotion of the urban night-space might call for the exciting energy overload of trance, techno or jungle dance music, say, but instead we hear a piano, solo cello and a series of bell-like sounds playing quiet, meditative music based around a repeating, falling three-note figure. The sound component of the ident incorporates the whooshes of passing cars, the echoed squeals of brakes, suggesting the splashing through puddles depicted in the 2's mirror. While the main portion of the visual field appears to have been shot in one take, as we would expect, the traffic behind the car, mirrored in the 2, seems to be moving at a normal pace and is revealed through a series of dissolves.

Zoetrope

A futuristic city teeming with flying cars is revealed to be the illusion constructed by a zoetrope, viewed through a series of spinning 2s that constitute the slits cut into the side of its cylinder. Here we do find the ready equation of dance music and urban space as a swelling break structure built out of looping musical fragments and repeating, percussive rhythms evolves cumulatively. The explicitly electronic nature of the music points towards a sense of futurism, while, visually, the city may also, in a paradoxical move, return us to the past by evoking Fritz Lang's vision of the future in *Metropolis* (1927). This sense of an ambivalent time frame is perhaps encapsulated by the ident's central conceit: the outmoded, old-tech zoetrope offering a vision of a future living space. The sound effects we hear are the synthesised sounds of the passing flying cars.

At a glance – and at first hearing – there seems to be no similarity between these 'Main' idents. However, this analysis reveals deep structures that they have in common. BBC Two is thereby able to present itself simultaneously as being vibrant and diverse while suggesting a core brand unity. Further diversity is provided by a secondary stream of idents that the channel refers to as

BBC Two, Zoetrope (2007)

the 'Tent' sequence. Visually and aurally, these appear to have little in common with the 'Main' idents. For one thing, this group share a lifestyle and leisure theme, offering representations of life in the great outdoors, at a pop festival and on the beach.

'Tent' idents: 'Arctic', 'Festival', 'Beach'

Unlike the main strand, the 'Tent' idents are not shot in one long take. Instead, we find a five-shot structure with the fifth shot revealing a view through a 2-shaped tent door, offering clear continuity with the screen device of the 2s in the 'Main' (and 'Tagging' idents discussed briefly below). The 'Tent' idents are linked visually by the colour of the tent and its zip (yellow and red respectively), and all feature the verisimilitude of foreground in-tent clutter as well as the view to the outside world beyond. They are also linked musically. Although, like the 'Main' idents, each has its own soundtrack, all three feature guitar-based cues with relaxed backing. As with the main strand, harmonic movement is limited – typically, here to a four-chord progression – and music and sound effects are both present on the soundtrack. Like the groups of idents above,

then, visual and aural differences are primarily surface in nature, and deeper structural elements linking each ident pull the series back in the direction of unity.

In 'Arctic', the unzipping of the 2-shaped tent door reveals a mountainous landscape beyond. The camera is situated in the tent looking out, but clutter (sleeping bags etc.) implies that life goes on in front

BBC Two, Festival (2007)

of the 2 as well as beyond it. As with the other two 'Tent' idents, the audible unzipping of the 2 is constructed from a brief montage of four shots before the fifth shot of the landscape is revealed: the remainder of the ident comprises this long fifth take. In a way, this can be seen as a visual analogue of the living-hold sequence of the 'Main' ident soundtracks, with fast-cut visuals front-loaded before a longer, static take. The music is a simple and laid-back repetition of a four-chord sequence given to electric guitar, acoustic drum kit low in the mix, electric bass guitar, strummed acoustic guitar and reverbed organ – somewhat surreal considering the supposed location of the tent. In the midst of the dramatic vista, sublime in the proper sense, the music sounds a note of comfort, familiarity and warmth.

In the second 'Tent' ident, 'Festival', the unzipping 2 opens out on a sea of other tents, evoking the communal living experienced at many live music events of long duration. Again, the full vista is kept until the fifth shot, and once more the foreground is occupied by sleeping bags, rucksacks and so on. This time, the music is given to layered electric guitars, some shiny and using a chorus effect, others distorting a little and feeding back. The sound element includes the familiar unzipping noise, along with distant cheering, the whistling crowd and the voice of an MC over a public address system. The music here, then, is much more in keeping with the space of the visual action.

In the third and final 'Tent' ident, 'Beach', after the standard four shots of unzipping, a beach scene at sunset is revealed, showing people gathered around a campfire with a placid sea, tide out, in the background. Again, the music is laid-back and guitar-based, its acoustic-guitar arpeggiated chords accompanied by a shaking tambourine. Laughter emanates from the small group on the beach as an acoustic guitar is presented to the only figure we can see clearly, a man sitting facing us in the middle distance. Before he can begin strumming, the ident is over.

An expedition into the great outdoors, a communal adventure in a pop paradise, an evening spent with friends in a remote coastal location: these three idents work to create a sense of escape from the quotidian, the urban, the stressful and a flight towards a series of destinations, each in their own way idyllic and utopian. Suggestive of breaks from the hustle and bustle of daily life, they present situations that putatively allow us to shake off our everyday existences, to de-stress, to convince ourselves that here, amid the extraordinary, we are actually most ourselves. The 'Tent' idents would thus be suited to leading into 'something light' (Davies, 2010). By extension, of course, and on a daily basis as we unwind from work and domestic duties, the channel suggests through these idents that it can offer us that sense of freedom, relaxation and identity, can put us back in touch with ourselves. Indeed, we could read every shot of these idents as a point-of-view shot (of the unzippings and through the 2), something which seems to suggest that the channel is whispering: 'Imagine yourself here'.

'Tagging' idents: 'Gallery', 'Football', 'Policemen', 'Skatepark', 'Graffiti'

While in many respects the 'Tagging' idents mark themselves out as different from the 'Main' and 'Tent' idents, featuring a far less polished fashioning of sound and image, they are also linked on a deep structural level by recurring features of their own. Conceptually, they all depict cheekily subversive instances of direct action: spray painting the walls of an art gallery (rebelling against high culture); using pink paint on a football (satirising the competitive masculine orthodoxy of the sport); painting on policemen (baiting authority figures); defacing newly canonised modes of street expression (graffiti-ing graffiti itself).

This suggests that one aspect of BBC Two programming is assigned an if not iconoclastic then certainly transgressive brand, undermining the channel's traditional reputation as the high-culture strand in the Corporation's programming, as opposed to the more populist BBC One (a function which in any case has largely been taken over by the digital channel BBC Four). In each instance, the camera is handheld, the operator a palpable presence in the scene; the idents are shot through a stencil 2, which is then used as a frame for the spray-painting; music is absent and the sound effects rough, chaotic and, though elements of collage work may be incorporated, spontaneous source recordings. Nevertheless, the 'Tagging' idents also share some strands of visual DNA with the more 'orthodox' current of idents, in that the 2 appears repeatedly as a screening/framing device and all are shot in one long take. To give a brief flavour of these idents, we now discuss one example called 'Gallery'.

In this ident, there is no ostensible music. Instead, the soundtrack is filled with the sounds of a gallery in which a lurid green 2 is stencilled on the wall between two more orthodox paintings. The handheld camera offers the point of view of the 'artist', and the entire scene is shot through the 2 cut into his/her stencil. The sound is very raw, suggestive of VHS home movies: we hear the camera motor, the excited breathing of its operator, the security guard's walkie-talkie crackling in and out, the ambient sounds of the gallery space and the shocking hiss of the spray paint. There is no sense of carefully crafted sonic perspective: everything sounds suffocatingly close to the microphone. This all offers a compelling sense of actuality and of the living moment, and while once again we are offered an ident shot in one take, conforming to the visual substructure of the channel, the rough

BBC Two, Football (2007)

spontaneity of the images and sounds works as an antithesis of the smooth, fluid, poised, carefully constructed beauty of the 'Main' and 'Tent' idents. Here, then, the contrast seems to extend itself to the visual track (lack of control, ugliness) as well as the soundtrack (the absence of music, chaotic and unpolished soundworld).

Conclusion

It is clear from the analyses above that the BBC Two idents have progressed far beyond the relatively simple manipulation of graphic elements that historically characterised much of the early ident output of both the BBC and the UK's commercial channels. The idents discussed above move beyond the straightforward visual statement and fanfare-based musical model that typified the genre in the past, certainly on commercial stations (Brownrigg and Meech, 2002). The present generation of idents represents the latest step the network has taken away from simple station identification towards articulating a sense of station identity, with the contraction 'ident' easing the slippage between the two concepts.

While BBC One offers a similarly rich palette of idents, the other channels comprising the Corporation's output (for instance, CBeebies, BBC Three, BBC Four) range their ident styles at a variety of earlier points along this evolutionary timeline, from the plain logo-based statement to the complex audiovisual feast. This does not mean that traces of the 'old', graphic, logo-based branding model do not persist: the uniform use, and indeed font, of the 2 attests to this. However, the visual and aural pleasures now surrounding this simple graphic element surpass those of previous generations of 2s. Though linked, as we have seen, by deep structures on both image and soundtrack, the idents launched in 2007 were more diverse, and more intricately planned, shot and put together, than ever before.

This developmental process underlines the sense that a space has been opened up in the junctions between programmes for a creative statement to be made, visually and musically, regarding channel image, tone and branding. Of course, idents have always, from their inception, comprised meaningful corporate and textual statements, but the crop of BBC Two idents examined here are highly suggestive in nature and, in many ways, appear as objects of beauty: they are richly conceived and constructed texts that seem quite self-consciously to demand decoding, not least given their often enigmatic nature. There used to be an adage, relating to commercial television in the UK, that the adverts were the 'best bit', superior in terms of execution and entertainment value to the programming they punctuated. Here, it seems that BBC Two's idents have moved to occupy a similar space, high in concept, comparatively big in budget.

This audiovisual exuberance is compounded by the idea that the main strand of idents, diverse as they are, was never conceived of as being 'enough'. The additional two groups, 'Tagging' and 'Tent', are themselves augmented with special, stand-alone idents for channel theme nights and to mark specific calendar events such as Christmas, Hallowe'en, Burns Night and so on (a practice that dates back to the 2 idents of the early 1990s). However, far from diffusing the sense of brand identity, the common elements, the deep structures, that organise the sonic and visual tracks of the idents operate to pull the various statements together, suggesting unity among the diversity, something we seem invited to project, in turn, onto the surrounding flow of programming. This amounts to a cumulative statement of singularity on the one hand (a strong sense of channel identity) and a corresponding celebration of difference relating to the variety of programmes on offer on the other. One senses that the unifying structural factors are particularly important in this respect, given that, alongside its own output, the channel broadcasts shows that also run on other commercial and satellite channels, and, indeed, shows that originally aired on BBC channels such as Three and Four, but which have been considered suitable to cross over to the more mainstream Two. This heterogeneous and, indeed, volatile model of programming, then, is ameliorated by the strong, yet malleable, sense of brand identity that the BBC Two roster of idents suggests.

From this analysis of BBC Two's idents of the late 2000s, it is clear that they are the result of a great deal of strategic and creative thought as well as a variety of technical skills. Each has been carefully designed to fuse visuals and sound into a satisfying whole, yet the complementarity of the two elements nevertheless tends to be overlooked in any discussion of idents. According to one BBC producer, 'Music is half the picture' (Simpson, 2010), but music, along with sound effects, is all too regularly ignored in favour of visual elements. Despite the wide diversity of approaches, there is an overarching artistic unity to the channel's idents that exemplifies what Roly Keating, then Controller of BBC Two, referred to as '[the] distinctive humour, creativity, playfulness and surprise' of the channel (BBC, 2007b). In addition, together with other BBC idents, they help to highlight the quality and range of the output of the Corporation as a whole. In doing so, they make their own distinctive contribution to the work of justifying its unique funding arrangement to government and the viewing – and listening – public.

Bibliography

Barenboim, Daniel. (2006) 'The Neglected Sense', <www.bbc.co.uk/radio4/reith2006/ lecture2.shtml> accessed 15 March 2009.

Bartholdy, Björn. (2007) *Broadcast Design* (Cologne: daab).

BBC. (2007a) 'BBC One Launches New Channel Identity', <www.bbc.co.uk/print/ pressoffice/pressreleases/stories/2006/09_september/26/idents.shtml> accessed 15 March 2009.

——. (2007b) 'BBC Two's New "Window on the World"', <www.bbc.co.uk/print/pressoffice/ pressreleases/stories/2007/02_february/13/two.shtml> accessed 15 March 2009.

——. (2007c) 'Citizen Idents', <www.bbc.co.uk/bbctwo/noise/?id=citizen_idents> accessed 20 January 2009.

Born, Georgina. (2004) *Uncertain Vision: Birt, Dyke and the Reinvention of the BBC* (London: Secker & Warburg).

Brownrigg, Mark and Peter Meech. (2002) 'From Fanfare to Funfair: The Changing Soundworld of UK Television Idents', *Popular Music*, 21 (3), pp. 345–55.

Collett, Peter and Roger Lamb. (1986) *Watching People Watching Television*, Report to the Independent Broadcasting Authority, London.

Davies, Andrew. (2010) Email correspondence with author, 2 November.

Fanthome, Christine. (2003) *Channel 5: The Early Years* (Luton: University of Luton Press).

Grainge, Paul. (2010) 'Elvis Sings for the BBC: Broadcast Branding and Digital Media Design', *Media, Culture & Society*, 32 (1), pp. 45–61.

Lambie-Nairn, Martin. (1997) *Brand Identity for Television, with Knobs On* (London: Phaidon).

Meech, Peter. (1998) 'Survey of Promotions Managers, Creative Directors and Promotions Producers' (unpublished).

——. (1999) 'Watch This Space: The On-Air Marketing Communications of UK Television', *International Journal of Advertising*, 18 (3), pp. 291–304.

Simpson, Claire. (2010) Email correspondence with author, 15 September.

Weissmann, Elke. (2010) *The Forensic Sciences of CSI: How to Know about Crime* (Saarbrücken: Verlag Dr Müller).

Winchester, Simon. (1997) Interview with author, London, 20 August.

5 TV Promotion and Broadcast Design: An Interview with Charlie Mawer, Red Bee Media

Paul Grainge

During the 1990s and 2000s, the junctions of broadcasting were distinguished by an ever-expanding range of promotional texts. This included teasers and trailers for coming TV shows, graphic pointers and end-credit menus announcing the network schedule, and stings and idents branding particular channels. As television companies sought to capture and manage attention within a competitive multichannel environment, promotion became a major component of TV output and broadcast design. In the early 2000s, for example, the BBC Creative Department responsible for promotional work became the third-largest provider of BBC content after news and sport in terms of hours of material produced (Mawer, 2009). While the preceding chapters focus on the function and aesthetics of interstitials as ephemeral forms, this chapter concentrates on the people and companies involved in their making. Through an interview with a leading industry practitioner, it connects the discussion of idents and interstitials to contexts of media work (Deuze, 2007).

Charlie Mawer has been at the forefront of developments in broadcast promotion in British television for over two decades. He was one of a number of professional marketers to move into the UK broadcast industry in the early 1990s, and worked in every area of the BBC's 250 strong in-house Creative Department before becoming its Executive Creative Director in 2003. Part of a BBC commercial division that was subsequently sold in 2005 and renamed Red Bee Media, Mawer is currently Executive Creative Director of Red Bee and has worked with numerous channels and brands internationally, producing channel identities, complete network rebrands, as well as branded content, interactive advertising and even pop promos. In the following interview, Mawer reflects on the creative and professional challenges of television branding specifically, providing a vantage on the way that media promoters have sought to communicate with audiences and 'bring people to shows' in a fast-paced media world.

Following its launch, Red Bee Media became central to the outsourcing of a wide range of operational, editorial and promotional processes in the UK television landscape. Based in the BBC-funded Broadcast Centre in London's White City, and with strategic regional offices in Germany, Spain, France and Australia, Red Bee is indicative of the growing role of technical and creative service companies in the transactional markets that support media industries (for a detailed analysis, see Grainge, 2010). Together with media brand work for corporations such as Nike, IKEA and AOL, Red Bee was responsible in the first decade of the twenty-first century for many of the idents, trailers and programme title sequences seen on British television screens, as well as in other markets such as Greece, Belgium and Japan. This would include channel branding for terrestrial broadcasters such as the BBC and ITV, and for digital channels such as Dave, Blighty, Virgin One, Living, Sci Fi Channel and Discovery International. Red Bee was also responsible for a number of high-profile promotional campaigns for Comic Relief, BBC World News and Formula One, and for the entire Olympic branding of the 2008 games for the host broadcaster, CCTV.

Promoting itself as a visionary boutique able to provide proprietary imaging skills, Red Bee argued in 2007 that 'organisations are being forced to find new ways of reaching and engaging increasingly fragmented audiences' (Red Bee Media, 2007). Mawer reflects on the creative and strategic challenges this presents for the discipline of television branding. Drawing on a portfolio of work for mainstream channels such as BBC One and niche channels like BBC Three and Dave, all of which 'editorialise' BBC programming through distinctive brand frames, the following interview concentrates on promotional communication in the 'between' space of television in the 2000s. As we have seen, this was a decade marked by heightened promotional activity among channel and programme brands (see also Johnson, 2011). Capturing a particular moment in the history of UK television promotion, the interview throws into relief the creative work of a strategic industry sub-field, and illuminates how idents, interstitials and other kinds of interactive content were used and discussed in a period where questions about how to 'navigate' viewers through a rich and complex media terrain were coming to the fore. The interview took place in March 2010 in the offices of Red Bee Media.

PAUL GRAINGE: *Let's start with a personal perspective. How did you get into broadcast design?*
CHARLIE MAWER: I started off working in advertising for J. Walter Thompson, who are often described as the university of advertising; they're one of the places that used to take a lot of graduate trainees, so there's a whole generation of people who went through there at some point or other. I was actually a slight rarity in that I didn't go in as a creative. Traditionally, advertising hires 'creatives' out of art college who've done

advertising copywriter courses and then they hire people with degrees to be 'suits', as they're pejoratively called, facing clients and strategic planners. I actually joined as a grad trainee expecting that I might end up being one of those suits, but actually wanting to write. Occasionally, somebody manages to jump the fence and I was one of the people who managed to jump the fence and start writing. Before that, I'd actually done some comedy writing, so I'd got a bit of a track record. But simultaneously when I was on the account-facing side, I was desperately trying to get into the BBC.

It was a lifelong desire to work for the BBC and then fortunately I saw there was an opportunity to join a relatively fledgling promo team that was for the first time starting to look for people with an advertising background. This was in 1994 and it was at the moment that the BBC had gone from treating trailers as being something that was simply about taking a small section of a programme out and putting a caption at the end of it – where you just informed people that a programme was on and assumed they would turn up because there was nothing else on – to a point where the BBC realised, with the advent of a competitive ITV and Channel 4 and the future of digital on the horizon, that they were going to have to persuade people to watch programmes. And so I was the first wave of people who were brought in with a very different mentality to what trails were. This was a bumpy ride to start with, because programme-makers weren't used to people telling them what was going to sell their programme for them. The department at the time was responsible for the presentation of the channels, and even that word 'presentation' suggests how it was viewed. You made a nice presentation of the programmes. It wasn't about selling and the way that we talk about identity now, which is very much as a marketing tool, as a branding discipline, and TV had to do a lot of catching up with other sectors in that.

PG: *In 1998, you said that the least rewarding aspect of the job as a creative director of promotions was the 'lack of recognition of our skills' (Meech, 1998). In terms of your relationship with programme-makers, you said that there was 'a gradual recognition from them of us as being more than an irritant'. Have attitudes changed at all?*
CM: They've both changed dramatically and not at all. What has fundamentally changed I think is the recognition of the importance of marketing and the importance of getting viewers to a show. What's not necessarily changed as dramatically is the recognition that there are people who have that as their skill set and are ruthlessly professional at doing it versus many programme-makers who still think they can sell their show. These are really broad generalisations, but I think it is still the reality compared to the United States where it's almost as important to get the marketing as to get the show right. I think the UK is catching up, however. What's interesting is that if you look at people in senior positions within the British TV industry, whether it's Andy Duncan, former Chief Executive of Channel 4 who was Head of Marketing at the BBC, David

Abraham who's replaced him who was the founder of St Luke's ad agency, or even Adam Crozier, formerly Chief Exec of Saatchi, who's taking over at ITV, these are people who understand the power of the brand. I think this represents a definite and subtle shift. People understand that it's not any more just about the quality of the content. You've got to have the quality of the content, but we talk about it being the era of the quick and the dead. With remote controls, you can't assume you've got people's attention; you haven't got the eyeballs to start with.

PG: *The quick and the dead is an interesting term. What do you see as the most effective means of capturing audience attention in the media environment you're describing?*
CM: In some ways, the same disciplines that you need to make an engaging programme you need to make an engaging thirty seconds – it's still about the craft of storytelling. It's still about engaging people from the first five seconds. In our world, it's about the first five seconds. Have you got a compelling image that is going to make people not hit the remote control button because they're in a junction and they can flick round for three minutes before something else starts? Are you telling them something they haven't heard before or asking them a question that demands them to think? I always give an example of a trail we did for *House of Saddam* [BBC Two, 2008] where the trail was a still photograph of the [Saddam Hussein] family melting. It would have been very easy to do a trail for the *House of Saddam* that was much more factually rich and complex in detail, but what we were saying was that this is a family meltdown, in the crudest sense applicable to *The Sopranos* [1999–2007] or *EastEnders* [BBC One, 1985–present]. The fact that it happened to be for an evil tyrant gave extra richness to it.

I used to make promos every week for the current affairs programme *Panorama* [BBC One, 1953–present] and it was a very interesting discipline, because the programme was rarely complete at the point that I had to make a trailer, because they make them right up to the wire. The process of making a trail often used to involve me phoning up the producer and chatting to them for half an hour about the programme. During the course of that conversation, I would be scribbling and doodling as he talked to me and usually at the end of that conversation I would know what to make a trail about, because it would be the most interesting thing that he'd said to me. Ultimately, it's *that* distillation. For example, I did a trail about the treatment of the elderly within the NHS, and the programme was actually a collection of thoughtful talking heads from hospitals and tragic experiences of people and their families. But he at one point said to me that it's the revolving-door syndrome – that it's all about getting people out even if you know that in two weeks' time they are going to be coming back, because it's not about fixing the underlying problems, it's about treating them. So, we took four elderly extras and marched them round a revolving door and filmed it. This basically said: this is the problem with the NHS that *Panorama*'s going to be exploring. It did so in a way that I think would have been impossible to do in thirty seconds and it certainly wouldn't have been as compelling as a visual or as a thought to get people to take notice.

PG: *Programme trailers are central to your work but so too are channel idents. What are the attributes of a successful channel ident in today's broadcast ecology? What does an ident need to do and how do you achieve this in audiovisual terms?*
CM: Idents are interesting, particularly coming from advertising, because they're probably in some ways the single hardest bit of creative work you'll ever be asked to do, because they serve a particular technical role within a television junction, the bits between programmes. In terms of their role, they have to literally identify which channel you're watching and to serve as a kind of mark, the equivalent of the badge on the front of a BMW that tells you it's a BMW not a Lexus. They also have to provide what I call a 'gear change' between very different types of programming. At its most extreme, on BBC Two let's say, you could be going from *The Hunt for Britain's Paedophiles* between nine and ten o'clock into a Paul Whitehouse comedy at ten into *Newsnight* at ten-thirty. The role of the idents can be to give you a bit of breathing space, but also to subtly shift you from first to third gear without feeling like these are really uncomfortable changes of view that you're going through. They've also got the practical value of being a moment in time that the continuity announcer of the channel can tell you both what's happening on the channel that evening, but also what might be happening on other channels within the family.

Often with idents, you're creating something where you don't know what sound is going to be used over it. For example, I didn't know when creating the 'Hippo Swimming in Circle' ident for BBC One [2006–present] that last night they might have been talking about who killed Archie in *EastEnders*. In this sense it's slightly surreal, all Dada. It's a film that you don't know what words will accompany it and also you don't know when it's going to end. Idents are usually made with what they call 'living holds' so that their time on screen can range from anything from fifteen to twenty-five seconds. If there's a longer piece of information, say a content warning that a programme contains scenes of violence or if we need to inform people that due to the overrun in the Formula One Grand Prix earlier, programmes are running half an hour late, idents need flexibility of duration. This differs from the commercial world where if you wrote a thirty-second script, you would know that it was going to run to thirty seconds, and have a beginning, middle and an end. You write it as tight as that. Idents have a slightly looser sense of pace but their fundamental role is as a piece of branding and positioning to say 'in this crowded marketplace this is the channel you're watching and this is what we're about'.

BBC One, Hippos (2006)

To take the example of the British digital channel Dave [specialising in reruns of BBC comedy and entertainment programmes], possibly the most celebrated channel rebrand in the UK in recent years, the spirit of that channel as embodied by a slightly extraordinary country-house weekend that you visit in every junction underlines the brand slogan 'the home of witty banter'. It encapsulates everything that the channel wants you to feel part of when you're a viewer and will make it feel as distinct from any other male-targeted channel like Bravo or ITV4. It's about defining yourself as clearly as Nike do with the Swoosh and 'just do it'.

PG: *Can you tell us something about the process of conceptualising and producing idents? For example, to what extent do you work with external agencies in generating ideas? Who is involved in their making? How much, on average, do they cost?*
CM: That's lots of different questions. In terms of who we work with, we're naturally fairly collaborative, but at the same time it's our specialist discipline so by and large, channels would work exclusively with us to produce a channel identity and the people we tend to work with will be in the technical professional skills domain. As you start to get into really specific craft skills that we don't have, we'll work with composers, 3D animators, illustrators, professional directors of photography, directors, etc. It'll tend to be more in the physical making. I'd say 100 per cent of the idea generation will be within our heads.

To talk through the process, if I take the BBC Three rebrand that we worked on that launched in 2008, a brief will be put out to pitch and half a dozen companies will pres-

Dave, welcome (2007), UKTV/Red Bee Media

ent. The brief will be: this is the challenge that this brand is facing at this time. Specifically, in this case, BBC Three was seen as having very little brand recognition with its target audience [of fifteen- to thirty-four-year-olds]; it was seen as a bit cold and distant and male and not young enough for the audience that they were being expected to bring content in. The challenge was simply, what would you do with our brand to alter those things? And so we pitched this notion of the island. We said that BBC Three has got a daytime environment and a night-time environment, and it's this extraordinary place full of young creative people like the stars of *The Mighty Boosh* [2004–7] and *Little Britain* [2003–6] and *Gavin and Stacey* [2007–10]. Because the channel only broadcast from 7 p.m. until 2 a.m., it didn't have a sense of continuity on air and so we said the most important thing is what you do with BBC Three online, so it became the first channel to stream live through bbc.co.uk and developed a really strong web presence with a lot of interactivity with its audience and lots of user-generated content which we proposed that they substitute within the junctions. User-generated continuity are intros to shows filmed by the audience, as peer-to-peer recommendations; this all came from the central thought of the island.

In terms of how much stuff costs, how long is a piece of string? You can have an ident that could be white type on a black background that I can do on PowerPoint up to the entire launch of the new identity of BBC One which was quoted publicly in 2006 as costing around £750,000. Anybody who's worked in commercials knows that that's less than you frequently spend on a single commercial, so it's anywhere in between those really. You'd be unlikely to get things that cost a lot more than that and a lot of the digital channels that we'll do now will be between £50,000 and £200,000 as a total project from logo design to all of the on-screen elements such as 'now next later' slides, trail packaging, dogs and bugs …

PG: *There's such a vocabulary …*
CM: Oh, there's a vast vocabulary. Dog stands for digital on-screen graphic. We also have stings and beops and eops or 'beginning and end of parts', moving pointers, in-programme pointers, which are the little crawlers that come on three minutes before the end of a programme to make sure you haven't flicked away. Again the quick and the dead! You only have to look at the TV channels in the States to see where things are going, and much as people protest about dogs and bugs and intrusive graphics, unfortunately trying to find a moment to talk to people is increasingly harder and every trick in the book is played.

PG: *You say that American television is in many ways a model of the future. Is that so in terms of an aesthetic of broadcast design?*
CM: No, absolutely not, not in my view anyway. I don't think you can generalise and I'm a massive fan of American TV, and I think if you look at title sequence design, all the title sequences that I admire, such as *Mad Men* [2007–present], *Six Feet Under* [2001–5] and *West Wing* [1999–2006], they're beautiful pieces of design and marketing and defining of a brand. But then if you look at the networks such as NBC, CBS and ABC, very rarely do they have the same strength of brand communication as the

networks in the UK in terms of genuinely defining themselves as being apart from their competitors and projecting what they stand for. FOX probably more so than the other three. I think cable and digital brands like HBO have absolutely led the field, but I still believe the UK is the powerhouse of motion graphic design. If you go, as I do, to Promax conferences around the world, which is the professional body that represents us, by and large if you distilled the quality of the work down, I would still take the UK over anywhere else in terms of leading the way and experimenting and discovering a richer variety of tones of voice that you can use.

PG: *Idents are peculiar in nature in that they are ephemeral but also repeated endlessly on television. Does the everyday repetition of idents shape, in any way, decisions about the style and shelf-life of your work?*
CM: Yes, it does. It's a really good point and it's one I should have made when I was talking about the particular challenges of idents, because it's almost the single biggest thing. Looking at two previous iterations of the BBC One idents, namely the hot-air balloons [1997–2002] and the dancers [2002–6], we worked out that, with a slight finger in the air, you can imagine that your ident is going to be seen roughly 3,600 times over its shelf-life. Trying to do something that you can watch 3,600 times without getting irritated by it is a particular challenge and it necessitates a particular type of storytelling and a particular type of engagement that is possibly less about grabbing you by the front of your jumper and shaking you and is much more about giving you something you can sit back and be immersed in, that you can take stuff from. It's a different level of engagement.

Interesting are the things that you learn. Something that audiences get tired of quickly, for example, are people's faces. To share a war story, one of the BBC One idents that we did involved people making the moon, floating out in boats and putting the moon together. This idea came from a wonderful French photographer who used an image of a girl carrying a piece of the sun. This inspired the story and we cast the ident full of interesting faces, in much the same way that if you were casting a TV show you'd be looking for engaging characters and people who you know. But there was one particular guy in it, and I don't know if this is just an example of 'gingerism', maybe because he was red-headed and bearded, everyone used to say 'God, I can't *stand* that bloke with the beard', literally after three months of it being on air. It is something to do with what gets attention in an ident. There are definitely things that you have to bear in mind when you're planning something that's going to be watched so often, in your own attention to detail. When people talk about the amount of money spent on idents, you can get away with a slightly dodgy bit of scenery in something that's going to be seen once, but when it's going to be seen 3,600 times, you can't – it's absolutely got to be picture-perfect.

PG: *Some idents are very compelling and complex in audiovisual terms and seem to invite audiences not only to enjoy them in the television moment but also, potentially, to re-watch them again on, say, YouTube. Are you trying to get audiences to engage and look again in this way?*
CM: Yes, we hope so. I think you can probably overinflate the impor-tance of what you do. I think the

BBC One, Penguins (2007)

best ads, the best bits of anything, will be watched again if people have really enjoyed them. I was hugely touched by the fact that the artist Tracey Emin in *The Independent* wrote that the hippos ident for BBC One had made her smile more than anything else that year, which might say more about Tracey Emin than the hippos (*laughing*), but I think that level of involvement is probably as much as you're going to get. We built into the penguins Christmas ident [2007: showing dozens of penguins skating between people on a festive ice rink] a huge number of little sight gags that would reward lots of viewing again and again if you wanted to. In the big circle of penguins going round, there's a little penguin that is a naughty penguin and goes between someone's legs, which you may not spot on ten viewings or twenty viewings. It's the sort of approach that Aardman or Pixar would take to making a film I guess, which is trying to reward things that you know are going to get watched and repeated more than in other genres. But at the same time, idents have got to work on a basic level.

PG: *Do you see promotional content as a form of art?*
CM: I think you have to be careful in that ultimately it's not an art form for its own sake, we are sales people. I think the point that you start to regard that what we do has a form without function is for me problematic, because most of us write or paint or take photographs or make films in our spare time and I think that's when you're cre-ating expression without a brief. Everything that we do has got an absolutely given role; for trails, for example, we are taking products that other people have made and we are showing them in the best possible light and trying to bring as many people to them as possible. When we launched Red Bee, we had to try and create a brand from scratch. It's always slightly uncomfortable when you are a business-to-business brand, but we talked about ourselves as being the company that brings stories and people together, because I think what we do is an incredibly important link in the chain to give the great artists who are the writers and performers in shows an audience.

PG: *There's a lot of talk about junctions and commercial breaks being imperilled by digital video recorders and other new media technologies. From your perspective, how has the multichannel, multiplatform environment shaped, or challenged, the function of the space between programmes?*

CM: Well, the space between the programmes doesn't exist obviously if you are searching on Hulu for an episode of *Heroes* [2006–10] and then watching it. So at its most blatant it doesn't exist, there is no such thing as a junction, there's no attempt to beautifully segue from one show to another and maximise the audience retention and flow them into something else. But what I will still argue is that the skills of bringing people to that show are as important if not more so in a non-linear world, in a multi-platform world. If you go back, it's the people who are putting playbills up for the Globe Theatre, getting an audience in there. The technology is not the bit that deter-mines the need. In a world of increased choice, the ability to bring people to those pro-grammes becomes all the greater. The ability to launch 'editor' brands that house content, and programme brands themselves, becomes all the greater; you need to have a really tightly defined sense of who and what you are. We talk a lot about the broadband world and I think we've probably been saying for too long that the era of the big commercial break is dead and it blatantly hasn't been, but there is going to be – I think with the advent of internet television services like Seesaw and, fundamentally, with IPTV starting to come into people's sitting rooms – a profound change in the way people watch. We're going to have to learn new skills which might be more about search engine optimisation in order to make sure if somebody looks for *Heroes* that they find it on your site and not anyone else's. But simultaneously, there is still going to be new content that people can't search for because they don't know what it is, and that's where, going back to channel identity, there's a crucial role for what we do in building what we call editor brands.

For example, to hark back to Dave, you can go out and ask everybody what Dave stands for in the UK and they will give you a pretty good idea of the sort of pro-gramming that ends up on the channel. If Dave is a broadband website and you're in the mood for a bit of comedy that's going to appeal to my sort of witty, banterish mind at ten-thirty in the evening, I'm going to try out a programme on there even if I've never heard of it before, because I've learned to trust the brand and the content it delivers to me. Recently, Dave launched a panel show called *Argumental* [2008–present]. If I saw a programme called *Argumental* sitting on a platform like Hulu and it doesn't have any other brand attached to it, why am I going to watch it? It means nothing to me. So the first experience of new shows I think is still going to be about the parent editor brand that it comes from, and that's absolutely what we do. We create strong editor brands and I think UKTV [a digital cable and satellite tele-vision network formed through a joint venture between BBC Worldwide and Virgin

Media Television] have really led the game in this way, at least in Britain, in preparing for multiplatform. If you launch a channel called Blighty, people know instinctively, both from the name and from the design that we've put around it, that it's going to be something that celebrates the wonderful modern eccentricity of our country and you instinctively know whether or not you're going to find stuff that you like there; whereas on a channel called UKTV People [Blighty's previous name before being relaunched in 2009], I don't know what I'm going to get there. We're learning in many ways from other sectors, like magazines and the strength of the masthead brand. For years, people have walked into a newsagent and been faced with infinite variety and in TV that's now what's starting to happen, but we're now moving to the stage beyond, which is the world of Amazon and the long tail and all the skills we need to learn from that.

PG: *Are there design or tonal or creative differences in doing work for a linear broadcast channel such as BBC One compared to a digital channel such as BBC Three or Dave?*

CM: No, the disciplines are all the same. BBC One is hard, because anybody who works in marketing will tell you that the toughest briefs are the ones that talk to everybody. There aren't many brands in the UK that talk to everybody and BBC One is one of them that is expected to have a tone of voice and an appeal that is literally totally pan-generational, that covers every age, sex, ethnicity. We talk about BBC One's mission as being bringing people together for major events and shared viewing experiences, and so you are naturally talking with that single mission in mind when you're writing every trail. In the same way, if I'm writing for a niche female-targeted, single-genre channel, it's a damn sight easier to write with that audience in mind, because you can really pitch them, you can do an incredibly detailed pen portrait and you know exactly what buttons to push, but you're still doing the same things I think for both of them. BBC Three is probably a halfway house in that it's quite a broad audience, but again it's got a very tight proposition as a channel which is never afraid to try new stuff. Everything that we write needs to try and reflect that spirit, and the rebrand that we did for them was very much about trying to create this slightly more populated place than it had been before. We talked about it being initially an island because, for me,

BBC Three (2008)

there's always a notion that whether it's Ibiza or Eel Pie Island in the River Thames, islands are places that encourage maverick experimenters and creative types, and so we then try to embody that feeling onto the channel.

PG: *In characterising its approach to broadcast design, Red Bee states on its company website that 'when you know the rules as well as we do, you can break them in ever more surprising ways'. What are the rules of broadcast design and how have you broken them in any specific ways or examples?*

CM: I think the greatest danger with anything is to think you know the answer and then to keep repeating it, and if I was being slightly controversial, I would say that our predecessors in terms of establishing the pattern of British TV presentation, in partic- ular Lambie-Nairn's work in the 1990s, believed in a formula of minimal graphic design and have stuck pretty rigidly to it. That's not how design and communication works for me. Going back to the Dave rebrand, the notion that TV channels had to be either numeric or descriptive pretty much existed until UKTV G2 became Dave in 2007–8. Channels were either One, Two, Three or Four, or they were descriptive like Discovery Home and Leisure, or Sky Classic Movies, or Eurosport – they did what they said on the tin. If you took the same model into the biscuit market, you'd have a biscuit called biscuit One, Two, Three, Four or double chocolate finger with caramel filling. It's just insane when you look at it that way; you think, why hasn't television had brands that can stand for more than the description of their parts? And so we absolutely broke that rule and since then you've got Discovery Shed, you've got Fiver, you've got a number of brands that I don't think would have existed if Dave hadn't been the suc- cess it had been.

I think you can also completely break the rules in terms of what an ident looks and feels like. For BBC World, we developed a thing called Dynamic Junctions, partly to deal with the complexities of regions and time zones opting in and out. This is a largely automated way of putting programme content in and out in a promotional way that is highly reactive and feels more like Bloomberg Television as a model. I think we've taken the characterisation or personification of the channel on a stage further and here I'd absolutely pay tribute to Lambie-Nairn's work with BBC Two in the 1990s, but I think if you look at the Virgin One rebrand we did in 2009 with Red as a character – a red puppet who embodies the spirit of Virgin and I guess Richard Branson ultimately – he's not just a face of the channel; his blog and Twitter pages are the most read sec- tions of the Virgin website. They parachuted 10,000 Reds into the V music festival last year and they became desirable items on eBay. It's about starting to take the channel out to people rather than just getting people into the channel; increasingly, it's break- ing the physical boundary of the TV screen, I suppose.

PG: *What level of importance does 'interactivity' have for media promotion and design?*

CM: It has been a fundamental game-changer when handled well. There were a lot of brands that were embracing interactivity without really having anything for people to care about. You've got to have a product and an environment and a purpose for engagement that people want to take part in. Competitions based on designing the next cat food colour for tuna, or the next biscuit slogan, are often just talking to a Facebook group of the marketer and three of their mates. There's a world of good content for people online; they're not sitting waiting for the benevolence of your idea to come and grab them. What interactivity has done is given us another whole new method of talking to people if you do it the right way.

I'll give you two examples from the last couple of years that we've done which should have harnessed interactivity in a very positive way. One was for the launch of a science show *Bang Goes the Theory* on BBC One [2009]. From the very naming of the show through to a two-minute live on-air experiment, which was one of the highlights of the promotional campaign, the entire process was driven by the notion of getting people to take part in science experiments. The poster campaign that we did challenged people to do things while standing at the bus shelter like 'is it possible to create the illusion that you've taken the end of your finger off?' or 'can your eyes be deceived by this simple stack of shapes?' This encouraged people literally to think, 'Oh, I can't work that out, text for an answer.' Here we're filling a moment in their lives when they're standing at a bus stop, we're giving them something entertaining to do and they're subtly getting across the message that you can approach science in a way that isn't dry and lab coated.

On another level, we launched the sixth series of *Red Dwarf* [BBC Two, 1988–1999; Dave, 2009–present] in 2009, which had been off the screens for ten years, and it was launching on Dave. So we had a historic but popular programme brand launching on a digital channel which had also never been heard of as a conceit. We launched it entirely with an Alternate Reality Game, which was absolutely appealing to the mindset of our target audience, where they could find their way through a treasure hunt online unlocking clues and breaking codes, helping each other out, finding bits of information and gradually zooming in through a succession of numbers which, if you got 3,000 people to unlock the code, gradually revealed a launch site where a space bug would land. This ended up getting over two million viewers and was the highest-watched multichannel show that year. I mean huge numbers for it in that environment and without spending a single pound in paid-for media.

But you can also do it on a mass level. We've just been working on the twenty-fifth anniversary of *EastEnders*, where the whole nature of the campaign was to get people to recreate their famous 'duff duff' moment [this refers to the distinctive drumbeats in the closing theme tune of the popular British soap opera, duly associated with cliffhanger moments] and uploading them onto websites. The whole nature of the campaign, whether or not you actually took part in it, was interactive; it was saying this is what BBC One's about, which is about stimulating national conversations around big moments.

PG: *When BBC Two unveiled a new set of channel idents in 2007, viewers were encouraged to download the '2' template from the channel website and create their own versions. What is the impetus behind this kind of audience involvement?*
CM: It's not a new thing. MTV did it with design colleges and animation colleges fifteen years ago; it's a great way of showing that you are an open-source creative environment. E4 has championed it over the years. We tried to do it in a different way with the user-generated continuity for BBC Three and it's a slightly more open brief which has led to equally extraordinary things coming back. I think it's got to be the right brand and I think you've got to be genuine about embracing it and using, in the buzz phrase, 'crowd sourcing'. When the snack company Walkers do it nationally to generate a new flavour of crisps, it's a huge proven marketing success when you really put weight behind it and do it on that kind of scale. I think if you don't have the scale and presence, you shouldn't try it, because you get a lot of people congratulating themselves on very moderate levels of interaction.

PG: *Are these strategies seen as free creative labour?*
CM: They can be. I don't know if you'll ever get MTV to admit it, but I'm *certain* that back in the day they found it a very cost-effective way of refreshing their identity and giving the sense of having their finger on the pulse without having to invest heavily in it (*laughing*).

PG: *What are the key challenges facing Red Bee Media as a company specialising in media branding and broadcast design?*
CM: As with everything, there are opportunities and threats for us as the world changes. The opportunities are suddenly the change in the web from being a fundamentally print-based design – which is what it was, they even talk about web pages; it was designed by people thinking in print terms – to one that is fundamentally now becoming televisual. I still believe that people will refer to 'TV' on the web. I think that phrase has stuck; it actually brings a whole load of clients and a whole load of work into the territory to which we are specialists, which is navigating audiences through rich visual environments with an aesthetic that is born out of cinema and television. So there's lots of opportunities and some of the brands that we've been working with, which are not what you'd normally consider media brands, like Nike, are promoting

themselves through events such as the Nike Deadly Five web experience in a way that is not profoundly different from a TV series that happens to exist online. The branding that they need to do and the work they need to do is very different from traditional brand advertising and one that comes into our skill set.

The pressures on us are the same that are facing lots of people in different industries; increasingly, a lot of what we do can be done by a single person sitting at their own computer and calling themselves a company. You get increased competition, what we do becomes highly commoditised, and the price becomes a pressure. More broadly, in the last couple of years the model for big media companies has really come under threat. People aren't used to paying for content on the web and, as much as it's keeping Rupert Murdoch awake at night (if it is), it's going to keep us awake at night, because we rely on our clients generating income from a creative product and needing our skills to bring an audience to it. That is still the billion-dollar question facing everybody. How much are people going to pay for creative content online given that there are generations that have grown up not paying for creative content online and expecting it to be free?

PG: *That seems a pregnant point to end on*.

CM: Scary, I've scared myself.

Bibliography

Deuze, Mark. (2007) *Media Work* (Cambridge: Polity Press).

Grainge, Paul. (2010) 'Elvis Sings for the BBC: Broadcast Branding and Digital Media Design', *Media, Culture & Society*, 32 (1), pp. 45–61.

Johnson, Catherine. (2011) *Branding Television* (London: Routledge).

Mawer, Charlie. (2009) 'Industry Perspectives', Plenary Lecture, Ephemeral Media Workshop, University of Nottingham, <www.projects.beyondtext.ac.uk/ephemeralmedia/index.php> accessed 10 January 2010.

Meech, Peter. (1998) 'Questionnaire: Promotions Managers/Creative Directors', Unpublished Questionnaire conducted by Peter Meech, Stirling Media Research Institute.

Red Bee Media. (2007) 'Interactive Design', <www.redbeemedia.com/interactive/index.shtml> accessed 22 October 2007.

PART3 BEYOND: ONLINE TV AND WEB DRAMA

6 The Evolving Media Ecosystem: An Interview with Victoria Jaye, BBC

Elizabeth Jane Evans

The emergence of digital technologies since the mid-1990s has had a significant impact on the television industry. Online or mobile phone content increasingly supplements, enhances or even replaces the ephemerality of television's 'broadcast moment' until that moment is only part of the television experience. The BBC has been at the centre of attempts to develop and exploit this 'beyond broadcast' space. Following on from its pioneering role in earlier television technologies such as colour, the BBC began experimenting with home computers in the 1980s and internet services in the mid-1990s (see Naylor *et al.*, 2000, p. 140). The Corporation's website, <www.bbc.co.uk>, was launched in 1998 and has since become a key BBC service, growing to include information services such as news, sport, recipes and history alongside programme information, gaming and the online television viewing service iPlayer. The 2006 Royal Charter review cemented this role, expanding the BBC's public service remit to include 'helping to deliver to the public the benefit of emerging communications technologies and services' (DCMS, 2006, p. 3).

The following interview with Victoria Jaye, Head of Multiplatform Commissioning for Drama, Comedy and Entertainment at the BBC, explores the Corporation's response to the challenges presented by digital technologies in the first decade of the twenty-first century. The first of these challenges concerned the nature of the BBC's content. In the 2000s, high bandwidth internet services opened up opportunities for new distribution avenues, allowing audiences to access television content via a permanent online 'library' of content rather than broadcasting's ephemeral 'flow' (Williams, 1974). At the same time, digital platforms allowed for the development of content such as games or social media-based services and YouTube began to normalise short-form content, challenging the dominance of the half-hour or hour-long episode format. Such platforms allowed for the alternative distribution of broadcast content, but they also opened up possibilities for the narrative worlds of television content to be expanded through transmedia storytelling (see Jenkins, 2006; Evans, 2011), offering audiences new forms of engagement. In this context, key questions emerged for the BBC. Specifically, what value does the broadcast moment hold when audiences are increasingly able to access content outside of broadcasting? To what extent should the BBC, as a traditional media producer, embrace the ever-increasing range of audiovisual content forms that new technologies are facilitating?

The second challenge concerned the impact of new media technologies on the BBC's key industrial relationships. The notion of the media 'ecosystem', and how that ecosystem has changed as a result of digital technologies, becomes particularly important here. The BBC itself functions as an ecosystem, consisting of a web of relationships between writers, producers, directors, performers, game designers and technology developers that must, as a whole, engage with an audience that is accessing media in an ever-growing variety of ways. At the same time, it sits within a broader media ecosystem, directly and indirectly interacting not only with other public service and commercial broadcasters but also with new media players such as YouTube and iTunes. The BBC occupies a unique position within this broader ecosystem. It is large enough to play a role in the global television market but is separate from that market, protected by the licence fee paid by all British television owners. However, it must justify that licence fee and, as Naylor *et al.* demonstrate, navigate 'an internal division between the licence fee-funded activities of the Corporation and its more commercial activities' (Naylor *et al.*, 2000, p. 140). The multiple opportunities for content dissemination that digital technologies brought about in the 2000s only intensified the BBC's need to negotiate this division, posing a different question. How could the Corporation fulfil its public service obligations and give licence-fee payers the full range of choice that digital technologies facilitate while simultaneously protecting both its own commercial interests and those of the independent production companies and personnel it works with?

Jaye's position at the centre of the BBC's multiplatform strategies offers insight into how the BBC was facing these challenges in the 2000s through both overarching philosophies and concrete programming strategies. The interview was conducted on 7 July 2010. Four months earlier, BBC Director-General Mark Thompson had launched *Putting Quality First*, a strategic attempt to reshape the Corporation's activities in a multiplatform media environment that promised 'a more focused BBC doing fewer things better' (Thompson, 2010). Two days previously, the BBC Trust had published their Strategic Review that endorsed a 25 per cent budget cut for BBC Online (see BBC Trust, 2010). How these political and financial issues will play out in long-term BBC practice and its use of digital technologies remains to be seen. The projects and services that Jaye discusses faced an uncertain future. The following interview therefore captures a moment of transition as it happens; it serves as a snapshot of the challenges facing a public service broadcaster within a constantly changing media landscape.

ELIZABETH EVANS: *How do you ensure you meet the BBC's public service remit in a multiplatform environment?*

VICTORIA JAYE: The last few months have really been about trying to understand what BBC Online comprises, how much we spend, what the key pillars are. We're constantly putting arguments forward for our different areas, but, frankly, I think we all totally agree that the BBC can give its most integrated account of itself online. Obviously the BBC is a public service and we have to deliver public value as detailed in our public purposes, so it's the same for multiplatform as it is for broadcasting: we have to deliver public value. We have to offer services and content that are distinctive, have a positive market impact and continue to connect audiences to each other around our precious stories, formats and events. It is also a BBC duty to take creative risks, especially in market impact failure genres,[1] for example comedy and drama. In the *Putting Quality First* paper, [Director-General] Mark Thompson outlines our five new editorial priorities, one of which is ambitious UK drama and comedy. Another is events that bind the nation together (Thompson, 2010). We need to be able to support that vision.

I think one of the key things coming through this period of change is looking at multiplatform opportunities as a way to refresh and renew how we approach storytelling, format generation and event coverage. At the same time, we constantly want to refresh the head end, at the broadcast moment. Increasingly, we have a view of our content distribution as a kind of ecosystem. The broadcast network is the lifeblood of that ecosystem; the whole thing really rests on it. So, the idea that broadcast is somehow losing its momentum in this environment is absolutely incorrect. In fact, perceptions of the healthy BBC are perceptions of a healthy BBC One, so we have to be renewing that broadcast. However, simultaneously, we are creating an open, permanent architecture for our programmes on the internet platform. So in its first burst, for example, we will be promoting the programme that's coming to air. While the programme is on air, it will be enriched with information about the programme, cast, synopsis and potential broadcast ephemera that are created through the production process such as storyboards or designs. We are also now asking that there will be a clip for every episode of every BBC programme.

The first level of investment in the online space is that we have a programme page for every episode of every TV and radio programme. We have, over the last year, made these much richer, but they are principally about our programming, how it was made, who was in it and so on. Over time, we'll build up the archive for the future, so this has a permanent presence. They will, over time, house 'commercial user journeys', so when the BBC public service is no longer offering that content, we are guiding the audience into commercial environments where they can purchase the episodes in full. It's very much about aiding discovery of and access to what we're already investing in, which is programmes.

The second level of opportunity in terms of multiplatform is stretching the form of some of those programmes – the storyworlds of our dramas, the formats of our entertainment shows, the events of our coverage. But that is a second level of investment and a much smaller investment. To even deliver the first level of multiplatform opportunity is extraordinarily resource-intensive. We're seeing 30 per cent increases in distribution costs from 2004/5 to 2008/9 as a result of simply converting assets to be placed online. It is very labour-intensive and as a business and an organisation, we weren't set up to do this. All sorts of production processes have to change, such as tagging, compliance and editorial, just to get that basic access to our programmes and information about our programmes in a permanent, fit-for-purpose state. So, when we get to that second level of what I'm calling the format renewal opportunities, that's a discrete enterprise. Of course we want to be on the front foot with it, because it is our duty to take these risks, to stimulate the market, but we can't put unwieldy amounts in that area, because our core business is fairly cost-heavy.

Simultaneously, this second level not only has to stretch the form of those shows, but somehow it also has to feed back into the ecosystem by finding the new faces of tomorrow or building our archive for the future. It has to deliver on the BBC's overall mission and I think that's probably the most difficult area to be really clear in identifying the opportunities, because it's a young industry. I think I keep dining out on this quote, it wasn't mine: 'The camera was invented thirty years before the film industry'. That's where we are with the internet platform. As a broadcaster, it's a new platform to be offering things on. What are we doing in that place? Is it about freshness of approach? Is it about targeting discrete audiences? What does success actually look like? We're only getting a project-by-project sense of this, so I think that is a big challenge for us. Of course, the BBC is leading the way, so you're having to take not only your own organisation along with you but also an industry and an audience with you, so that's quite a big challenge.

EE: *You talked about the public value of creating shared experience, something that has long been part of the BBC's remit. Is the internet as a platform uniquely capable of enhancing broadcasting's ability to do that?*
VJ: Yes, absolutely, and I think what's absolutely fascinating in that space are our event websites such as Comic Relief, Children in Need. On these sites, where the nation comes together for the greater good, we're seeing increases in web traffic between 30 per cent and 50 per cent from year on year. That's staggering actually, because those sites are doing very simple things like facilitating people fund-raising, or facilitating donation, or the sharing of event photographs. So, speaking to the audience team, they're convinced that this increase is really due to the public knowing that the internet platform is a place to organise, and coalesce, and come together, and share,

and connect, so that feels a really natural thing to do. I think we're beautifully craft-
ing the basics, really making sure we can deliver on the promise of those events in a
way in which the audience are very comfortable with. I think there is an expectation
that those events are beyond television, and they are, but we have facilities to bring
audiences together and participate, engage, in ways that we hadn't before, and so
that's absolutely a priority.

EE: *Have multiplatform priorities changed over your time at the BBC?*
VJ: Yes. I think we've always understood the potential for digital platforms to enable
audiences to participate in our events. The red button was absolutely about partici-
pating in programmes such as *Test the Nation* [2002–present].[2] But being part of the
entertainment experience itself and being something that's owned by the programme
is a growing endeavour in the sense that in the past it's been on the side. Now, it's
actually part of the armoury of the format, and I think one of the challenges we have
is actually making that evolution towards being able to communicate it with conviction and confidence to the audience via presenters and on-screen performers, and I
think that continues to be a challenge. It's still a little bit over there, but I think the
audience is absolutely ready for being told these things are available to them with a
lot more conviction, from the heart of the format or the show or the event.

EE: *What are the BBC's key strategies for using digital technologies?*
VJ: Well first and foremost, it's getting that first level right, which is a permanent,
public record of every programme or radio programme we've ever transmitted, which
is enriched over time not only through archive release or production content but
potentially by audience and social elements, whether that's reviews by the audience or
bringing in conversations they're having. So, that's using that first level to sweat the
assets of broadcast to their absolute maximum too. This is really important when you
think that our programming does end up on other channels, such as Dave, and ensuring the public has a strong sense of the value they get from public service, that we get
maximum credit for the creation of our output. The idea of content's original source is
absolutely crucial to our long-term survival in the sense that if people stop identifying
the BBC as a programme's origin, we can't sustain the ecosystem. So, while this seems
fairly modest, it's actually very fundamental and philosophically very powerful, because
that sets you up for everything else. So, you've got a broadcast head and then you've
got this long tail, or permanent archive, or cumulative presence, for what were transient moments and that's absolutely the most important thing to establish. Then on
top of that you layer other ways to cut entry into that content. It could be via aggregation. The Comedy Portal, for example, is an aggregation of things that were on air
or are totally original to the web. There's ways of positioning that content that are

audience-facing in their own right and are another way to enter into content outside of broadcast. So, on top of that sort of permanent, global programmes' architecture containing programme information, you get access to a wealth of archive content you could not access via just broadcast alone. *Wildlife Finder* [<www.bbc.co.uk/ wildlifefinder/>], for example, offers up archive from the BBC's Natural History Unit permanently online. We ensure the television programmes are supported with their online programme information, but there will be an aggregation of archive content as well.

What then happens is that the audience relationship over time begins to shift. It continues to be about 'appointment to view', big moments of television, but it's also about coming to an internet platform and exploring content in a way that is about your interest. The relationship becomes one of an enabler or a facilitator as well as a broadcaster; that's when you start seeing it as an ecosystem. So, getting that first, programme-information layer in there and releasing strategically into it, relating to broadcast moments, looking at the archive entry points, then you're looking at that second level which I'm calling that kind of genre renewal. How do you stretch the form of the show? It involves storyworlds where television just cannot contain the world; it flows over. *Doctor Who* [1963–present] and *EastEnders* [1985–present] are our two really premier brands in the drama space. Interestingly, they're from opposite ends of the spectrum. One is a world with its own rules which is the *Doctor Who* world; the other is a soap which very much lives its life as we live ours. One is on all year round, the other isn't, but both have an enormous young share. Now I'm not only chasing the young, but we have to also accept at the head end of our ecosystem, the BBC channels attract older viewers: fifty-five to fifty-seven is the average age of a BBC One viewer. So what better way to increase the value younger viewers get from the BBC than actively commissioning multiplatform content for those brands they're very comfortable with, to allow them to engage more deeply.

So, [online *EastEnders* spin-off] *E20* [2010–present] was conceived as Albert Square from the point of view of the young characters, to try and get a much more authentic portrayal of young Londoners into the soap. The whole process was about nurturing new talent; the music composer won an *E20* online mixing competition, for example. The whole of the *E20* project was facilitated by the internet platform and could not have existed without it. The way it was released and how it unfolded was absolutely built on what the internet platform does. Assets were released slowly online, building the story over time, allowing characters to be fleshed out in a way that they just couldn't be on television. The audience was feeding back with a lot of fan pages, and so the whole thing was a slice into that narrative that simply couldn't have come about if we were only thinking of broadcast moments. We've got a second burst of *E20* in September 2010 which will take this different point of view to another level with a new set of characters moving into the Square and we'll explore the challenges they face. So, that's very much the *EastEnders E20* story, and I think it's a very power-ful one. We had three million views over the two to three weeks it was first available around the twenty-fifth anniversary of the series.

The second example is *Doctor Who: The Adventure Games* [2010]. *Doctor Who* is a forty-year-old brand really for the BBC. It's an extraordinarily rich storyworld and has always pushed the boundaries of production technology and ways of telling its story. We were always spilling over broadcast whenever we could, whether that was Tardisodes, or *Attack of the Graske* on red button, or comic-makers, trailer-makers, and all the sorts of things that the audience can engage in the world. But with the arrival of the eleventh Doctor, we pushed the level that step higher and actually said, 'You can physically be the Doctor'. The *Doctor Who Adventure Games* are not about *Doctor Who*, they are *Doctor Who* in a new dimension, to quote the trailer, and they were an extraordinary coming together, an almost alchemist practice of bringing together established television writers, headed up by [series head writer] Steven Moffat, highly respected and revered games writer Charles Cecil and a very experi-enced games designer, Sumo, in Sheffield. This group took the adventure game format, which is not a particularly commercially exploited format, so again it's about stimulating the games industry, not trampling on it. BBC Worldwide[3] clearly has its own agenda in the games area for *Doctor Who*, so the *Adventure Games* are very much conceived as part of the TV series as four interactive episodes. We actually say there are not thirteen episodes of this series of *Doctor Who*, there are seventeen, four of them happen to be interactive and online. There are more cut scenes within the game than you would have in a normal adventure game – 50 per cent are cut scenes – so it's still very much of the *Doctor Who* canon. It's been amazing to hear the writ-ers – the TV and the games writers – talk about the process of how they came to create the adventure. The games writers could imagine worlds *Doctor Who* could go to that simply television could not, such as burning down Trafalgar Square or setting the whole episode underwater. Even thinking about the fact that the Tardis was bigger on the inside than on the outside, which actually is something the games people showed us when they first pitched and blew Steven Moffat away. They showed us a drawing of the Doctor's drawing room. We've never seen the Doctor's drawing room but the whole world was built out because of the capability of the canvas to do it.

I think that's something we're getting a lot richer ideas about and really focusing on the writers. What does this canvas allow us to do that television cannot? Beyond fiction, beyond television, what does that look like? And that doesn't mean you choose the endings all the time, but it can mean you can release content like we have with *E20*. We've got some other really exciting projects planned where just how you release it and how you allow the audience to patch together the story for themselves, and how you link out to the bigger connected internet, offers fantastically exciting opportunities. As a broadcaster, you simply would not have conceived of the *Doctor Who* canon like that had you not had that platform to begin to conceive it on.

In comedy we have a threefold agenda, but one important part of the comedy multiplatform story is origination of comedy. So, on telly there are a discrete number of opportunities and what you find is we don't have the big sitcoms we used to have, the family sitcoms, and there's a whole new audience of active comedy seekers online who we're potentially not reaching through our formal channels. So, how can we renew how we express comedy from the BBC? Again, the internet offers us wonderful opportunities of playing with form, duration, point of view, talent, and this is really what we're doing online. What's wonderful is not only does that comedy need to stand alone and be fantastically appealing for an online audience, as the BBC we clearly want to have that eye on the network 'head end', how are we moving the creative conversation forward for comedy as a genre from the BBC? So, another really important role for that original work is finding the new faces and the formats that we simply wouldn't have got had we continued to ask for thirty-minute, pre-watershed shows. If you keep asking that same question, you potentially might not find an interesting answer. So we have Jason Lewis, who was a talent we found online and is now going to a BBC Three series. Again, we wouldn't have found him otherwise, you know, so that's really important.

EE: *So creative personnel are changing as well? You're taking people who work in television such as Steven Moffat?*
VJ: Yes, but who completely gets this potential.

EE: *And bringing in people from outside of television?*
VJ: Absolutely. For me, having been in this space for a long time, the most exciting and successful projects have been when you have brought together people who would never normally have come together, whether that's marketers and comedians, or games writers and drama writers, or soap writers and social media experts. It's fusing ideas together and fusing teams together, where expertise collides and questions; I think that's when you get the creative spark. I think because it's such an unknown space, one of the responsibilities of a role like mine is to set out opportunity in the clearest possible way, removing it away from the kind of functional, 'What does the internet do? What is the software?' and instead asking, 'What is the potential for a writer? What is the potential for a format? What is the potential for the audience?' This content, for me, delivers when it's related to television; it simply makes TV viewing better. You can take that back to [the music festival] Glastonbury, which was one of the first services I launched. Pressing red just makes watching Glastonbury better, because I don't have to stick with a band I don't want. That's a very simple thing to do.

My ambition for *E20* would be that young audiences who love it, love *EastEnders* even more because of it. Increasing the love factor is a really important measure of success. It's a very simple ask, but it's very difficult to achieve, because, as I said before, it's not a mature area. It is a very young area. For most companies and producers, the opportunity is unclear, the rewards are unknown and, for many, entering this domain represents a loss of control. Broadcast has always been very much about being in control as a creative and managing scarcity at every level, whether that's spectrum at a technical level, or editorially teasing audiences with access to talent, plot, the funniest scene, etc. … 'We'll wait, we'll put that at the end of the show.' And we're potentially saying, 'We want that funniest scene on YouTube three weeks before transmission.' That took us some time with comedians, for example, and we were saying, 'We want your funniest sketch, we want to put it on YouTube and we'll use that to virally create interest in your new show.' There used to be a real sort of, 'Oh, no one's going to watch the show if they've seen that on YouTube,' and of course that's absolute nonsense. We're not seeing any cannibalisation of the network audience through more aggressive distribution or, indeed, iPlayer catch-up. There just isn't, it's just not happening, so I think that's interesting.

EE: *In addition to a greater love for TV, are there any other particular values, either for the audience or for the BBC, in using the internet?*

VJ: Well, simply for the audience, it gives them more opportunities to view and find out about programming and engage with information around it. At the level one, programme support stuff, it's very much about making sure that they don't miss out. 'Making the unmissable unmissable', that's what iPlayer's agenda is; you haven't got to be sitting on your sofa at a certain time to get *Imagine* [2003–present]. There are more opportunities to view what you've already paid for and more opportunities to find out what's coming up. To have your questions answered is another simple example. 'What was the music used in that show?' Constantly we used to have that kind of audience need for more information about our programmes. Now we've given them comprehensive information about our shows online. Who was in it? It's answered there; there's everything you ever wanted to know about the show, every opportunity we can offer you at a free-to-air, to watch it again. Increasingly, when we can't offer it to you for free, we're going to tell you where you can buy it or where you can download it.

We will also use online to creatively surface or aggregate information. So, for example, if *Doctor Who* covers Pompeii in one of its episodes, and suddenly your kids are all going, 'What is Pompeii?', we will make sure we're connecting *Dr Who* content with Knowledge content, thereby facilitating rich journeys around topics that just couldn't have been facilitated before.

Finally, I think new ways to connect with other like-minded people, new ways to come together as a nation and organise fundraising events at the very simplest level such as parties in your area around *Sport Relief*. So, for the audience, we can actually deliver public value even more effectively via these platforms in a way that we've never been able to do – ever. Our purposes really come to life in digital in a way that they couldn't before.

EE: *You mentioned linking to the BBC's archive. Is there a sense of making use of (and making available) material that you already have, rather than having it sit there on a shelf?*
VJ: Yes. That's right. Releasing the archive, the hundreds of thousands of hours of ephemera. There's an awful lot of work going on as to what the BBC itself digitises, how it has partnerships with the BFI or art galleries, e.g. the Tate, so the whole strategy for releasing the archive can only be done through partnership. The simplest stuff to clear that has the longest life, that the BBC feels like they totally own and should release, would be the kind of thing that we would release first. But there are other areas that are less public where the priority for it lies in more of a collaborative release through mutual interest with the BBC and other public bodies like cinemas. In terms of comedy, we're releasing small collections, but we're very clear that those are really tasters, if you like, of the long form which it would be right for you to acquire long term, because the artists and the writers that created that should be rewarded when we're outside of our public service halo.

I can't speak in detail about the whole archive strategy, but that's the principle of it. There's the release of certain collections where it's more straightforward to clear them, they're public service aligned, and then there's partnerships for the deeper archive which would absolutely require the deeper archive to be paid for or working through the partnerships to support the release and digitisation of that content.

EE: *The BBC obviously plays quite a big role in storing television as a permanent object, because you keep everything.*
VJ: Yes, that's right! But now we're republishing it.

EE: *You're making it non-ephemeral by giving it back to the audience.*
VJ: Yes, that's right. In fact this word, since last year, has really got some traction in this organisation thanks to the AHRC workshop on 'ephemeral media' at the University of Nottingham. Understanding the value of audition tapes, for example, is an area we're looking at in drama. When someone goes through an extraordinary metamorphosis to be Churchill or play John Lennon, what does that first audition of the lead give the audience? There's something very simple about releasing that onto the programme page which is simply about the show; you see the trailer and you may see that first audition tape. *Being Human* [2008], when we released the storyboards for the next

series online onto the blog, there were hundreds of comments from the fans, who were fascinated to unpick what might be coming up. Or David Attenborough's original expense claims, which have an extraordinary value when you piece them together with the long history of programme-making for this organisation, and give you a sense of the moment. They obviously contributed to a transient broadcast moment, but have an archive and cumulative value well beyond that moment, and I think that's what we're really talking about when we're thinking about the broadcast moment. It's a transient, powerful, mass audience, an enormous driver of appeal and interest, and then there's this beautifully crafted long-term/cumulative platform, harbouring the riches of how that was made, sometimes stretching the form of what that is, but also building this archive for the future.

Once you build this online body of programme information, broadcast ephemera, the archive, you can take these creative slices of it. Comedy is one of those; *Wildlife Finder* is another one of those interesting slices that an audience may come to quite independently of something going on there, but through that may discover something new.

Thinking of BBC content as a kind of ecosystem helps you make these connections and also helps us understand where it's absolutely critical that we maintain public service value and understanding, which is around that broadcast moment. If the public doesn't value us for doing that, we cannot support all of these commercial user journeys and all of the partnerships and archive release, because that's what's holding it up, and frankly, it's still what the audience generally believe the BBC is.

EE: *What other concrete multiplatform programming strategies have emerged out of the appropriation of digital technologies?*
VJ: With drama, there are two approaches. The first is extensions of TV brands where there's a programme with a young share in particular, because that's a low-hanging fruit, that's the active fiction-seekers, if you like. Then, in terms of the original fiction that we're creating, the question is TV output has to look like it just couldn't possibly had looked had we not done a multiplatform element, otherwise just go and pitch a fifty-minute show to BBC Two. The measure of its success is if you say: 'That is extraordinary television and that came about because of this process.' *E20*, *Doctor Who: The Adventure Games*, *Being Human* all have to deliver on making something happen that simply could not have happened without the platform enabling it to be thus, or to let the writers think the unthought beyond television.

With comedy, we don't have as much on air as we used to, so when we do have comedy, we amplify that broadcast window moment with bonus content and access to talent, for example via Twitter, something that makes it feel bigger than just a transmission, because, again, we want to ensure our reputation remains for being brilliant at comedy. So, one agenda for the multiplatform in that area is to amplify the impact of network comedy. There's another ambition to redefine what BBC Comedy can look like using the internet platform, finding the new faces and formats of tomorrow.

In the area of entertainment, it's about enabling the audiences to come together physically and share and celebrate. It's a facilitational tool, and in the entertainment area that's potentially the most potent thing we do. We can genuinely deliver on playing along, or getting involved through a digital platform. For example, with *Only Connect* [2008–present], a BBC Four quiz show, you can play the games online. It's like a bit of *University Challenge* [ITV, 1962–87; BBC, 1994–present], but you have to find the association between four sets of four words. We released a number of these grids online and for a BBC Four programme, which has limited visibility frankly, we got 1.6 million plays for these over the series window of thirteen weeks, which is a lot. If you also think about *Doctor Who: The Adventure Games*, which so far, over six weeks, have gotten a million plays. For something so big and high profile, we're not unhappy with a million, but *Only Connect*, which is a bit of a slow burn, it's very interesting.

There's something in our formats that lend themselves to ongoing play online, but again, this is an area under enormous scrutiny under *Putting Quality First*. We've had to rest many ambitions in the entertainment area online simply because they have not been seen to be the priority, or they seem to be areas the market is supplying handsomely across, for example, the areas of quizzes and games. I would argue vehemently against that in a sense that *Mastermind* [1972–present], *University Challenge* or *1 vs 100* [2006–9] are core BBC public service formats, but therein lies a challenge. But that's not to say we're not looking at big, live Saturday-night entertainment programmes and being able to offer exciting new ways for the audience at home to affect or participate in the jeopardy on air. That's where the entertainment opportunity really is for us; it's really delivering on format jeopardy and audience participation.

EE: *How do the meanings of the term 'ephemeral' (both as duration and lifespan) apply to the way you're using the internet to stretch the broadcast moment?*
VJ: Well, clearly everything is potentially permanent! But television is to be celebrated and feels special because it is transient, it comes and goes, and we create a lot of hype about it being transient. All our marketing effort is about that. But simultaneously and independently, we are also saying there is an archival value to that transience and there's a way of packaging all the content and the materials that went into the making of that transient experience. They have an archival value that we can publicly publish and gift back to the audience, and it can feel like a gift if we curate it properly. So, those ephemeral materials in various forms – I don't just mean video, I mean text, I mean image, I mean audio – they can be liberated and establish their own long-term potency when they're made permanently available and linked to in ways that they

couldn't be linked to before by the nature of the platform. They have a public value that they just didn't have on the dusty old shelf.

So that's the programme-making and about the programmes. In terms of stretching the form, this is something we're being challenged by really. We are commissioning bursts of digital endeavour around *Doctor Who* so we can release four games, or we will have done a burst for *E20*, but now those are sitting there online. They were created to support specific broadcast moments, but now they're going to bank up online, so we might have more *Doctor Who: Adventure Games* or we might have *Torchwood* ones and how well do they hang together as a permanent presence? We now have a body of fiction online that hasn't necessarily been considered in its portfolio permanent presence. This work exists on a connected platform in which fans are still oscillating and chatting around it, so there's a challenge for us to creatively corral and make sense of the forms we've given birth to happily related to specific broadcast moments, but now their lifespan has increased, the life value is different, it's shaped differently. The big-value moments are big audience numbers around the broadcast head end. There are smaller numbers, in truth, around the digital endeavours, but they're trickling on. So we had three million views during the twenty-fifth anniversary [of *EastEnders*] for *E20*, but every week 30,000 are still coming in. That's quite interesting. *Doctor Who: The Adventure Games* had a million downloads around transmission, but those games are still playable for the next ten years. So, it is forcing us to re-evaluate the measures of success. The numbers in truth, compared to broadcast, for all of this are small. You know, you can get eleven million viewers for one *EastEnders* episode; it takes you a number of weeks to get any number of millions for digital content.

So, are we comparing the wrong thing? Are we measuring it over the wrong time period and actually, how do those two things oxygenate each other? How does stuff going on in a game affect the next bout of series episodes? So it's stretching the assets of programmes as well as stretching the storyworlds in which they are built or the format play on which they're also established beyond transmission. So, even with the *Only Connect* walls, multiple walls are available to play by audiences well beyond the broadcast moment. The show will come back, but it's still oxygenating itself over here, online. Nothing is ephemeral, it has bursts of life orchestrated highly here at broadcast and ongoing presences. I think that's what we're beginning to get a sense of.

EE: *Is there a value for something that's short in duration as well?*
VJ: Definitely. *Eurovision* this year blew the minds of the Television Audience Insight team in a way that they always go, 'The numbers are a bit small, aren't they, to do all this?' But this year, it was an aggressive short-form strategy and it got 8.6 million views of the short-form around the event. The BBC's YouTube channel beat *X Factor*

[2004–present], *Britain's Got Talent* [2009–present], everybody else, because everyone was looking at short-form. So, reliving those moments, it's a no-brainer: the last breath of the Doctor; Maid Marion dying in *Robin Hood* [2006–9]; Peggy having a fight with somebody in *EastEnders*; the Jacksons returning. These moments are absolutely what people continue to want to share and talk about. It's about sweating the assets, getting those moments out there immediately to fuel the social currency. In the entertainment space, where there's such talkability around the shows, it's absolutely essential to get short-form out immediately and for it to be the best moment.

EE: *What about the broadcast moment itself? What value does that hold now?*
VJ: I would argue it's almost heightened in a way. The stakes are high and it's more exciting than it's ever been, because so much of life is not event any more. I think, in a way, you're seeing the renaissance of event television, which potentially makes it harder for smaller channels to fight in this space. But I still think, as a public, we love events and gathering round each other. It seems very much in the DNA of being human, and I think there are more opportunities for how that might look. But live television is really coming back on a Saturday night in a way that we haven't seen before, potentially invigorated by digital play-along and audience engagement. The broadcast moment is still what we strive for, celebrate and cherish, definitely, and that's absolutely delivering centrally to public purpose. That's exactly what the BBC is hitting; if we cannot do that, then that's a really big problem. So I think the broadcast moment is precious, to be cherished and is what's driving this ecosystem.

But we're seeing that broadcast moment even more broadly. The premiere moment we're even considering as transmission plus seven-day catch-up. So, we're even taking iPlayer as the broadcast premiere now and are beginning to consider this as a public service transmission period very slowly.

EE: *So the moment itself has changed?*
VJ: We still do overnights,[4] but actually, they're beginning to put iPlayer catch-up as part of the performance of the transmission, which clearly sets us apart and sets a sort of temporal line in the sand for when to hold back content from becoming commercial. We've got to hold stuff back from the commercial environment to get as much public value out of that original investment. For example, if we give an asset to Dave too early, it's not associated with the BBC, so we absolutely have to max out on that, and that's where we crucially stand in front of the audience and go, 'This is from the BBC; this is what you've paid for.' So, I think that moment is still really important, it's where our relevance is and, interestingly, on the BBC Online platform the high-value audience-facing things are the iPlayer, which is television catch-up, news and sport, which is moment-intensive content.

And interestingly, with the iPlayer, which philosophically those running it thought would lead to all sorts of serendipitous discovery of other content, what we're witnessing is, 'I've missed *Top Gear*, I'll watch *Top Gear*, I'm out of here,' you know! 'I've missed *EastEnders*, I'll watch *EastEnders*, I'm out of here.' It's totally driven by the broadcast moment. People are mostly catching up on programmes the morning after broadcast or later that night. After the sixth day post-transmission, not a lot happening, so again, the moments are still driving it.

EE: *So is it more important to create a particular moment or to create something permanent?*
VJ: It's about creating that moment. We create those moments, that's what the BBC does, moments. But now those moments are no longer just gone. While we're maxing out on their momentariness, we will also ensure that they will never have to be forgotten, so you're giving them a permanent place or record of the passing of that moment, but it's still a moment. You definitely still want to create hit moments of jeopardy and hilarity, and that's absolutely what we're doing. We are driving moments, but those moments have a lasting value and we can support that lasting value through these endeavours.

EE: *You've mentioned the challenge of negotiating the BBC's public service role and its commercial enterprise. Is that a key challenge facing the BBC?*
VJ: It definitely is and redefining commercial boundaries is important, because we have to have positive market impact. We go through a market-impact assessment with all of our significant commissions, because we don't want to trample the market. But even if we enter the market with a high investment, like in the area of online drama, we can shape the market by doing that, so we have to be very aware of that. So it would have to be a win-win situation whereby we are given the premiere moment, we establish audience public value from that moment, we have a permanent presence or public record of those moments in short-form, but wouldn't have a whole programme there beyond its seven-day life. By the same token, the rights holders have to be free to then exploit that, whether that's through distribution to other networks or DVD. That's the whole philosophy of the holdback, how do you hold things back and when's long enough?

Building that permanent architecture is significant in the sense it enables us to link, for the audience, the public moment they have seen that has passed with the commercial life it now has via iTunes or via a big commercial game website, whatever they've built around that format. So, you can see where we are doing things like *Doctor Who: The Adventure Games*, that very much brings us into quite sharp relief. What's the difference between a public service interactive episode and a worldwide game? There's an enormous creative difference, but the questions are being asked as to why would you do a public service game? Why is the BBC looking at the internet platform to renew itself? Well, one of the grammars of the internet platform is game mechanics. Alongside webisodes, blogs, social media, short-form, these are the grammars of the web. Not to bend our purpose and look at those is cutting off our relevance for the future, so that's why we feel quite strongly that games of our formats have a role in the public service space. The level of it and the shape of it are still to be discussed, and I think it's an area of tension for sure. That whole area has never been conceived in an environment where you're permanently connected to a global platform and traditionally you are about momentary stuff.

In terms of business, all of our rights and commercial windows run through temporal and geographical time, which, on a global connected platform, presents us with a lot of challenges. That is why we are now beginning to see this as a kind of ecosystem whereby there's a public service and then it's heavy linking into deep archive which you maybe pay for or commercial opportunities to purchase. We're working a lot with our rights holders, and independent companies, and partners to unpack what this really means for a win-win situation.

EE: *Are there platforms you won't go onto because of this commercial tension?*
VJ: Yes, there's ways we express ourselves on consoles. For example, at the moment, the only way BBC will appear on a console is via the iPlayer product. So, *Doctor Who: The Adventure Games* were conceived for PC and Mac, not for the console. That's what Worldwide will do, that was the agreement, they do the console market.

But actually then, a lot of platforms like Sky don't want to take iPlayer once you get into Internet Protocol TV (IPTV), so there are really fundamental challenges ahead with the world of IPTV and our most basic product, iPlayer. All of this is just a complete distraction from some of the basics of how do we get our programme information on IPTV, who's delivering it? Is it in EPG? Is it here? Is it there? A whole set of other challenges that are all unknown. Everyone's feeling their way and all you can ever do in these sort of roles is ask the best questions you can based on what you already know. I think that's the fundamental responsibility, to ask the decent questions rather than why aren't all dramas games? That's not a helpful question. It's what is it about this canvas that allows us to enrich stories and also deliver output on telly that simply is extraordinary?

EE: *Are there any other challenges that you're facing?*
VJ: We continue to face challenges with respect to talent buy-in and permission to produce beyond broadcast content that features them. There may be legacy rights agreements in place which are prohibitive, or even when we do have the rights, for example to create a talent-fronted quiz, that talent may not agree to take part and we have to respect these moral rights. This is a real challenge for us as we negotiate our place in this new media environment.

Notes

1. This term refers to genres that the commercial sector finds to be unprofitable (see Bennett, 2009).
2. The 'red button' refers to the BBC's digital television services. By pressing the red button on their digital television remote control, BBC audiences can access a range of additional services including text-based news, sports and traffic information, alternative coverage of sports events and interactive 'play-along' features (see Bennett, 2008).
3. BBC Worldwide is the Corporation's commercial arm. It runs international channels such as BBC World and BBC America, sells BBC formats to overseas markets, produces programme-related magazines and licenses content for merchandising and home distribution (see <www.bbcworldwide.com>).
4. Overnights equate to the number of people watching the original, 'live' broadcast of a programme.

Bibliography

BBC Trust. (2010) 'Lyons Sets Out Initial Conclusions on Future Direction of the BBC', Press Release, 5 July, <www.bbc.co.uk/bbctrust/news/press_releases/july/strategy_review.shtml> accessed 3 August 2010.

Bennett, James. (2008) 'Your Window-on-the-World: The Emergence of Red Button Interactive Television in the UK', *Convergence*, 14 (2), pp. 161–82.

Bennett, Jana. (2009) 'Not Dead, but Different: Public Service Broadcasting in the 21st Century – Safeguarding the Cultural Commons', Speech given at the London School of Economics, 27 October, <www.bbc.co.uk/pressoffice/speeches/stories/bennett_lse.shtml> accessed 19 July 2010.

DCMS. (2006) Copy of the Royal Charter for the Continuance of the BBC, <http://www.bbccharterreview.org.uk/pdf_documents/Cm6925_BBCRoyalCharterFinal.pdf> accessed 28 June 2010.

Evans, Elizabeth. (2011) *Transmedia Television: Audiences, New Media and Daily Life* (London: Routledge).

Jenkins, Henry. (2006) *Convergence Culture: Where Old and New Media Collide* (New York: New York University Press).

Naylor, Richard, Steven Driver and James Cornford. (2000) 'The BBC Goes Online: Public Service Broadcasting in the New Media Age', in David Gauntlett (ed.), *Web Studies* (London: Arnold), pp. 137–44.

Thompson, Mark. (2010) *Putting Quality First*, <www.bbc.co.uk/pressoffice/speeches/stories/thompson_ft.shtml> accessed 19 July 2010.

Williams, Raymond. (1974) *Television: Technology and Cultural Form* (London: Fontana).

7 Beyond the Broadcast Text: New Economies and Temporalities of Online TV

J. P. Kelly

Online distribution became a significant part of mainstream television culture in the late 2000s. *Wired* magazine reported that the BBC iPlayer had increased in popularity by 150 per cent in 2008 alone and by mid-2009 was estimated to account for approximately 7–10 per cent of all UK online traffic (Chibber, 2009). Likewise, Hulu.com, a US-based aggregator of film and TV content, experienced a similar degree of success. Launched in March 2007, Hulu was ranked by *Businessweek* as the United States' second most popular online video distributor in August the following year, trailing only YouTube (Lowry, 2008). It was also voted as one of the top five inventions of 2008 by *Time* magazine.[1] The site is currently available to US audiences only, but despite this geographic limitation, viewing figures have been substantial. As *Variety* reported in May 2010, Hulu streamed 1.17 billion videos to 43.5 million unique viewers, each of whom spent an average of 164.1 minutes on the site (Littleton, 2010).

Although the internet grew in popularity as a legitimate destination for watching television in the 2000s, the revenue and distributional models for this nascent medium were, and remain, in a state of transition. Many online distributors are still figuring out how to most effectively organise, circulate and monetise their goods within a largely untested but certainly profitable terrain. Hulu, for instance, has trialled numerous different promotional and distributional techniques, including the pre-broadcast premieres of *30 Rock* (2006–present), extended versions of *The Office: An American Workplace* (2005–present), exclusive web-only digital shorts of *Saturday Night Live* (1975–present), as well as commercial breaks that viewers can decide when and how to watch. In each instance, the logics of online TV indicate a significant departure from the temporal regimes that structure its broadcast equivalent.

With broadband penetration and the ownership of personal computing expected to grow, so too will the popularity of online television. Such a development calls for a consideration of how the traditional logics of broadcast 'flow' (Williams, 1974) are adapting within this new media environment. This chapter considers the consequences of transferring television into an online environment. In doing so, I identify the various textual, economic and temporal practices that have developed during this initial period of 'hypercast' TV, addressing several key questions in the process: What kind of economic models are being developed in order to support and capitalise upon online distribution? In what ways do new promotional and distributional opportunities disrupt or otherwise reconfigure the original broadcast narrative? To what extent does online television reproduce particular kinds of ephemerality, both with respect to the brevity of television's promotional and paratextual surround and in terms of programme availability and evanescence? Rather than a radical break from the commercial models of yesteryear, I argue that online TV is an amalgamation of both old and new media logics, extending established practices of broadcast flow while capitalising upon the new promotional, economic and textual possibilities inherent in digital media.

Hulu is a particularly useful example through which to explore the distributional and economic issues facing television as it moves into this alternative terrain. As a joint venture of NBC Universal and News Corp. – and with investment from Disney/ABC from April 2009 – it offers an insight into how the majority of the major commercial US networks were anticipating and attempting to shape the future of online television in the first decade of the twenty-first century. Despite this high-profile backing, Hulu was relatively unknown until the broadcast of *Huluwood*, a sixty-second advertisement that appeared during the commercial break of Super Bowl XLIII in February 2009. The spot begins with an establishing shot of the landmark Hollywood sign. From here, the camera zooms swiftly into a secret entrance positioned at the base of the letter 'H' where we are greeted by 'TV star' Alec Baldwin. 'Hello Earth', he cryptically quips before stepping inside an elevator that brings us deep beneath the hillside. Once below, we are taken on a trip through a laboratory filled with test subjects glued to computer screens which endlessly loop clips from popular television series such as *Family Guy* (1999–present) and *30 Rock*. Meanwhile, X-rays reveal the immediate and damaging effects of this incessant repetition, with the subjects' brains shrivelling to a fraction of their original size within seconds. Addressing the viewer candidly during this brief guided tour of the company's premises, Baldwin admits that Hulu's real intent is to take over the world, using online TV as a way to reduce the population's brains to an easily controllable 'mush'. The sequence ends with the actor positioned in front of a giant matrix of screens as he salivates at this prospect. Confirming our deepest suspicions, a green tentacle emerges from beneath his suit, and while dabbing his mouth he remarks, 'Because we're aliens, and that's how we roll.' A final tag line appears, reiterating the company's not-so-hidden agenda: 'Hulu, an evil plot to destroy the world.'

While the commercial's literal depiction of the internet's capacity for 'dumbing down' invites consideration of the relationship between brevity, repetition and memory loss, it also draws attention to the different distributional strategies of 'old' and 'new' media. Debuting during an ad break of the Super Bowl, the most costly commercial spot of the entire broadcast calendar, the *Huluwood* promo neatly illustrates the fundamental difference between broadcast and hypercast television. On the one hand, it highlights the rigid temporal regimes that have long structured the form and economy of broadcast TV (primetime, daytime, seasons, liveness, appointment viewing), while on the other hand it draws attention to the contradistinctive logics of online, on-demand distribution, where, in the words of Alec Baldwin, content can be accessed 'anytime, anywhere'. While Super Bowl spots are highly valued because of the precise moment they appear in the broadcast schedule, this model fails to translate to an online environment where time is much more fluid. The atemporality of the internet poses a potential problem for the economic viability of such a venture – in offering a service that transcends the temporal regimes of the broadcast spectrum, how is Hulu to value commercial time and structure the flow of online texts?

Flows, files and streams: the temporal regimes of twenty-first-century TV

In order to fully understand the emerging economic strategies and distributional logics of online television, it is first necessary to consider the specificity of the medium itself, to identify the unique technological, textual and temporal features of TV as digital media. To this end, Derek Kompare's distinction between 'flow' and 'file' is a useful starting point (Kompare, 2002). While the former refers to the programmed sequences of texts characteristic of broadcast media (when we switch on a TV set, the content will 'flow' until switched off), Kompare describes the file as a discrete, user-controlled and increasingly popular unit of contemporary media culture (Kompare, 2002, 2005, 2006). Elaborating upon the specific temporal attributes of this new cultural form and how it differs from broadcast media, he explains that 'the file is the opposite of flow. As flow creates large synchronous audiences over long stretches of time, the file is made available directly to individuals in small packages on an ad hoc basis' (Kompare, 2002, p. 4).

Whereas broadcast television is characterised by patterns of temporal regularity (daily, weekly, seasonal), file-based media circulates in a much more unpredictable manner. Admittedly, time-shifting technologies such as TiVo and Sky+ may have blurred the definitional boundaries between flow and file, but broadcast schedules have remained fairly consistent over the years. In the US and UK in particular, the vast majority of programming (particularly during primetime) is structured around thirty- or sixty-minute blocks. This gives schedules a certain temporal neatness, and viewers have come to expect that shows will begin at regular intervals on, or at thirty minutes past, the hour. The economy of broadcast television has been built upon this kind of temporal standardisation, with advertising space sold according to the time of day. For instance, television networks have historically treated the 'daytime' period as primarily female-oriented, with commercials and programming targeting this particular demographic. However, this kind of temporal logic is absent in an online environment, where (with certain limitations) consumers can begin watching content at any time of the day. Evidently, the highly routinised logics of broadcast flow do not adapt well, if at all, to a medium comprised of files and characterised by temporal fluidity.

As well as affecting the broader temporal regimes of television distribution by making content permanently available for 'acquisitive repetition' post-broadcast, the file also engenders a different temporal relationship between viewer and text at the point of consumption (Kompare, 2006). As Kompare points out, a key attribute of the file is its malleability, which allows consumers to interact with the individual text in more temporally diverse ways. In contrast to the once ephemeral and irreversible stream of broadcast flow, with the file we can 'stop it, repeat it, rearrange it, edit it, catalogue it, and discard it' (Kompare, 2002, p. 1). Thus, the temporal affect of the file extends well beyond the initial disruption of broadcast flow (dis-embedding the text from logics of primetime, scheduling, liveness) to enable more complex and liberated modes of viewing (time-shifting, fast-forwarding, pausing, repetition).

This flow/file distinction is a useful way in which to explain some of the key temporal differences between broadcast television and its more recent file-based iterations. However, a further distinction should be made when talking about online television, one that acknowledges the combination of flows *and* files that underpin its distributional logic. While DVD box sets, episodes purchased via iTunes and digital recordings stored on DVRs are all permanent copies (until we choose to discard them), online television is ultimately transient. Although files by definition, online videos are rarely, if ever, stored locally but tend to be 'streamed' remotely. Thus, online television retains the temporal flexibility of the file (we can still pause or fast-forward through episodes), but not the permanence that is associated with DVDs, purchased episodes or home recordings. In other words, television sites such as Hulu or the BBC iPlayer permit their visitors a file-like interaction with the text, but do so within flow-like windows of accessibility. Simply put, streaming is the application of the logics of flow to a medium of files.

As a medium composed of files, the internet can be seen to embody the temporal flexibility of this twenty-first-century media form. Online audiovisual content can be accessed at will and on an ad hoc basis (with certain restrictions). It can be stopped, repeated, rearranged, edited, catalogued and discarded (again, with certain restrictions). In contrast to television's extended durations of flow, the internet has emerged primarily as a venue for short-form content, as exemplified by the time constraints placed upon YouTube videos (which, with the rare exception, is limited to ten minutes) or the popularity of sites such as *Thirty Second Bunny Theatre* in which entire cinematic narratives are condensed and re-enacted in record time.[2] As a medium then, the internet is predominantly one of fragmentation, of hyperlinks and non-linear flows, and where a vast array of audiovisual files sit side by side often pulling our attention in several different directions at once. It has produced what YouTube CEO Chad Hurley has called 'clip culture' (cited in Helmore, 2006). And while the internet has the potential to offer a more sustained and lasting experience in which content can be gathered and archived for future use, its interface is constantly evolving, with no two visits ever the same. Moreover, access to these video archives and their remotely hosted texts is never guaranteed, as demonstrated by Viacom's decision in March 2010 to remove two of Hulu's most popular series, *The Daily Show* (1996–present) and *The Colbert Report* (2005–present). Thus, the web is semi-permanent at best. Once transferred into this space, television must assimilate with a medium characterised by ephemerality, fragmentation, brevity and temporal fluidity.

Don't touch that mouse, we'll be right back after this break …

In examining the more transient and abbreviated aspects of online TV, we might begin with a consideration of one of the medium's most ephemeral elements, the commercial break. Although often overlooked in scholarly analyses, these in-between texts are an intrinsic part of the overall televisual experience, shaping the rhythm and tempo of commercial broadcasting. They are the principal source of revenue for commercial networks, and the most consistent, most repeated and most viewed element of our TV diet.

In terms of their technical capability and material composition, broadcast television advertisements have remained fairly consistent throughout the medium's history. Genre, style, duration, frequency and positioning may have changed over the years, but the core definition of what constitutes a commercial break has remained the same: a short audiovisual sequence, usually no longer than a minute, which is simultaneously broadcast across the airwaves at specific intervals. This is not the case with online advertising, which, given the versatility of the file, can come in many different guises. Indeed, in a typical visit to the web we are confronted with a range of innovative and diverse commercial forms: banner ads that expand when our cursors hover above, short interactive games or pop-ups that require clicking before we can continue browsing. However, as the promotional literature of one online advertising specialist explains, initially:

most marketers did little more than repurpose their TV spots for use in video advertising. While this behaviour reinforced branding and campaign messaging, it did little to actually expand the campaign, or to take advantage of what could truly be done online. As the medium evolved, so did ad implementation. Over the years advertisers and creative agencies grew smarter about how they used video in online campaigns. Video shot specifically for the web or with tailored user experiences for interactive spots has allowed for impactful and visually arresting display ads. (Palumbo, 2009)

While many were slow to realise the new possibilities of online advertising, Hulu embraced the commercial idiosyncrasies of the web from its very beginning. Using the dynamic potential of digital media, they have been able to diversify their promotional efforts in several innovative ways. In 2010, the site offered nine different promotional options to potential sponsors. These included 'branded slates' (static promotional images that appear before programming and run for around five seconds); 'pre-roll' or 'in-episode' spots (which resemble typical television advertising and range between fifteen and thirty seconds); 'ad selector' (an interactive commercial which allows the viewer to choose from a number of different products); and 'branded entertainment selector' (an option to watch commercials up front, or periodically dispersed throughout the content that follows). While each option differs in the way it delivers advertising to the user, their one common feature is that commercials cannot be skipped.

Perhaps the most noteworthy development in this area has been Hulu's proclivity for shorter commercial breaks, a model that advertisers have labelled 'attention-for-content' (O'Leary, 2009), in which the heightened attention of viewers is rewarded with fewer and shorter commercials. Such a transaction is more appropriate, or perhaps even necessary, within the fragmented context of the internet. Rather than the usual four-minute slots allocated during broadcast programming, online viewers need only sit through fifteen- or thirty-second breaks. This means that during an 'hour-long' show, Hulu viewers will watch around two and a half minutes of commercials, whereas viewers of the broadcast text will watch up to eighteen minutes, almost eight times more. Put another way, viewers can watch nearly one and a half hours of online content for every hour of broadcast material. Although not entirely free from commercials, this 'less is more' revenue model compresses the viewing experience, allowing consumers to work through a much greater volume of content if they so wish.

Given the multifunctionality of the computer, and the various distractions offered online, it is hardly surprising that Hulu has opted for these short-form commercial segments. Within such close proximity to the numerous other competing windows of a computer screen, viewers might be tempted to shift their attention elsewhere – to quickly check their email, to update their social networking status or to interact with any of the various other files that sit just one click away. The brevity of these promotions is thus one way to curtail the encroachment of the computer screen's many other potential distractions. At the same time, the reduced duration of these commercial interruptions conforms to the internet's existing proclivity for short-form content where consumer concentration can be scarce, and where attention is thus a highly valued commodity. Of course, it should be noted that the duration of advertisements themselves hasn't necessarily been reduced. Rather, the strategy for a continuous sequence or flow of promotional texts has been rejected in favour of individual spots. Ultimately, Hulu has developed its commercial opportunities in a way that capitalises upon the flexibility of digital media, opting for a model of short-form advertising tailored to the fragmented and fleeting kinds of viewership that the internet invites.

As well as brevity, another distinct feature of online advertising is its potential for interactivity. For instance, visitors to Hulu can interact with commercials through thumbs up or thumbs down gestures, a system that encourages viewers to 'stay tuned', to borrow the parlance of broadcast TV. On the one hand, it makes visitors to the site feel more valued, as they get to participate by providing feedback on their viewing experience, while on the other hand, it delivers targeted content more relevant to their interests, an arrangement that benefits viewer, distributor and sponsor alike. Importantly, this heightened level of engagement with the commercial text might also suggest a potentially greater level of investment in the accompanying televisual narrative. As a study by Experian Simmons, a US-based consumer research group, reported in 2007, 'consumers are 47 percent more engaged by ads that run with television programmes viewed online than those watched on a TV set' and, as a consequence, are '25 percent more engaged in the content of TV shows that they watch online' (cited in Riley, 2007). Although such findings should be treated with some scepticism, they do correlate with popular conceptions of television and computing as 'lean-back' and 'lean-forward' technologies, respectively.[3] Similarly, it highlights the different viewing dispositions that are commonly associated with logics of flow (passive) and file (active).

These features of brevity and interactivity are not unrelated. Hulu may stream fewer (and usually shorter) commercial breaks than its broadcast counterpart, but this is balanced by the fact that it is able to 'engage' viewers, gathering precise feedback for sponsors (through thumbs up and thumbs down gestures), tailoring each commercial experience and, in the case of registered users, delivering specific demographic data (age, gender, generic preferences). Whereas the economy of broadcast advertising is built upon assumptions about who is watching and when, Hulu can deliver commercials specifically targeted to each individual user. These opportunities for interactive and targeted advertising might entitle the site to charge sponsors more for less.

However, it should be noted that this does not necessarily compensate for the sizeable gulf in viewing figures between broadcast and streamed episodes of a show. Full episodes of popular series such as *The Simpsons* (1989–present) receive millions of views per month on Hulu, but will draw tens of millions in a single night on broadcast television. That said, Hulu's financial model appeared to be working in the late 2000s. Within two years of launching, it had already posted a net profit, with revenues exceeding $100 million in the first half of 2010 alone (Major, 2010).

In addition to promotional brevity and interactivity, another noteworthy feature of these online advertising texts is their potential to be programmed in flexible ways. Although Hulu stresses its fidelity to the placement and frequency of commercials as they appear during the original broadcast, in January 2009 the company trialled a more flexible strategy for the season seven premiere of *24* (2001–10). Visitors to the site could either watch several thirty-second spots within the show, or they could opt to begin with a two-minute trailer up front in exchange for an uninterrupted commercial-free episode. After the initial trial of this model, in which Hulu reported that 88 per cent of viewers chose the latter, the company used the strategy for a number of other selected programmes. To reposition commercials in this way is to potentially alter the narrative experience. Commercial television is produced with the ad break in mind. Narratives are written as a series of act breaks that work in anticipation of the inevitable commercial interruption. Quite often, writers will utilise moments of heightened suspense (or 'cliffhangers') prior to these breaks in order to ensure the viewer will return, and of course to keep the sponsor happy.

Once commercials are removed from the equation, it can make the experience of watching television somewhat strange. This is particularly pronounced in the case of *24*, a show premised upon a 'real-time' narrative structure. Those who watched the programme as part of a DVD box set would no doubt have noticed the on-screen clock leap forward at several points throughout each episode. Although most viewers would understandably prefer to watch content in this way (as Hulu found when it initially tested this option), in this instance ad-free viewing may have a negative effect, with the lack of commercial interruption undermining the temporal order of the text.

Whatever the effect for the consumer, the emerging forms of online television advertising are ephemeral in a number of ways. Commercials are brief and infrequent, blending seamlessly with the internet's penchant for audiovisual brevity. Due to their interactive design and their ability to target specific viewers, online commercials have taken the ephemerality of their broadcast equivalent one step further. While the duration, format and frequency of television advertisements are tailored to their own particular broadcast environment, the attention economy of the web demands a different kind of strategy in which ads are still fleeting but are even shorter in duration and fewer in number.

Windows of opportunity

Online television is just one of a growing number of technologies that have displaced regimes of broadcast flow. Armed with a laptop, a DVD box set or a DVR, consumers no longer have to tune in at specific times dictated by the network. This shift from industrial to user flows has caused a profound change in the spaces, times and rhythms with which we consume our media. Even the advertising models I describe above have played their part in this transformation, reconfiguring the commercial experience so that advertisements have become shorter and less frequent. As a result of the brevity of these new promotional strategies, visitors are able to condense their viewing of individual episodes. Even with commercial breaks, it takes significantly less time to watch an hour-long programme on Hulu. However, this compression not only works at the level of the individual episode. Indeed, as an archive (albeit, a temporary one), the site permits more diversity in the frequency and volume of our viewing so that multiple episodes of the same series can be watched in just one sitting.

Writing about another iteration of the television archive, the DVD box set, Amanda Lotz has noted that having access to entire seasons often results in 'compressed consumption' or, as it is more colloquially known, 'binge viewing' (Lotz, 2007). Rather than waiting for the allocated weekly airing of a particular show, during which time viewers may forget key narrative details, fans can quite literally 'binge' on several episodes at a time, one after another and without the usual interruption of commercial breaks. What would have quite literally taken 'seasons' to watch can be, and from anecdotal evidence very often is, condensed into the space of just a few days. To return once more to the example of *24*, there has been a growing tendency among dedicated fans to watch the series in 'real time' – in other words, to begin at the exact hour a given season commences, and to consume an episode every hour in tandem with the show's diegetic timeline. These *24* marathons may only constitute a small percentage of the contemporary television audience, but consuming even just a few instalments at a time can exert a dramatic effect upon the viewing experience. As Lotz explains, 'the opportunity to compress viewing allow[s] for better memory of meaningful details that might be forgotten if viewing was stretched over months and suggest[s] the new potential viewing pleasures that might develop from the possibility of condensed viewing' (Lotz, 2007, p. 62).

In comparison to the DVD box set, the opportunity for binge viewing online is more limited. Like a lot of audiovisual content on the web, television series on Hulu are subject to limited availability, with only a select number of episodes from currently active series made available for streaming – at present, the standard has been set at five episodes. This paradox of Hulu as a 'temporary archive' highlights the site's potential for permanence but preference for ephemerality. Replicating the transient availabilities of broadcast television in which content is never permanent but always fleeting, Hulu strikes a careful balance between flow and file. The site's extended window of availability is meticulously timed so as to supplement, rather than replace, broadcast television. On the one hand, Hulu offers a degree of flexibility to ensure viewers will not fall behind on a series, particularly useful in the case of 'narratively complex' serials which require a much more committed level of viewing (Mittell, 2006). On the other hand, these windows of availability are short enough so as not to impede the industry's various other revenue streams. After all, if entire seasons were available online for free, for ever, who would buy DVD box sets or watch broadcast television with all those annoying commercial interruptions?[4]

Going viral: 'unbundling' the TV text

Short-form, targeted commercials and temporary windows of availability are not the only ephemeral aspects of online TV. Given the inherent mutability of digital media, full episodes on the site are also prone to temporal reconfiguration. For instance, Hulu openly invites users to create their own customisable clips. By dragging their cursors to position in and out points on a timeline, consumers can then distribute these extracted segments via email, or embed them within social networking sites such as Facebook. In this way, programmes themselves act as discrete promotional texts, further reinforcing the popularity and dominance of fragmented and short-form content across the net. Although this editorial control is rather basic and somewhat restrained (viewers, for instance, cannot edit together different scenes or material from different sources), it nevertheless encourages an increased production and circulation of even more televisual ephemera. From a financial perspective, this viral strategy works in favour of Hulu, as any extracted content comes embedded with its own commercial support. Meanwhile, viewers get to watch promotions previewed by promotions.

The abundance of short-form audiovisual material available on Hulu is not simply a consequence of user creativity. Rather, the site hosts a wide range of officially produced ephemera, the majority of which run under five minutes in length. These abbreviated texts are organised so that visitors can browse through categories that include 'clips', 'excerpts', 'web exclusives', 'digital shorts', 'trailers', 'interviews', 'previews' and 'recaps'. Like the user-defined clips, these ephemeral narratives act as promotional texts, increasing the visibility of a show and, especially in the case of recaps, offering a point of entry to potential new audiences. In this regard, Hulu is not just a venue for watching TV but is a tool through which viewers can discover new shows.

While broadcast television strategically places trailers and forthcoming previews of series within the commercial breaks of similar programming, the wide range of promo texts available on Hulu enable users to sample and discover a more diverse selection of shows.

As well as shaping the ways in which we might discover, recommend and share television series, there are other potential implications that accompany these instances of textual reconfiguration. For instance, certain genres may lend themselves to narrative extraction, or, as Max Dawson (2007) has termed it, 'unbundling'. As a result, particular kinds of programming will receive greater exposure on the site. There is evidence to suggest that this is indeed the case, with self-contained 'sketches' from comedy shows such as *Family Guy*, *30 Rock* and *The Simpsons* among Hulu's most popular clips of all time. Meanwhile, scenes from more narratively complex serials such as *Lost* or *24* feature far less prominently.[5] In fact, of the twenty most popular clips of all time on Hulu, seventeen of these come from just one show, *Saturday Night Live*.[6]

In addition to 'unbundled' episodes, 'clips' and commercials, the site is a haven for a different kind of ephemera – discussion. Capitalising upon the participatory nature of the internet, Hulu actively encourages and facilitates this activity. Using *Lost* as a case study, Will Brooker (2009) argues that watching television as files on a computer enables and even invites the viewer to perform a kind of 'forensic analysis' on the text. When watching TV as discrete downloaded files, users can pause, review and scrutinise every frame. Following this, they use internet forums to post their findings in 'real time'. Catering to this participatory impulse, Hulu positions discussion boards – the online version of the 'water-cooler moment' – beneath each individual stream. Within the spaces of these forums, viewers can debate, seek answers, share opinions or simply rate the accompanying video. While the temporal flexibility of watching television online may have undermined the necessity or likelihood for the 'water-cooler moment' (we are less likely to discuss a plot point if we are all watching at different times), these forums are yet another instance of online television's ephemerality. In fact, these materials are especially transient, as once the broadcast window of their related content expires, they too disappear into the digital ether.

Watching television online is thus ephemeral on several fronts. In just one sitting, online viewers can watch any given combination of texts. They can build a playlist of videos solely comprised of ephemeral 'clips', 'trailers', 'promos' or 'recaps'. Alternatively, viewers may come online in search of a more sustained television experience, watching episode after episode, or perhaps even an entire season of programming. Others still may prefer a combination of the two, mixing long- and short-form content as it suits them. On top of this, viewers themselves participate in and help proliferate various forms of textual brevity, from customised clips to temporary discussions.

The aesthetics of online time

In moving towards a conclusion, I would like to reflect on some of the potential formal and experiential consequences of watching television online. Although lacking the meticulously structured temporal regimes of broadcast TV, time is especially visible on the internet. In his discussion of this conspicuous temporal presence and of the various clocks and countdown timers embedded within digital media, Daniel Chamberlain observes that:

> Regardless of the display technology, software platform, or content delivered, the prominence of temporal metadata associated with watching video in these emergent contexts alters one's relationship to the video itself. When watching television in this manner the obvious temporal cues make it difficult to get lost in the story. (Chamberlain, 2007)

Indeed, one of the most striking things about watching content on Hulu is the prominent progress bar, which appears on screen and indicates total running time, time elapsed, as well as the precise points at which viewers should expect commercial interruptions. Not only this, but even the promotional breaks themselves include countdown timers informing the viewer of how long they must wait before their chosen show resumes.[7] Thus, while we might initially assume that time plays a less significant role in the structures of online TV (especially in contrast to its centrality in the logics of broadcast flow), these examples suggest that it remains a pronounced feature of the televisual experience, albeit in a different iteration. Whereas time is concealed in the continuous stream of broadcast flow, it emerges as a prominent and defining feature of the online stream.

As Chamberlain notes, watching TV online, with all its accompanying temporal cues, can make the process of viewing profoundly different to that of broadcast TV. Watching content in this way, the viewer is more conscious of the text's narrative construction and impending commercial breaks, as constantly reminded by the various on-screen metadata. However, these kinds of temporal cues are often already embedded within the text itself. Consider, for instance, the expository dialogue of *Prison Break* (2005–9) in which lead protagonist Michael Schofield would constantly announce his deadlines ('We only have thirty minutes left until …') or the assortment of digital clocks and on-screen graphic timers that appear throughout *24* and act as a constant reminder of the show's narrative urgency and real-time premise.

Chamberlain's observations may also help to explain not just the structural and aesthetic but also the thematic preoccupation with time (and timers) in a wide range of contemporary shows including *24*, *Day Break* (2006), *FlashForward* (2009–10) and *Prison Break*, to name just a few. In a culture where time increasingly pervades our daily lives, not just as part of the metadata attached to digital media but across a broader spectrum of the everyday (digital countdown schedules on bus stops, automatic time and date stamps in emails or the omnipresent clocks lurking in the corners of our computer screens), it is no wonder that this motif has come to feature so prominently within contemporary television narratives.

While brevity, transience and the visibility of time may be the key temporal features of online television, sites such as Hulu also have the capacity to offer a more extended narrative experience. Although I have suggested that Hulu tends to prioritise ephemeral texts, equipping its users with the necessary tools to 'unbundle' and embed videos themselves, it also attempts to emulate more flow-like aspects of traditional television programming. As Joshua Green notes in his study of two earlier online ventures, Innertube (now CBS.com) and Miro, 'while the individual program is the core unit traded', both sites 'attempt to re-embed this programming within some semblance of the flow logics of broadcast television' (Green, 2008, p. 97). Indeed, online distributors may trade in files, but they do so by building upon established practices of flow. As Green goes on to explain of Innertube and Miro, 'each of these new television sites attempts to negotiate an identity as an evolution of broadcasting television, rather than necessarily positioning itself as an object that breaks from it' (ibid.).

Like most other online video sites, Hulu has integrated a number of flow-like strategies within its user interface. For instance, at the end of each video, viewers will automatically receive recommendations for other related content or can simply click 'replay' to review the current clip. There are also options to build custom playlists of content, enabling visitors to the site to effectively create their own schedules. They can subscribe to particular series, a feature that automatically adds new episodes to the user's playlist as they become available. Another flow-like feature is 'recommendations', in which registered users can build a list of their own personal preferences, rating a range of different genres such as 'action and adventure', 'comedy', 'family', 'music' and 'sports'. Based upon this information, Hulu then pushes content specifically targeted to each user. Although flow is absent in this environment, these strategies of streaming serve the same purpose – to retain the viewer. Visitors to the site may not follow 'branded flows' in the way they might if watching broadcast television, but are perhaps more likely to follow 'generic streams'.

Conclusion

As television continues to diversify into different spaces (and times), we must update our methodological tools accordingly. Whereas Raymond Williams' (1974) concept of flow remains pertinent to the temporal and economic structures of broadcast television, Kompare's notion of file (or, as I have also suggested, 'streaming') is a more accurate model through which to describe and examine the temporalities of online TV. As I have shown, online distribution is exemplary of this twenty-first-century media form. Through its inherent flexibility, it enables a range of new promotional and distributional opportunities, offering a very different experience of TV than that of its broadcast counterpart. Online television is ephemeral in its particular, new media conflagration of promotional brevity and programme evanescence. Not only does it contribute to an ever-increasing body of ephemeral texts (commercials, discussion boards, 'unbundled' clips) but it is also ephemeral in the way it 'streams' TV content (limited windows of availability, fragmented consumption and tailored commercial experiences).

Of course, broadcast television is also a highly ephemeral medium. Content flows relentlessly and (without the aid of a DVR) irreversibly. Like its online successor, it too is punctuated by various ephemeral texts including promos, idents, trailers, recaps and commercials. But while both broadcast and online television are fundamentally ephemeral, their evanescence and brevity manifest in different ways. Indeed, as I describe above, watching television online engenders a potentially different viewing disposition, with the medium's 'lean-forward' design and interactive commercials producing a heightened level of engagement. Similarly, the 'unbundling' of texts and the proliferation of various televisual ephemera on Hulu encourage a more diverse and fragmented kind of consumption. But despite these differences, online TV builds upon existing logics and commercial strategies of broadcast flow. For instance, while distributors such as Hulu have extended the broadcast window, content tends to be made available as temporary streams rather than permanent archives. Moreover, online TV relies on broadcast television for the very content it supplies to its internet users. Rather than replacing broadcast television then, online TV complements its sibling medium, embodying the transience and ephemerality of flow as well as the brevity and mutability of the file.

Notes

1. Although Hulu came second, it is worth noting the significant difference between these two rankings. For the month of October 2009, internet market research company comScore reported that Google sites (including YouTube) accounted for 37.7 per cent of online video traffic in the US (just over 10.5 million views), while second-place Hulu accounted for only 3.1 per cent (or 855,559 views). See <http://www.comscore.com/Press_Events/Press_Releases/2009/11/Hulu_Delivers_Record_856_Million_U.S._Video_Views/(language)/eng-US>.

2. Also, see Jason Mittell's (2009) discussion of the YouTube user-made recaps for *The Sopranos*, which condense key narrative details from several seasons into just a few minutes.

3. These terms refer to the different viewing dispositions associated with these technologies. Television requires very little interaction and once it is switched on, we quite literally assume a passive 'lean-back' position. By comparison, technologies such as the personal computer require much more interaction, resulting in a 'lean-forward' engagement.

4. More recently, Hulu has used windowing to differentiate between its basic service and its newly launched premium service, Hulu Plus. This latter option is a subscription service, which, for a monthly fee (currently $9.99), extends the broadcast window indefinitely, providing more high-definition material, and giving users more mobility by allowing access to the service through a wider range of devices such as Apple's iPhone and iPad or games consoles such as the Xbox 360 or Sony Playstation.

5. The shows do fare well when it comes to 'recaps', but their popularity still pales in comparison to self-contained scenes 'unbundled' from other series.

6. This list was correct as of June 2010. Incidentally, the other three 'clips' are all from *Family Guy*, a series that is similarly comprised of self-contained sketches. In fact, the show is particularly known for its frequent use of 'cutaway' gags and for this reason is especially susceptible to the strategy of unbundling.

7. It is worth noting that this strategy of timing commercial breaks has also been carried over into broadcast television. For instance, in the UK, MTV utilise various watermark timers in the top left corner of the screen, providing the viewer with an indication of time remaining until their programme resumes. More recently, they have begun to use this strategy within the programming itself so that both episodes and individual music tracks on a range of MTV-branded channels now come with their own timer.

Bibliography

Brooker, Will. (2009) 'Television Out of Time: Watching Cult Shows on Download', in Roberta E. Pearson (ed.), *Reading Lost: Perspectives on a Hit TV Show* (London: I.B. Taurus), pp. 53–76.

Chamberlain, Daniel. (2007) 'Watching Time on Television. *FlowTV*', 19 July, <http://flowtv.org/?p=615> accessed 6 July 2009.

Chibber, Kabir. (2009) 'The Man Who Saved the BBC', *Wired* (UK edition), May, pp. 54–8.

Dawson, Max. (2007) 'Little Players, Big Shows: Format, Narration, and Style on Television's New Smaller Screens', *Convergence*, 13 (3), pp. 231–50.

Green, Joshua. (2008) 'Why Do They Call It TV When It's Not on the Box? "New" Television Services and Old Television Functions', *Media International Australia*, 126, February, pp. 95–105.

Helmore, Edward. (2006) 'Just How Many Billions Is YouTube Really Worth?: The "Broadcast Yourself" Website Is Riding a Wave', *The Observer*, 27 August, p. 9.

Kompare, Derek. (2002) 'Flow to Files: Conceiving 21st Century Media', Conference Paper, *Media in Transition 2*, Cambridge, MA, 11 May.

Kompare, Derek. (2005) *Rerun Nation: How Repeats Invented American Television* (New York: Routledge).

Kompare, Derek. (2006) 'Publishing Flow: DVD Boxsets and the Reconception of Television', *Television and New Media*, 7 (4), pp. 335–60.

Littleton, Cynthia. (2010) 'Hulu Bows Paid Archives', *Variety*, 30 June, <http://www.variety.com/article/VR1118021227.html?categoryid=1009&cs=1> accessed 12 July 2010.

Lotz, Amanda. (2007) *The Television Will Be Revolutionized* (New York: New York University Press).

Lowry, Tom. (2008) 'NBC and News Corp.'s Hulu Is Off to a Strong Start', *Bloomberg Businessweek*, 25 September, <http://www.businessweek.com/magazine/content/08_40/b4102052685561.htm> accessed 18 October 2010.

Major, R. (2010) 'Hulu's International Launch Again in News', *Rapid TV News*, 12 July, <http://www.rapidtvnews.com/index.php/201007127057/hulus-international-launch-again-in-news.html> accessed 12 July 2010.

Mittell, Jason. (2006) 'Narrative Complexity in Contemporary American Television', *The Velvet Light Trap*, 58, Fall, pp. 29–40.

Mittell, Jason. (2009) 'Previously On: Primetime Serials and the Mechanics of Memory', *Just TV*, 3 July, <http://justtv.wordpress.com/2009/07/03/previously-on-prime-time-serials-and-the-mechanics-of-memory/> accessed 15 September 2009.

O'Leary, N. (2009) 'Searching for Life on Hulu', *Ad Week*, 25 May, <http://www.adweek.com/aw/content_display/special-reports/other-reports/e3i15f4e2b3b4a487b3cbb6ddcfb338c9e7?pn=1> accessed 6 July 2009.

Palumbo, P. A. (2009) 'Online Video Advertising 2009: Point Roll', <http://pointroll.com/downloads/Video_Advertising_Guide_2009.pdf> accessed 14 July 2010.

Riley, Duncan. (2007) 'Online TV Ads Suck Less Than TV Ads on TV: Study', *Tech Crunch*, 24 December, <http://www.techcrunch.com/2007/12/24/online-tv-ads-suck-less-than-tv-ads-on-tv-study/> accessed 6 July 2009.

Williams, Raymond. (1974) *Television: Technology and Cultural Form* (London: Fontana).

8 Time Slice: Web Drama and the Attention Economy

Jon Dovey

While the preceding chapters consider the impact of new media technologies on television culture and its modes of online distribution, this essay provides a vantage on the temporality and aesthetics of 'web native' media forms. Specifically, it is an analysis of the relationship between the emergent cultural form of the web drama and the attention economy. Combining critical, creative and applied modes of research to discuss the kinds of temporalities in play in the attention economy, this chapter argues that web native forms of interruptible content are the constituents of new narrative genres and offers an analysis of how they are the function of the monetisation of Web 2.0.

In cyberspace, no one can hear your scream

Like many academic endeavours, this chapter begins in enthusiasm and ends in complexity. Its roots lie in a number of unsuccessful attempts I made to finance a web drama project through 2007–8. My enthusiasm was based on the explosion of new moving image forms afforded by the spread of online media. As a long-time media activist and theorist, I am particularly susceptible to the Web 2.0 rhetorics. The kind of arguments for plural public spheres that have underpinned serious media criticism since its inception now mutate as celebration of participation and co-creation. In the 'Play and Display' zone of culture, our deep play with social media offers a sense of agency in the mediasphere. Our photos, graphics, videos, podcasts and blogs share everyday feelings, pleasures, pains and enthusiasms; these sharings obviously create community. Our lip-syncs, mash-ups, swedings, collabs, animations, parodies and video blogs are new shared symbolic experiences often based on acting out in the forms of mainstream media. I defy any viewer to see a selection of the best of this work and not be affected by the compelling experience of human creativity, ingenuity, joy and empowerment that they convey.

Sadly, while this wave of video creativity was, as we will see, widely reproduced in commercial online media forms, the reality of attempting to finance a production that could inhabit the digital media ecosystem as a successful professional practice was another matter altogether. I found myself undertaking a crash course in the mechanics of the attention economy. Everyone liked the pitch for our web drama concept, it worked. But it became clear that to produce it we either needed to bootstrap the project, to make it for nothing until it built an audience, or find sponsors with deep pockets who would stay with it until it found a regular 100,000–250,000 viewers online. The problem was finding an audience. In the olden days, getting a TV commission guaranteed an audience. Television, as traditional media political economy argued, is a mechanism for delivering eyeballs to advertisers. The problem is that the 'long tail' (Anderson, 2006) of cyberspace has too much content to attract attention in numbers that are meaningful to mass media advertisers. Attention is itself the premium commodity of the long tail. The competition for attention out there made the pitch harder than usual to sell. The problem can be usefully understood in terms of networks. In their paper 'The Emergence of Scaling in Random Networks', Barabasi and Alberts (1999) argue that the network is a basic principle of the organisation of all kinds of systems, human, biological and chemical. However, because of the principle of 'preferential attachment to already connected nodes', there is every chance that a few nodes in a network will become highly connected while most will remain loosely connected or disconnected. A new node in a network (e.g. a new Facebook page) is more than likely to link to popular users with many friends, to an already highly connected node. A few big internet trees get to grow strong in the sunlight of audience attention, while there are a myriad of tiny ephemeral organisms that remain invisible to an outside observer of the system. Barabasi argued:

> the most intriguing result of our Web mapping project was the complete absence of democracy, fairness and egalitarian values on the Web. We learned that the topology of the Web prevents us from seeing anything but a mere handful of the billion documents out there (Barabasi and Bonabeau, 2003, pp. 56–7).

These experiences and considerations led me into an ongoing investigation into the attention economy that underpins this chapter. Through the example of the web drama, which emerged as a form in the mid-2000s, I want to look at the aesthetics, economics and temporality of web native media 'beyond' traditional broadcasting regimes.

Time and attention

Any consideration of media temporality might begin with the assertion that media have always, by their nature, been ephemeral – radio signals passed on the airwaves, today's newspaper became tomorrow's fish and chip wrappings, cinema was a fleeting moment in the dark. The VCR and DVD were technologies pointing us toward a temporality that is now the opposite of ephemeral. Online media can be accessed repeatedly, revisited, replayed, downloaded, forwarded, recycled and mashed up. YouTube, Vimeo and TV on-demand liberate us from TV schedules and create increasingly re-watchable and reusable media. The whole principle of user-generated content and its viral means of transmission are reliant not upon its ephemerality but upon its 'always-on' availability.

And yet this is not an archive in any settled, stable sense of the word. If not exactly ephemeral, online media are both pervasive and ambient, like a weather system – dynamic, mutable, complex, airborne. One day the internet is faster than another, items disappear or reappear somewhere else, I never follow the same hyperlinked journey twice. The internet today is a different internet from the internet yesterday; our media co-constitute a system that is anything but stable (see Elsaesser, 2009, for an account of the instability of online media navigation). The perpetual innovation afforded by the operation of Moore's Law, the principle that data density will double every eighteen months, has created a permanent 'upgrade culture' in which novelty itself has intrinsic value (Dovey and Kennedy, 2006, p. 52). Upgrade culture has a kind of ephemerality built into it, where interfaces, platforms, licence agreements, user profiles, tweets, favourites, likes, Google rankings all change, like the weather, on an hourly basis. The speed and connectivity of the net afford many opportunities for the expression and recording of our affective engagements, hence the application of new swarm-based aggregation algorithms that create the new verb to 'trend'. Google Trends and Twitter's 'Trending now' features are softwares which sieve the viral dynamics of the web to produce live attention maps. Permanently updating has given the present moment more currency than ever before.

It's not just the software systems and user profiles that are permanently upgrading. Data is becoming ubiquitous; wirelessness brings permanent connection into the day-to-day spaces of our lives, which in turn affects our experience of time. As communication becomes mobile, media becomes mobile in the sense that it is not only 'always on' and 'always available' but 'always present', everywhere. The pervasive media slogan promises to deliver 'the right media at the right time in the right place'. To do this the delivery devices will be context-aware and platforms will be mobile social networks that facilitate easy exchange of all kinds of user-generated content, from viral video to restaurant rankings, dance floor updates to bus timetables. We no longer catch up with media, it catches up with us.

So the temporality of online media has this quality of always on, not exactly ephemeral but often insubstantial in an almost throwaway mode given its context of social network communication rather than broadcast. Understanding or defining these precise temporalities necessitates an understanding of the temporalities of attention. At one level, the sheer amount of online media content means that we have less time for all of it; it comes at us thick and fast filtered by search engines and user recommendation rather than the relatively stable TV listings guides. In the age of media abundance, perhaps it is *our attention that becomes more ephemeral* rather than the media themselves. 'Common-sense' experiences of online media (Carr, 2010) argue that our attention *has* to be ever more fleeting as it is made the object of intensified competition. This everyday feeling has its explanation in the astonishingly simple question that lies at the heart of the 'attention as commodity' paradigm. What is it that information consumes? Attention (Simon, 1971). The more information or media, the less attention we have for it. If we assume that attention is zero sum, that there is a limit to how much attention a set population can give, then as media events proliferate, they will perforce command smaller and smaller attention segments. This is the position from which leading web polemicist of the idea of the attention economy, Michael Goldhaber, begins:

> [O]urs is not truly an information economy. By definition, economics is the study of how a society uses its scarce resources. And information is not scarce – especially on the Net, where it is not only abundant, but overflowing. We are drowning in information, yet constantly increasing our generation of it. So a key question arises: Is there something else that flows through cyberspace, something that is scarce and desirable? There is.
> No one would put anything on the Internet without the hope of obtaining some. It's called attention. And the economy of attention – not information – is the natural economy of cyberspace. (Goldhaber, 1997)

At a simple level, this can be read as a restatement of the idea that a media ecosystem delivers attention to advertisers, brands and therefore to consumption. In this reading, attention and time are the same. Indeed, the television ratings system for pricing advertising made this assumption; if the TV was reported to be on, then it was assumed that it was being attended to. If the advertisements whose income was the essential system nutrient were getting into the living room, then the CPM (cost per thousand viewers) was assumed to be the same; the *quality* of attention was assumed to be neither here nor there. (Advertising cost variation on TV and elsewhere is differentiated by the class or buying power of the viewer/consumer.) The fact that viewers were distracted, bored, looking after children, doing housework or making love while the ad was screened made no difference to its price as long as the TV was predicted to be on.

However, the increased competition for our attention and the decline of the oligopolistic control of the attention markets of mass media brought about by digital connectivity mean that we are now being forced into thinking far more about the *quality* of attention not just its quantity. Like Goldhaber, Davenport and Beck argue that we are in an era-defining shift from time (as labour) as the basic economic measurement to attention, but that the two are different:

> Certainly something to which people allot a good deal of time in practice can receive minimal attention. Anyone who has been in school probably knows the feeling of sitting through a lecture for what seems like hours on end, while thinking about something totally unrelated … Conversely, a huge amount of effective attention can be given to something in a small amount of time. One blinding flash of insight or a compliment to a co-worker may not take much time, but may result in focused attention worth a whole year's worth of work. (Davenport and Beck, 2001, p. 28)

As is often the case, the vantage point of digital culture produces new archaeologies of media which have also revised the history of attention (Lanham, 2006). Jonathan Beller has taken the 'attention as scarce commodity' paradigm and argued compellingly that twentieth-century mass media has been producing attention as a commodity since the birth of cinema and mass media advertising. For Beller (2006), the intensification of competition for this capital producing attention is a commodification that goes way beyond the commodification of time as labour: new media 'are the viral penetration of the logistics of capital into the life-world that turns revolutionary desires (for self-realization, for survival) into the life-blood of a growing totalitarianism'.

This insight goes to the heart of the ambivalence that critical theorists experience when confronting the vast human labour constituting the World Wide Web. On the one hand, it is an awesome expression of human ingenuity, creativity and cooperation (our 'revolutionary desires'). On the other hand, its very exploitation of desires for self-actualisation and agency trap us ineluctably within capitalist value production; a trap where every ingenious innovation produces another opportunity for commodification of desire and accumulation. To fully grasp this point, we must just pause for a moment and think about what we do when we are online. How do we make the choices that drive our interaction? What drives our click journeys through the web? We used to celebrate the simple notion of 'interactivity' but all our interactions are driven by affect, by desire, by curiosity, by pleasure, by consumption, by epistephelia. When we are 'surfing' the web, we spend a lot of time, like actual surfers, waiting for the wave, waiting for the series of connections that will turn the heart/brain/eye/mouse/database/router/server assemblage into a wave of discovery that gives us the surge of satisfaction at finding what we didn't know we were look-ing for. This realisation is one of the driving ideas behind Web 2.0. When Tim O'Reilly made 'Data is the new Intel inside' one of the precepts of his 2005 Web 2.0 prescrip-tion, he was emphasising that for business the ability to capture data about our desire-driven click journeys on the web is a huge asset (O'Reilly, 2005). Knowing about us through the data produced by our interaction is one of the factors that makes Google one of the most powerful corporations on earth in the early twenty-first century. We produce value for new media economies through the expression, attention and co-creation of our subjectivity.

What is at stake here is indicated by Tiziana Terranova when she talks about the *bios* of attention, underlining that attention is a neurophysical quality, necessary to the satisfactory development of the infant brain. Recent advances in the idea that the brain carries on being plastic, affected by different stimuli for much longer than was previ-ously thought possible, underline the importance of the quality of attention we pay to the subjects that we become. However, Terranova (2010) draws attention to the vari-ability of 'multiple and heterogenous values' derived from attention, defined 'neither by work, scarcity or the market, but by the powers of memory and by actions as they express themselves in the social powers of association [and] in the circulation of flows of desires, beliefs and affects' that run over the social body. This offers an argument against Beller's totalising commodification.

It is clear that lower barriers to entry into the media market mean an exponentially widening field of availability of media all competing with each other for the attention, and therefore the necessary capitalisation, to reach profitability. These enterprises are competing very heavily for users, so marketing and promotion are key. *These eco-nomic conditions have a direct effect upon the media form and the user experience.* The web media user constantly finds herself hailed, solicited, invited to connect. Community management has become the starting point for web marketing. Web media invite the user to join, to create a profile, to post blogs or other announce-ments, to make links, to invite other friends and so on. This is not because media providers just want us all to play nice and have lots of warm friendships. It is because they are seeking, in a crowded, transient marketplace characterised by a nomadic audience, to create *brand engagement*. For users, this means that our web media experiences are interrupted by, suffused with and sometimes nearly drown in a sea of advertising and sponsorship content. Pop-ups, banners, sponsorships, product place-ments, interactives and virals that pretend not to be ads are all characteristic of this media ecosystem. Our behaviour becomes data that can be sold on without our knowledge and then be used to maintain consumption in whatever segment of the long tail our habitus is identified with.

Web drama: designing transmedial narrative

I will now move on to show how the temporalities of the attention economy are producing new cultural forms by focusing on examples from web drama. Web drama is one of the sites where televisual narrative form meets new practices of social networking. It is a fruitful site for investigating how TV mutates in the digital media ecosystem. In this instance, we might think about how television's appeal to liveness is being transmuted in the 'user-generated' diegetic worlds afforded by webcams, mobile phone footage and home movies. We can also see the traditional segmented forms of television narrative transmuted by the new rhythms of online attention flow. Web dramas take a serial form, appearing in short five- to ten-minute episodes, sometimes on a regular schedule of two or three times a week or more usually on a more sporadic basis. They therefore depend not on the discipline of the TV schedule to find an audience but on the 'always-on' temporality of viral communication which depends on the user to like, recommend, store and transmit. There has been a wide range of experiment and funding models. The earliest experiments were bootstrapped, produced with tiny budgets but finding audiences through viral serendipity and assiduous self-promotion. The indie series made as a calling card for TV crossover followed experimenting with sponsorship and income from product placement. Finally, the 2000s saw fully funded FOX, Disney or BBC productions running online. The emergent form of web drama has become the site of some notable experiments in digitally native popular narrative which I want briefly to consider through some indicative early examples.

The form first attracted attention in 2006 with the production of *lonelygirl15*. *lonelygirl15* achieved a level of web notoriety on its launch by appearing to be the real video blog of a 'Lonely Girl' which gradually became a more and more compelling story, as Bree, the main character, seemed to be recording her descent into a dark and cult-like urban nightmare. It became a YouTube hit, gathering an active and speculative fan base. The Lonely Girl was eventually exposed as an actress by journalists and the whole project revealed as a brilliantly staged promotion by a group of aspiring filmmakers and producers. The ambiguous status of the reality of *lonelygirl15* is typical of web aesthetics. The webcam blog carries the feel of authenticity and one-to-one communication that makes a strong dramatic 'proposition' to the viewer sitting at home on their own in front of the computer screen. The question 'is this real or is it fiction?' is at the heart of the Alternate Reality Gaming (ARG) experiences that are an equally significant web native cultural form and which often spin off from web dramas, offering engagement potential for audiences and advertisers. This promise of engagement is crucial for understanding what follows below in our analysis of the economics of attention. Posting narrative segments in the social media context of YouTube affords comment and community-building. Characters can comment back in role; fans can respond, create their own forums for discussion and get involved in solving the mystery. Attention is thus commanded way beyond the borders of the five-minute story segment; the web drama is 'sticky' with opportunities for more in-depth engagement. The team behind *lonelygirl15* went on to produce *KateModern*, discussed below and at more length in the next chapter.

Happy Slip (2006–present) is an example of a different kind of series based in home-made ethnic comedy. Written, directed and performed by Christine Gambito, an American Filipino actress, *Happy Slip* uses a deliberately amateur low-tech style in which, for instance, Gambito will play several roles in one episode, creating humour out of the continuity cutting as she acts with herself in multiple personas. Later on, the series evolved to incorporate other performers, friends and family members as she developed her own soap opera pastiche. The series' humour is based in a classic second-generation migrant experience of trying to establish a life across two sets of cultural norms. By the end of the 2000s, Gambito had become a self-made web personality. Her YouTube channel had 645,000 subscribers and nearly eighty million upload views. This successful attention-gathering created income through commercial work in promotional video campaigns as well as work for the Philippines Embassy and fronting a health awareness campaign. *Happy Slip* became a comedic brand complete with merchandising virally transmitted through YouTube, Gambito's posts developing her characteristic style of crossover between real life and performance. For example, a post on 7 October 2010 featured her performance of the different styles of greeting a newborn that she had encountered in the previous few months following the birth of her second son. Again, her Tumblr and YouTube sites had opportunities to comment and to get involved with other members of the *Happy Slip* world, member profiles appearing like friends on a Facebook page. It is not hard to see how such a community could well constitute an environment for generating sales leads for particular products that might fit with the *Happy Slip* 'cute' style.

The anonymously produced *Human Pet* (2006) was a much darker concept. A series of what look like authentic ransom videos were posted online and the audience were invited to help save the victim through their interactions. The videos showed a bound victim in a bare room; the viewers of the clips had to solve puzzles to keep the victim alive. The storyline is that Sam Deercot (aka Codemaster) has kidnapped Eric Taylor. Codemaser states online, 'If my identity is ever revealed or compromised, Eric will die. This is my masterpiece, and you will play by my rules. Codemaster p.s. – art is a mystery to be unraveled.' Again, a community is built up around the site, speculating as to its reality status and supporting one another in the ARG-type puzzling activities that would drive the plot forward. This was a very low-tech production which exploited the popular tropes of so-called 'torture porn' and the grainy ransom videos posted by terrorists.

The Guild's 2007 crossover hit occupies another kind of web culture. An award-winning sitcom featuring the members of an online gaming guild clearly based on *World of Warcraft*, the project was self-financed by *Buffy* actress Felicia Day after television turned it down for being too geeky. Some of the first series was funded by fan donation and then the second was picked up by Microsoft advertising, who partnered the production with the Sprint phone company to deliver *The Guild* as exclusive content for the Xbox Live platform. (Exclusive in web contexts usually means a time-limited exclusive release to a particular platform or network before general availability.) The sponsorship thus facilitated the Sprint, Xbox and Samsung brands involved in the funding package to reach a niche target audience of young male gamers, early adopters who would respond positively to the phone company pitch. The excitement and enthusiasm generated by discovering your own community affectionately parodied on the web is clearly one of the pleasures that *The Guild* has in common with *Happy Slip*; moreover, this pleasure is enhanced by the sense of agency delivered when the user feels that they have somehow discovered the series themselves, either through viral friend recommendation or through their own serendipitous navigation. In this sense, we can see the process whereby our own desires constitute us as consuming subjects; *we* seek out the material and volunteer ourselves to Samsung and Microsoft as particular kinds of people with particular kinds of tastes, in particular kinds of networks that can be tracked through our online behaviour.

There are numerous examples online. The selection above from the emergence of the form in 2006–7 is intended merely to give the general reader a sense of the range and style (see Lander, 2010a, for further web links and references). These instances of web drama have constituted a media lab where experiments in new forms of narrative and crucially new forms of monetisation are conducted. They are at the cutting edge of what television will become in the post-scarcity media era; they are the contemporary archaeology of transmediality.

We begin to see ways that user-generated content has created its own aesthetic; a set of stylistic tropes and social networking conventions that are drawn from the behaviours of non-professional media-users. The world of UGC has become the context for new forms of web-based entertainment fiction. Here, for instance, the wobbly-scope first-person address of the camcorder becomes the webcam confessional that now constitutes the 'mastershot' of many web-based video forms. The burgeoning field of web drama and online '360-degree' TV spin-offs have developed a new diegetic world where there has to be a reason for the camera to be present. The mark of the user, of presence and of technology, has become a precondition. The narrativisation and commodification of UGC in these emergent forms exploits the history of 'vernacular video'. Vernacular video is demotic, promiscuous, amateur, fluid and haptically convenient, technology at hand and in the hand. I derive the idea of vernacular video from Jean Burgess' 2007 doctoral research and subsequent work with Joshua Green on YouTube where she defines vernacular creativity as 'the wide range of every-day creative practices (from scrapbooking to family photography to the storytelling that forms part of casual chat) practiced outside the cultural value systems of either high culture or commercial creative practice' (Burgess and Green, 2009, p. 25). The online forms of vernacular video also develop from what I have discussed elsewhere as the 'camcorder cultures' of the 1990s (Dovey, 2000, p. 55) and display many of the same characteristics. The grammar of this vernacular is characterised by affect, intimacy, desire and display. Like any demotic, it is mercurial, endlessly inventive, driven by the self-replicating memes of web culture. The ubiquity of the video camera in everyday life creates a fluid subject position: the camera can simply be handed back and forth and turned on by whomever, facilitating an intimacy and ease of address. This demotic visual style has an immediacy and an appeal to users; it is the visual grammar of the everyday. Its potential for participation is therefore significantly higher than it might be if the work was characterised by mainstream TV or Hollywood production values. The fact that a lot of the material looks like an average YouTube post or mobile phone movie makes it a lot easier for me to comment, in my vernacular, than it would be if the material had a traditional TV or cinematic finish. The cultural constitution of the subject through 'our vernacular' therefore becomes a value-producing process whereby the demotic becomes the grammar of brand engagement. No longer does 'everyday creative practice' lie 'outside the cultural value systems of … commercial cre-ative practice'; on the contrary, it becomes a new visual grammar of consumption driven by the self-constituting practices of its creators.

Salami-slicing attention

We now turn to the precise methods through which the demotic creativity of the web can be monetised within the context of the attention economy. However, it's worth pointing out before we do so that the majority of YouTube material that falls into the category of vernacular or non-professional is not produced or uploaded with the inten-tion of making money. Patricia Lange (2007) has used the idea of 'fractal distinction between the public and private' to analyse the processes whereby our YouTube posts are cast on the water of the shifting tides of net traffic, pitched at many different pos-sible destinations between the 'privately public' affinity group of friends and family and the 'publicly private' viral hit. Most amateur posts are aimed at an immediate social network audience of mostly known friends and family, with the vague awareness that you too could go viral in the lottery of web celebrity. This chapter is more concerned with those semi-professionals or aspiring producers who seek to take advantage of the lower barriers to entry afforded by digital cultures in order to create new kinds of work and new kinds of media companies.

The problem for media companies with ambitions to professionalism starting up on the web is finding an audience. The paradox of Barabasi's principle of 'preferential attachment to already connected nodes' is made manifest as soon as you launch your site. You may have a great idea but how do you achieve the scale to find an audience? Most of the ways that media producers can monetise their talent rely upon selling attention in tiny measurable units. Essentially, a media company provides content for free by harvesting the potential for users to purchase a product in the future (brand engagement), by selling advertising space, by sending potential purchasers to shopping sites or by delivering the viewer, via free content, to a subscription service (the freemium model). In order to sustain any of these income streams, the media producer needs to have deep pockets that afford the patient building of audiences. As we will see, compared to those of broadcast 'big media', the audience numbers are tiny. However, if your audience segment is specific, has spending power, is reliable (i.e. returns over time) and most important of all is *measurable*, then your small audience numbers may be valuable to media buyers.

The costs a producer is able to charge for the attention they deliver to brands depend on online advertising metrics. In the past, advertising costs were calculated as 'cost per mill' (CPM), a figure calculated on how many thousand people would see the advertisement. Online brings the ability to measure not only CPM but, also, how long does your mouse 'hover', how long do you spend on a site, how often do you 'click through' to a product site from a sponsorship logo and how often an ad leads to purchase? Here, the attention economy is salami-sliced into high-value layers that can be packaged up and sold to advertisers at differential rates and in a bewildering variety of packages. Advertising and sponsorship have developed myriad new forms in order to measure our attention. Cost per thousand has become cost per action (CPA), commanding a higher price because it implies *engagement*, the holy grail of brand marketers; the user has taken an action (share, comment, like) and these actions can be aggregated into a figure that can have a financial value attached to it.

A brand's media buyers will need to know not only how many monthly visitors and viewers the web drama has but also how often these users actually upload or participate by commenting, Tweeting, 'liking' in Facebook, and how many of these actions can be turned into monetisable actions (purchase, subscription). Web 2.0 is built on the simple realisation that the web will record all of these actions anyway, if we ask it to. In order to facilitate this process, new forms of advertising and sponsorship are being devised all the time. The spaces and connections of the network are for the social marketeer just so much real estate, tiny dynamic billboards waiting to be exploited. As a media buyer looking for advertising space online, you can pay for a variety of formats, each one designed for specific kinds of product or market segment. For example:

- an 'expandable hub' – a banner ad that when clicked plays a video
- ad boxes with video already embedded
- expandable video players with different branding boxes available
- ads that allow the user to sign up to a Twitter stream or a Facebook group where they can discuss the product or service being advertised
- simple overlay ads that take the user straight to a purchase point
- overlay ads that allow you to see what other users have said about a product
- ads that look like possible questions to ask about a service that then offer answers from a Twitter stream.

Many of these services seek to leverage the power of social networking to encourage consumption. In October 2010, Seth Goldstein's Social Media.com launched a new product called 'Social Re-Engager' with the straplines:

> In the first 4 seconds, a user decides whether or not to interact with your ad.
> More than 99% of users become DISENGAGED.
> Get them back with the Social Re-Engager!
>
> Social Re-Engager detects disengaged users, and gets them re-engaged with the power of social pressure. Get them back with the Social Re-Engager!
>
> Increases clickthrough rate by up to 800%! (Goldstein, 2010)

What does all this mean to the producer and to the form of web drama? First, that your story has to be constructed in such a way that it will appeal to particular kinds of audiences with particular kinds of buying power. In fact, this is no different from any other form of commercial media production. It just so happens that the generalised field of upgrade culture produces particular kinds of young, mobile, socially networked subjects as its 'preferred technicities' (Dovey and Kennedy, 2006, p. 64). They are the idealised consumers for whom most online media producers are competing and who are allegedly leaving television in favour of the web. (According to the Internet Advertising Bureau, 2009, total ad spend on the web surpassed ad spend on TV in the UK for the first time in 2009.) Second, your chances of success will be enhanced by the more opportunities you offer your user to interact with and participate in the experience. So at the very basic level, all your characters will have their own Facebook pages, they will email, text and tweet, encouraging a community to build up around the show. All of these potential sites of engagement are potential sites of attention monetisation: saleable events. Third, your storylines should have the temporal quality of being permanently interruptible – online media exist in overlapping windows usually open at the same time, all commanding slightly different attention modes. So your storyworld has to reflect these medium-specific qualities of temporality. Then the experience of 'expandable hubs', media players with permanent advertising overlays or Twitter interruptions are all par for the course. Fourth, you should be prepared for your story to exist in that liminal space that is both demotic digital realism aiming for viral impact *and* sponsored fiction. In other words, to set a story in the domain of the viral ad – advertisements that look like home-grown demotic video but are actually agency-produced. The series *My Sister Freaks Out* (2006), for instance, looked like the real video diary-based account of a very spoilt Californian teenager in the realm of *Beverly Hills 90210* (1990–2000) but turned out, after a short run, to be an ad for Domino's Pizza. Finally, you should be ready to accept sponsorship and product placement at all levels of the production. Sponsorship can be in the form of selling 'branded wrap-arounds' for your whole site, or selling particular parts of it to sponsors. It might also involve selling narrative space inside the story by integrating products into a storyline. Here, sponsorship segues into product placement. So, for instance, the web drama *Where Are the Joneses?* (2007), sponsored by Ford, had the eye-catching (but terrible) idea of having the fans write the script; the script wiki was locked each day at 4.00 p.m., shot the following day and uploaded the day after. The story starts from the proposition that Dawn Jones discovers that her father was a sperm donor, and that she has lots of siblings whom she decides to trace. It became a picaresque journey round Europe in – guess what? – a Ford Ka.

Upgrade buzz

Finally, I want to turn to the value of the attention generated by upgrade culture that is above and around the functional mechanics of farming attention in the emergent ecosystems of online media. I want to argue that the dynamics of upgrade culture produce novelty as an apparently intrinsic value. This line of inquiry draws on more recent research I have conducted with digital media start-ups working with new narrative forms, context-aware delivery systems, augmented reality and interactive public spectacles. (See, for example, Hazel Grian's *Traces of Hope* for the Red Cross, PIAS Mobile's *Plastic Beach* Augmented Reality Campaign for the band Gorillaz, Seeper's Interactive Projection Mapping for *Nokia Ovi Maps*.) In these cases, the value of novelty was explicit: the fact that producers were offering a new format that could make a brand look 'cutting edge' was of more value than any metrics showing engagement or purchase intentions. If the campaign itself attracted column inches in the advertising press, this was *as valuable* to the brands concerned as a rise in sales. This is a point at which the attention economy can be seen to be ramifying itself way beyond a mere restatement of the old 'eyeballs to advertisers' principle. Here, the attention of the 'attention farmers' themselves has a premium value that is actually never monetised in any conventionally comprehensible way. Its value is as 'buzz', cultural capital that becomes actual capital through the complex processes of cultural practice and hegemonic influence that Bourdieu (1986) has established but here transposed into the techno-cultural milieu of the early twenty-first century.

The ideological force of the value of buzz in upgrade culture can be measured in the money spent investing in techno futures. The first dot.com bust taught us this lesson, and since Web 2.0 we have been in the grip of a further manifestation of technological desire based in part on online media. Despite the intensification of attention farming described above, the jury on the conventional profitability of web media is still out. YouTube was forecast to actually lose $470 million in 2009–10 despite its wild success (Johnson, 2009). The ad revenue just doesn't balance out the high operating costs (in bandwidth and storage terms) of serving a video clip to each user. Despite this, Google was prepared to pay $1.6 billion for YouTube in October 2006. This exemplifies the value of attention. It doesn't matter that your income stream doesn't match your costs if you can create enough press attention and buzz to attract a buyout. This is one of the real meanings of the 'attention economy': if you can focus attention on your brand, you will make money even if there is no actual cash flow. Media start-up business plans are characterised by an argument that revenue will match costs at a certain point but at five or ten years all investors will have exit options based on the idea that the company IP will be bought up by a much bigger player like Microsoft or Google. That's actually one of the ways that new Web 2.0 entrepreneurs are making big money – through speculation on unproven future income – exactly as they did in the good old Web 1.0 crash.

These strands are all in play in the story of the social network Bebo and the role of the web drama *KateModern* in creating attention capital that became real cash. Launched in July 2005, Bebo was a social network aimed at the teen user between children's social media (for example, *Club Penguin*, *Habbo Hotel*) and Facebook, and had grown to more than five million users worldwide by 2009. As discussed in detail by Elizabeth Evans in the following chapter, *KateModern* launched in July 2007 on the Bebo social network and ran as two series totalling 240 episodes. Each episode ran as an exclusive for twenty-four hours on Bebo and was then made available on other networks such as Veoh and YouTube. Although the work can therefore circulate virally, Bebo hopes that all those users who want to know more or to participate in the community will be driven back to the original Bebo pages.

KateModern follows the story of Kate, an east London art student whose life takes a turn for the dark and mysterious when she becomes the victim of a shadowy organisation who want her 'trait positive' blood supply (which they believe holds the secret to eternal life). The narrative follows events as her friends get drawn into the mystery plot and Kate is kidnapped and eventually found dead in the series one climax. The second series followed Charlie, Kate's best friend, as the group attempt to solve the murder mystery only to discover that they are harbouring a gruesome serial killer who is also at odds with the original suspects 'The Order'. The story is set in the twenty- to thirty-something social milieu typical of *Friends* (1994–2004) that is the aspirational generation for the Bebo teen demographic.

Throughout 2007–8, Bebo was all over the press with reports of its groundbreaking web drama, which was the first in the UK to attract crossover attention through its innovative mix of product placement, advertising and sponsorship. Bebo claimed that the first series of the show attracted thirty million total views, with an average of 200,000 views per episode (see Lander, 2010b). One of the ways it achieved this was by ensuring that the *KateModern* videos ran automatically on the Bebo homepage. The other was to have an effective PR operation which stressed the power of this form of web experience to deliver engagement to brands looking for that young, mobile, 'taste-forming' demographic. The audience is here a fan to be cultivated and 'engaged' in online advertising. As one of the first into the field able to argue that it had large and loyal audiences, the production company LG15 was very successful in attracting sponsorship through product placement by major brands such as Microsoft, Orange, Disney, Paramount, Kraft Foods, Procter and Gamble, and New Balance. On the basis of the *KateModern* experience, in 2008 Bebo was offering sponsorship packages for its new series *Sofia's Diary* that broke down the value of its supposed audiences. Two major plotline integrations, a minimum of two video inclusions per plotline and twenty product placements/mentions plus branding across character profiles were on offer at £425,000 for six months. For £100,000, a brand's media buyer could have bought bespoke integration consisting of one major plotline integration, a minimum of two video inclusions and two product placements.

In the meantime, at another level, online tech gossip was beginning to circulate the idea that the company was worth £1 billion. In March 2008, it was sold for $850 million (£417 million) to AOL, and its numbers have been in decline since. AOL announced its decision to seek a buyer or close it down in April 2010. Column inches, press attention and buzz here create economic value way beyond the value of advertising to individual sponsors. In the process, LG15 was also able to leverage the attention, relaunching itself as EQAL with a $5 million investment dedicated to promoting online brand engagement.

The very public process of monetising attention in its commissioned online web dramas attracted the attention of the global investment community. Upgrade buzz became an $850 million deal for Bebo's founders. The reality was more complex, however, as Bebo's eventual demise was to prove; engagement was still hard to monetise compared to banners and logo flashes (see Lander, 2010b).

There is no 'outside'

The creative, critical and applied methods at work in this essay create their own tensions that prevent easy conclusions. The critical perspectives on the attention economy offered, for instance, by Beller and others suggest compelling arguments that our identities are being colonised by the constant intensification of our work as 'audience commodity'. These processes come into focus when we examine how a demotic online form becomes drawn into professional media production. However, in the context of creative and applied research methods, or from the point of view of the media producer wanting to take advantage of the transformed means of production and distribution made available by online, this situation is not new. Media producers have always worked within an attention economy. There has never been 'an outside', where we could work without recourse to funding tied to attention. For producers, the ethical choices of 'whose money will you take?' and 'at what price?' remain the same. It's just that there are many avenues between the 'everyday production of symbolic value', intrinsic value and economic value than ever before. Further research will explore how the methods of value co-creation common to peer-to-peer networks, freemium or social gifting systems might offer radical reformulations of the attention economy in practice.

Bibliography

Anderson, Chris. (2006) *The Long Tail: Why the Future of Business Is Selling Less of More* (London: Hyperion).

Barabasi, Albert-László and Réka Alberts. (1999) 'The Emergence of Scaling in Random Networks', *Science*, 286 (5439), 15 October, pp. 509–12.

—— and Emil Bonabeau. (2003) 'Scale Free Networks', *Scientific American*, 5 (60), pp. 50–9.

Beller, Jonathan. (2006) 'Paying Attention', <www.cabinetmagazine.org/issues/24/beller.php> accessed 5 May 2010.

Bourdieu, Pierre. (1986) *Distinction: A Social Critique of the Judgement of Taste* (London: Routledge).

Burgess, Jean and Joshua Green. (2009) *YouTube: Online Video and Participatory Culture* (Cambridge: Polity Press).

Carr, Nicholas. (2010) *The Shallows* (New York: Norton).

Davenport, Thomas and John Beck. (2001) *The Attention Economy: Understanding the New Currency of Business* (Boston, MA: Harvard Business School Press).

Dovey, Jon. (2000) *Freakshow* (London: Pluto Press).

Dovey, Jon and Helen Kennedy. (2006) *Game Cultures: Computer Games as New Media* (Maidenhead, Berks.: McGraw-Hill).

Elsaesser, Thomas. (2009) 'Tales of Epiphany and Entropy: Around the Worlds in Eighty Clicks', in Pelle Snickars and Patrick Vonderau (eds), *The YouTube Reader* (Stockholm: National Library of Sweden), pp. 166–86.

Goldhaber, Michael. (1997) 'The Attention Economy and the Net', *First Monday*, 2 (4), <http://firstmonday.org/htbin/cgiwrap/bin/ojs/index.php/fm/article/view/519/440> accessed 5 May 2010.

Goldstein, Seth. (2010) <http://blog.socialmedia.com/index.html> accessed 18 October 2010.

Internet Advertising Bureau. (2009) 'Internet Ad Spend Grows 4.6 Per Cent', <www.iabuk.net/en/1/adspendgrows300909.mxs> accessed 18 October 2010.

Johnson, Bobbie. (2009) 'Does YouTube Actually Make Any Money'?, <www.guardian.co.uk/technology/blog/2009/apr/07/youtube-video-losses> accessed 18 October 2010.

Lander, Rick. (2010a) *VonViral*, <http://vonviral.ning.com/> accessed 12 October 2010.

——. (2010b) 'The Truth about Bebo', <http://vonviral.ning.com/profiles/blogs/web-funding-part-two-the-truth> accessed 18 October 2010.

Lange, Patricia. (2007) 'Publicly Private and Privately Public: Social Networking on YouTube', *Journal of Computer-Mediated Communication*, 13 (1), article 18, <http://jcmc.indiana.edu/vol13/issue1/lange.html> accessed 10 May 2011.

Lanham, Richard. (2006) *The Economics of Attention: Style and Substance in the Age of Information* (Chicago: University of Chicago Press).

O'Reilly, Tim. (2005) 'What Is Web 2.0: Design Patterns and Business Models for the Next Generation of Software', <www.oreilly.com/pub/a/oreilly/tim/news/2005/09/30/what-is-web-20.html> accessed 5 October 2010.

Simon, Herbert. (1971) 'Designing Organizations for an Information-Rich World', in Martin Greenberger (ed.), *Computers, Communication, and the Public Interest* (Baltimore, MD: The Johns Hopkins Press).

Terranova, Tiziana. (2010) 'The Bios of Attention', Unpublished Conference Paper, 'Paying Attention' conference, Linkoping, Sweden, September 2010.

Web citations

Grian, Hazel. (2009) *Traces of Hope*, <http://tracesofhope.com/> accessed 18 October 2010.

HappySlip. (2006) <http://www.happyslip.com/> accessed 18 October 2010.

Human Pet. (2006) <http://www.youtube.com/profile?user=thehumanpet1> accessed 18 October 2010.

KateModern. (2007) <www.bebo.com/katemodern> accessed 18 October 2010.

lonelygirl15. (2006) <http://www.lg15.com/lonelygirl15/> accessed 18 October 2010.

My Sister Freaks Out. (2006) <www.youtube.com/user/MacKenzieheartsu> accessed 18 October 2010.

PIAS Mobile. (2010) *Plastic Beach*, <http://pias.com/mobile/?p=101> accessed 18 October 2010.

Seeper. (2010) Interactive Projection Mapping for *Nokia Ovi Maps*, <http://vimeo.com/groups/1313/videos/11188067> accessed 18 October 2010.

The Guild. (2007) <http://www.watchtheguild.com/> accessed 18 October 2010.

Where Are the Joneses? (2007) <http://wherearethejoneses.wikidot.com/> accessed 18 October 2010.

9 'Carnaby Street, 10 a.m.': *KateModern* and the Ephemeral Dynamics of Online Drama

Elizabeth Jane Evans

Film and television are temporal media. Unlike 'static' storytelling forms such as painting or photography, they are experienced through time, constantly changing alongside the lived experience of their viewer. They are, in essence, defined by a sense of ephemeral experience. This chapter explicitly considers the term 'ephemeral' and its application to our understanding of the relationship between audiovisual technology and audience engagement. While the last chapter establishes a basis for examining the professional media production of web drama as linked to economies of attention, this chapter uses the case study of *KateModern* (Bebo, 2007–8) to examine, in detail, how online drama series have used technology to complicate and encourage particular forms of audience engagement. In doing so, such dramas simultaneously call on traditions of cinema/broadcast media that centre around notions of 'event' and liveness *and* emerging customs of online communication that centre around notions of community and agency. The resulting experience involves modes of engagement that are both 'anti-ephemeral' and 'hyper-ephemeral'; they create a permanent media object that can be watched whenever the viewer chooses but also privilege engagement with a particular moment that can never be replicated.

Audiovisual ephemerality before the internet

The history of audience engagement with audiovisual entertainment forms can be seen as involving a negotiation between ephemerality and permanence. Harold A. Innis, in his historical study of the role written and print media played in the development of empires, argues that media forms either 'emphasize time … [and] are durable in character, such as parchment, clay and stone' or 'emphasize space [and] are apt to be less durable and light in character, such as papyrus and paper' (Innis, 1972, p. 7).

The former were made to endure through time, to be available to later generations; the latter were concerned with crossing space and accessing a wider population quickly and as simultaneously as possible. While the development of a new medium of communication does not obliterate the usefulness of previous forms, Innis maintains a clear division between this 'bias of time' and 'bias of space' (Patterson, 1990, p. 3). This division and the notion of a shifting in media technologies between those aimed at creating permanent artifacts and ephemeral, temporary objects is useful in considering the technological development of audiovisual media. However, as the following discussion will explore, the emergence of the internet as a platform for audiovisual, fictional communication requires the need to complicate any clear division between technology as either permanent or ephemeral.

Innis argues that the emergence of audiovisual technology signals a shift back towards time-based media (Innis, 1972, p. 170). However, as Roger Silverstone points out:

> This shifting media-based phenomenology of time and space is not without its contradictions in Innis' account. For while it is clear that radio (and television) create a transforming environment for empires based on print, and appear to be providing something of a return to a time-based culture, it is a time-based culture paradoxically based on this occasion not on the durability of parchment, clay and stone, but on the dramatically enhanced ephemerality of the widely broadcast spoken word and visual image. (Silverstone, 1994, pp. 93–4)

Notions of a fleeting, ephemeral moment are central to the experience of many popular narrative forms. The pleasures of performance-based narrative, such as theatre, opera or ballet, are founded on notions of ephemerality – each performance is unique, the moment of engagement fleeting and unrepeatable; you have to be there to get the atmosphere and buzz of seeing the performance. The true experience, sitting within a particular crowd of strangers with the performers right in front of you, in the flesh, giving a one-off performance, is impossible to record or recreate. Film allowed the capture and display of 'real' events with a certain degree of permanence, but this permanence is incomplete. For the audience, film is not actually a physical, durable object. Performances are at set times; if you aren't in a certain space at that time, you miss out; individual experiences of watching film (the sounds of fellow audience members, the comfort or discomfort of seats, the general 'atmosphere' of a specific group of people in a specific space at a specific time) in the cinema are unique. Since, as Siegfried Zielinski discusses, '[a]ll the artefacts [of cinema] that were required to realise this communicative process, including the machines for copying the films, stayed with the producers, laboratories, and those who ran the cinemas, including the object of desire, the film itself' (Zielinski, 1999, p. 188), the permanent object of film remained outside of the viewer's grasp. Although they could return and see the film multiple times, they could only do so on the cinema's terms and each experience would be different. While film allowed for the permanent recording of real or staged events, its true permanence for the audience was limited.

Television continued an emphasis on ephemeral experience in ways that became central to its cultural and critical understanding. Both Zielinski and William Uricchio have argued that the development of cinema technology involved the desire to share a specific moment simultaneously with many viewers across the globe, rather than store a record of that moment (see Uricchio, 2004, p. 127; Zielinski, 1999, p. 34), something that television would provide. As has been discussed previously in this volume, broadcasting's central experience is ephemeral; images vanish as soon as they appear and the related concept of liveness has long been argued for as a central, ontological characteristic of television broadcasting (see Ellis, 1992 [1982], p. 132; Gripsrud, 1998, p. 19; Carroll, 2003, p. 268; Hills, 2007, p. 43). Concepts such as Raymond Williams' flow (1974) or Newcomb and Hirsch's viewing strip (2000 [1976]) underscore the conceptualisation of television as fleeting. Elana Levine argues that this sense of liveness 'represent[s] the epitome of "television" itself' (Levine, 2008, p. 396), something that is 'predicated upon the belief that television is at its best when it broadcasts live' (ibid., p. 397). Liveness and its accompanying ephemerality, a sense that the viewer is experiencing something that can never be experienced again, has been seen as so central to the definition of television as a medium that without it, content is somehow lesser.[1] For audiences, cinema and television broadcasting initially shared a sense of impermanence. Although the technologies allow for the storing of content for the industries that produce it, the experience for audiences was primarily fleeting.

However, both cinema and television have seen the development of technologies designed to transform the viewing of film or television from an ephemeral, fleeting experience into permanent objects that could be watched (and of course sold) over and over again.[2] Home cinema systems such as the Birtac camera projector were available as early as the 1930s and wealthy middle-class families could create a library of film, with the earliest versions of video shops appearing at the same time (Chalke, 2007, pp. 226–7). More recent developments such as the VCR and DVR have transformed these elitist activities into common daily practices. As Camille Bacon-Smith writes, addressing the use of videotapes to introduce science-fiction fans to new programmes, 'moving onto the video circuit, the neophyte must change attitudes and perceptions of the very nature of mass-produced entertainment. The ephemeral, throw-away nature of television changes, as programming becomes frozen in time at

the will of the viewer' (Bacon-Smith, 1992, p. 123). The development of such technology is evidence of an increasing desire throughout the history of film and television
to capture content and make it a permanent object, to 'de-ephemeralise' it for the
viewer. Film can now be a box on your shelf which can be accessed whenever you
choose, as many times as you choose. Television is no longer a flow of images and
sounds that are impossible to hold down. While the ephemeral experience does not
go away or cease to be important, audiovisual engagement's pure ephemerality, its
'unrepeatable-ness', is undercut. Modern technological developments have created a
contradiction within the nature of media engagement through a tension between the
permanence of the media object that sits on the viewer's shelf and the ephemerality
of the viewing experience.[3]

Ephemerality and the internet

This tension, between permanent object and fleeting experience, is epitomised in the
development of the internet as a medium for both personal and mass communication.
The internet can be both 'anti-ephemeral' and 'hyper-ephemeral', something that has
been recognised by scholars investigating various forms of online content.
Alvan Bregman and Caroline Haythornthwaite, for example, in their discussion of
online communication, argue that '[t]he permanence of the final posted presentation
may vary from near ephemeral, for example, as email is sent and quickly deleted, to
near permanent, for example, as messages, web pages, etc. are archived' (Bregman
and Haythornthwaite, 2003, p. 124). The complexities of online ephemerality extend
into the internet's appropriation as a platform for audiovisual narrative and offer a far
more complicated relationship to notions of ephemerality and the historical shift
towards permanence.

On the one hand, the internet takes the moves begun with the Birtac camera projector and developed in the VCR even further, transforming the experience of audiovisual content from one defined through a fleeting temporality to one defined through
archival permanence. This is most evident by focusing on engagement with television
content. While, as argued above, the VCR or DVR allow television to be transformed
into a permanent object that could be viewed at the viewer's discretion, access to that
content is still defined through the temporal structure of the schedule (see Evans,
2011, p. 149). A viewer no longer has to ensure that they are sitting in front of their television set at a particular time, but they still have to ensure that they have set a piece of
machinery by a particular time. In the case of both the VCR and DVR, the viewer is, to
a greater or lesser extent, still bound by a schedule that flows through time and cannot
be captured retrospectively. With downloading, however, a television programme can

now exist permanently as a file that can be accessed via a home computer at any time. As with the VCR, each programme becomes a physical, though virtual, entity. Like a book or a DVD, it can be taken off a (virtual) shelf and watched whenever the viewer wants to watch it. Content loses any sense of being 'transmitted and received in the same moment that it is produced' (Ellis, 1992 [1982], p. 132). The downloading audience is not tied to the television schedule at all, beyond having to wait for a programme or film's initial release. To an even greater extent than the VCR, it gains instead a more permanent existence in downloading than in the fleeting, momentary nature of broadcasting (see Evans, 2008). In this respect, the internet has completed the move towards anti-ephemerality that has been present in the technological development of audiovisual content since the late nineteenth century.

On the other hand, however, in addition to having the capacity to store information, many functions of the internet, such as email, instant messaging, social networking sites and chat rooms, depend on notions of instant or near-instant communication. The social and cultural use of the internet in this way stems from an inherent potential for ephemerality within its technological structure. As Schneider and Foot argue, not only is 'web content … ephemeral in its transience, as it can be expected to last for only a relatively brief time', it is also ephemeral in that 'a website may destroy its predecessor regularly and procedurally each time it is updated by its producer' (Schneider and Foot, 2004, p. 115). This is evident to a certain extent in the structures of broadcasters' downloading services that privilege recent content. In the UK, services such as the BBC's iPlayer or the ITV Player only allow access to content for a limited period of time after its initial broadcast; the viewer does not actually have permanent access to it. Viewers are equally unable to save such content on their hard drives, so the extent to which content on these services comprises truly permanent objects is limited.[4] This indicates a tension within the appropriation of the internet as an audiovisual platform: it can both recreate the ephemerality of older media forms and transform their texts into permanent objects. In short, it is as capable of being a hyper-ephemeral, broadcast medium as much as a storage medium.

KateModern: negotiating anti- and hyper-ephemerality

This negotiation is epitomised in the original online drama *KateModern*, which was released through the Bebo social networking site between June 2007 and July 2008. The series was a spin-off/sequel to the infamous YouTube series *lonelygirl15* (June 2006–August 2008) in which a sixteen-year-old girl named Bree seemed to post video blogs about her life. The videos were ultimately revealed to be fiction and the story evolved into a fantastical narrative involving the quest for eternal life (see Burgess and

Green, 2009, pp. 27–9). *KateModern* recreates the video blog style of *lonelygirl15*, consisting of short videos, normally of Kate (Alexandra Weaver) or one of her small group of friends talking directly to the camera. The narrative arc of the first season (which ran from June 2007 to January 2008) tied closely to the narrative of *lonelygirl15* and involved Kate's discovery that she had an unusual blood type, called 'trait positive', which a quasi-religious group called The Order believed held the secret to eternal life. The central mysteries of what Kate's blood type means, who the members of The Order were and whether they would succeed in kidnapping her in order to steal her blood underpin each of the individual videos. When Kate is murdered at the beginning of the second season, the narrative shifts to the hunt for her killer and the protection of other girls with 'trait positive' blood.

To a certain extent, *KateModern* perpetuates the kind of 'anti-ephemeral' engagement that emerges through the history of older media forms and the technological developments that have surrounded them. While individual videos are short, normally only two to three minutes long, the whole series is vast, totalling almost fourteen hours over the two seasons. This may not be as long as a full television series but it is significantly longer than a film and far from brief in terms of duration. When this series is added to the others in the 'LG15' universe, including, in addition to *lonelygirl15*, a Polish spin-off, *N1ckola*, and two sequels, *LG15: The Resistance* and *LG15: The Last*, the amount of time required to engage with the full text becomes equal to, if not more than, that of a television season. Similarly, the website epitomises the permanent, archival potential of online video discussed above. Both seasons are archived and listed in order on the official website; it is still possible to watch the whole series at any time, years after its initial release. The series is a permanent (albeit virtual) object that to watch in its entirety takes up a significant amount of the viewer's time. In this respect, it fits into the recent technological developments that focus on a desire to turn previously ephemeral content (broadcast television) into physical objects.

At the same time, however, the producers of *KateModern* used the capability of the internet to encourage modes of engagement that work against this historical move towards permanent audiovisual objects. As much as the series promotes anti-ephemerality, it simultaneously promotes *hyper*-ephemerality, a form of engagement that is just as fleeting as the constant flow of television broadcast images or unrepeatable theatrical film performances. This hyper-ephemerality is manifested in a number of interrelated 'interactive' narrative and scheduling decisions throughout the series' run that can be categorised in three main ways: distribution, audience–text interaction and audience–text integration. These three methods of promoting hyper-ephemerality offer distinct pleasures to the audience while at the same time creating a relationship between audience and text that is based on communication, community and agency.

i) Hyper-ephemerality through distribution – marathons

The first way in which *KateModern* emphasises a sense of hyper-ephemerality is in two 'marathons' in which videos were posted at set times over a period of twelve hours. These marathons function as an intensification of the series' narrative format. Most of the series takes a 'flexi-narrative' approach (Nelson, 1997) involving a combination of videos that progress a single serial narrative and individual 'stand-alone' moments that have little bearing on events seen before or since. The marathons, however, consist of a single, serial arc, with each video leading on from the next; they must all be watched sequentially in order for the narrative to make sense. While the narrative does not follow a strict 'real-time' format, there is a sense of story time roughly following the twelve-hour posting time, with sunset occurring at the correct time and each video detailing events that have occurred prior to its posting but since the previous video. The narrative of the series is adapted in these moments in order to promote engage-ment with them over a period of twelve hours, as they are released. They also appeared at key moments within the series' narrative when suspense or intrigue is brought to the forefront of the viewer's experience. The first, 'Precious Blood', which took place on 5 April 2008, reveals the identity of Kate's killer. The second, 'The Last Work', was posted on 28 June 2008 and concluded the series through a confrontation with Kate's killer and the group's decision to stop posting video blogs (via the symbolic destruction of a camera). Both of these points of the narrative function in similar ways to the 'sweeps' episodes of US television, when producers encourage viewers to watch live through techniques such as stunt casting, cliffhangers and the dramatic culmina-tion of long-running storylines (see Lury, 2005, pp. 124–5; Lotz, 2007, pp. 102–3).

The marketing material of these marathons further emphasised their temporally specific nature. Each marathon was advertised separately, as a distinct unit of narra-tive. Posters proudly declared '12 videos in 12 hours', with the start date and time fea-turing prominently. Trailers placed similar emphasis, consisting only of graphic screens stating the date and reiterating the '12 in 12' motif, followed by a few short bursts of images from the forthcoming episodes. Video titles confirmed this twelve-hour struc-ture. Rather than having individual, descriptive titles as the other videos in the series do, they are labelled with the marathon's overall title and then the time that corre-sponds with when they were first posted, for example 'Precious Blood: 2 p.m.'. This naming has the twin effect of connecting each of the twelve videos together as an overall story arc and reiterating their time-specific status.

These marathons share certain characteristics with what Daniel Dayan and Elihu Katz term 'media events'. These events are principally defined as being 'not routine', as a break from the norm of television broadcasting (Dayan and Katz, 1992, p. 5). Dayan and Katz focus on factual programming such as coronations and large-scale sporting events. However, this emphasis denies the usefulness of 'event' as a concept for considering the distribution and reception of fictional texts. Mimi White's discussion of 'television of attractions' echoes many of Dayan and Katz's sentiments but suggests their potential application to fictional programming. While she too begins with a study of catastrophic events, she goes on to argue that the 'ongoing co-articulations of liveness and historicity' characteristic of these moments are 'not restricted to catastrophe coverage, but permeate all sorts of special event, "live" programming' (White, 2004, pp. 78–9). Through the example of the series finale of *Cheers* (1982–93), White indicates the importance of 'attracting audiences at the moment [such a moment] was aired' (ibid.). The recent abundance of midnight screenings for films such as *Star Wars* (1977–2005), *Harry Potter* (2001–11) and *Twilight* (2008–12), or the heavy promotion that broadcasters place on season openers and finales, is a clear indication of how such a planned and orchestrated sense of event status is regularly conferred on works of fiction.

KateModern posters for 'Precious Blood' and 'The Last Work'

The key implication of the event model, and its usefulness for understanding fictional programming, is an emphasis on hyper-ephemerality and sharing a 'moment'. While the content may be recorded (and so become 'permanent'), the moment of release takes on a special significance. You may be able to watch a race during the Olympics the following day, see *Twilight* a week after it is released or record the finale of *Lost* and watch it after it has aired, but you will have missed the *event*. The same can be said of the *KateModern* marathons. They are distributed in a pattern that is explicitly 'not routine' in comparison to the rest of the series, and it is one that is not only focused on releasing more videos during a shorter space of time but also on releasing them *at a specific moment in time*. The series producers explicitly tied this to the distribution patterns of television, with producer Kelly Brett describing it in its press release as a 'traditional TV broadcast technique' and demonstrative of *KateModern*'s 'credibility and creativity' (EQAL, 2008), again further emphasising not only the episodes' 'remediation' (Bolter and Grusin, 2000) of older media but the fact that they were different and special. Marketing techniques and the use of specific arc titles only set these episodes further apart from the 'normal series'. Viewers are encouraged not to watch the videos whenever fits their day best, but to watch them together, as a collective, as soon as they are made available. It is clear, from the distribution, narrative and marketing of these videos that engagement with them as they are released is key; if you are not part of the marathon as it happens, you have missed out on something special.

ii) Hyper-ephemerality through audience–text interaction: blogs, chats and quizzes

While the event status created through these marathons calls on traditions of television broadcasting to promote a sense of hyper-ephemerality, elsewhere the series uses the communicative facilities of the internet to encourage hyper-ephemerality via audience–text interaction. Neil Mossey, a writer on season two of the series, describes how a primary appeal of using the internet as a platform for audiovisual narrative is 'the potential for two-way communication with the audience while the show is running, unlike film or TV where you are completely divorced from the audience' (personal email to author, 9 July 2009). He goes on to discuss how the specific production structure and narrative techniques used by the series facilitated this communication:

> A member of the production team would actually post, and answer comments 'in character' – an 'Interactive Coordinator', or 'Community Manager'. They would ask the writing team for guidance in steering what each character would choose to upload (for example, what pictures or information they would place on their Bebo profile), and the writing team looked to the Interactive Coordinator for guidance in how the fan community were reacting to character or story developments. (ibid.)

Each character had an individual blog on the Bebo site where they would describe themselves, link to other characters they were in a significant relationship with and post photos. These sites would also feature the videos that they had diegetically created, giving the impression that they really had been made and uploaded by the characters themselves.[5] Viewers could then befriend them and leave comments, which, as Mossey explains, would be responded to 'in character'. Viewers were encouraged to form the same kind of online relationships and communications with the characters from the series that they may have with each other.

This emphasis on two-way communication with the audience filtered through into the on-screen narrative. The character of Sophie (Pippa Duffy) was positioned throughout the series as their direct link to the narrative events of *KateModern*'s diegesis. She featured in the online community long before appearing on screen, being credited as the founder of the *KateModern* website and writing regular blogs about videos as they were posted. Not long into the series, she began to function more explicitly as a way to encourage viewers to take part in a number of interactive moments. The first of these was in the form of a puzzle part-way through the first season. Kate visits a mysterious doctor in an attempt to find out more about her condition but wakes up the following morning with no memory. She finds a series of photos on her phone which her friend Steve posts online in an attempt to find out where she had been. Sophie then encouraged viewers to write in with their suggestions for the photos' locations. Those viewers who did were rewarded with an in-text message of thanks from Kate. Such quizzes continued throughout the series, often in association with the marathons discussed above. One quiz during 'Precious Blood' again served a narrative function (identifying where one kidnapped character was being held) but also offered a real prize in the form of a Toyota Aygo. Not only do these quizzes privilege direct communication between the viewer and the narrative world (and a sense of competition between viewers), they also privilege a hyper-ephemeral mode of engagement. If you watch the relevant videos now, you can still answer the questions and solve the puzzle, but you will not get a diegetic thanks or a new car.

During the final marathon, 'The Last Work', the hyper-ephemerality foregrounded through communication with the diegesis was combined with that foregrounded by an 'event' distribution approach. Live chats took place whereby viewers could write a message or send a question to Sophie and various other characters (who all appeared in a small video box in the top left-hand corner), which she would then respond to. While Sophie's responses were oriented around clarifying recent narrative events, audience questions also included non-narrative issues such as why the feed quality was poor and intertextual comments relating to the cast's other roles. As with the quizzes, viewers could insert their virtual identities into the narrative of the show but, unlike the normal blogs where they could contribute at any time, they could only do so if they were at their computer at a particular moment in time. The live chats had event-like build-up, with the feed of audience responses going live before Sophie's video link and participants expressing their growing excitement by exclaiming, 'COME ON SOPHEEE [sic]' ('Live Chat 2 p.m.') or running a countdown until it started.

These moments of hyper-ephemerality are distinct from the use of marathons in that rather than calling on the kinds of distribution models familiar from broadcasting, they exploit the communicative facilities of the internet. These moments share the aesthetic of online communications far more than that of television or film. From the use of multicoloured text to distinguish between different participants and the 'textspeak' adopted by contributors, to buttons inviting viewers to 'upload media' and the often jerky video feed featuring Sophie in the top left-hand corner, these episodes do not attempt to recreate even the handheld visual style of the rest of the episode. Instead, they emphasise communication as a form of narrative engagement, a communication that, in its

'The Last Work: Live Chat 8 p.m.', *KateModern*, Season Two

instantaneous nature, is hyper-ephemeral by definition; if you're not there between 8.00 p.m. and 8.05 p.m., you can't take part.

Each of these forms of audience–text interaction use their hyper-ephemerality to build on the sense of community established by the marathon 'events' and twin it with a sense of increased agency over not only how a viewer engages with a text but also what the text actually becomes. Viewers do not have to ask characters questions, answer the quiz questions or contribute to the live chats but if they do, they not only help create the series' narrative, and so appear to be contributing to its progression, but also become part of a more visible *KateModern* community. Benedict Anderson's (1983) notion of the 'imagined community' has long been associated with the television audience. John Hartley, for example, argues that 'one unwarranted, invisible fiction – the imagined community of the nation – is used to invent and explain another: the television audience' (Hartley, 2003, p. 57). Television audiences are positioned as a community through shared awareness, rather than physical proximity. We may not know that anyone else is watching what we are, but we have a sense that they are. Moments of audience–text interaction in *KateModern* make its audience community less 'imagined'. The most extreme version of this are the live chats that make both this agency and the community visible on screen, and so an integral part of the series' aesthetic. Community, twinned with agency, are key components of the series' construction of a hyper-ephemeral mode of engagement.

iii) Hyper-ephemerality through audience–text integration: meet-ups

The association between a hyper-ephemeral mode of engagement, direct involvement with the storyworld and the establishment of a strong viewing community is taken even further in the creation of moments in which the viewer is invited to integrate themselves more fully into the on-screen narrative. On a number of occasions throughout the series, viewers were invited to meet the characters and witness part of an episode within the real world. Echoing the flash mobs of social networking sites, in which large numbers of individuals are brought together in the same physical space through web and mobile connectivity, these moments called for viewers to meet in a physical location at a specific time. There, they would not only meet other fans of the series but also in-character actors who would then guide them through a particular episode. In the first of these, following on shortly from quizzes concerning Kate's lost day discussed above, two of Kate's friends, Charlie (Tara Rushton) and Gavin (Ralf Little), discover that Kate is planning to go to London's Carnaby Street the following day and confront the doctor. After getting trapped in a basement office, they post a video pleading with viewers to go to Carnaby Street and stop her. The next day, a video entitled 'Carnaby Street, Saturday 18 August, 10 a.m.' was posted showing Sophie meeting up with fans, all of whom then witnessed Kate attempting to see the doctor but in fact discovering that he had been killed. In addition to the footage filmed by the *KateModern* cameras, fans were invited to upload their own videos and reports of the day's events.

These meet-ups promote a sense of ephemerality that is simultaneously familiar from older media forms, and exploitative of the unique capabilities of the internet. As discussed above, there is value is seeing something such as live sport or the final episode of *Lost* when it is broadcast, a value that persists despite time-shifting tech-nologies and is evident in the quizzes and marathons of *KateModern*. The syn-chronicity involved in the Carnaby Street episode, however, takes this even further. The moment of broadcast (or release) is already too late; it is the moment of produc-tion that is privileged in a way that is not present in film and present only occasionally in broadcast television that involves live studio audiences. This is only made possible through both the technological capability of the internet as an instant (or at least semi-instant) communication tool, allowing word to spread of such meet-ups in less than twenty-four hours, and through the social use that has been made of these technolo-gies, as a space in which the organisation of such meet-ups is acceptable. Since its inception, the World Wide Web has been associated with notions of community, with inventor Tim Berners-Lee's hope 'that the World Wide Web would be built through collaboration' (Gauntlett, 2004, p. 6). In the 2000s, flash mobs changed their style and status from a mode of unauthorised (sometimes infamous) community-gathering to something commercially endorsed.[6] Judith A. Nicholson (2005) discusses them as 'deliberately ephemeral', and so they have a natural alignment with the hyper-ephemeral modes of engagement seen in *KateModern*. While the Carnaby Street meet-up is focused on witnessing and creating a fictional universe, rather than con-ducting a prank or stunt, it shares the key element of community with flash mobs. By utilising not just the internet as a technology but the social uses to which it has been put, *KateModern* aims to transform the invisible 'imagined community' of the broadcast television audience (Anderson, 1983; see also Hartley, 2003, p. 57) into a visible physical community that shares a geographical location, even if only for a short period of time. By integrating the audience into the construction of the text (as extras), the importance of 'being there' extends beyond that seen in broadcast television or even theatrical film viewing, of being in front of a screen or in a specific location at a specific time. The sense of hyper-ephemerality in this case is both temporal and geographic and is focused around creating not only a sense of audience agency in the creation of the narrative but also strengthening a sense of community.

Conclusion: ephemerality, community and agency

KateModern demonstrates that while the internet calls on and perpetuates a long history of ever more permanent forms of storing and experiencing moving images and sounds, it simultaneously offers the potential for a sense of ephemerality that is as much bound to a moment in time as television broadcasting and theatrical performance. In its use of distribution techniques such as marathons, audience–narrative interactions like live chats and quizzes, and audience–narrative integration via meet-ups, the series constructs layers of engagement which are based around a shifting balance between anti- and hyper-ephemerality. It is of course possible for someone to watch the series now, making use of the archiving capacity of the website to engage with the series in a traditional way, as they would engage with a television series or a film. It was also possible for viewers to watch the series at the time it was released, and experience the sense of immediacy and liveness worked into the narrative, but not to take part in any of the interactive or community-building elements. They would experience it as a traditional form of content but be tied to the moment of production and distribution in the way that television audiences were tied to the moment of broadcast pre-VCR. However, it is also possible for viewers to have become enmeshed at the moment of distribution and in the communication and agency provided by the internet's technological capabilities to the point where the experience of watching *KateModern* can never be replicated. For the viewer who answered the quiz questions, stayed at their computer for the twelve-hour marathon, asked characters (and each other) questions and went to Carnaby Street at 10 a.m. on Saturday 18 August 2007, the pleasure of community and agency is predicated upon a strong sense of hyper-ephemerality – they were there *in the moment*. They've experienced something with only a few other people, something they'll never experience again. At this far end of the scale, experiencing the text involves an ephemerality that is akin to live theatre or, arguably, real life (there are equally those who 'experience' the series merely by being in Carnaby Street for other reasons at 10 a.m. on 18 August).

To return to Harold Innis, unlike earlier audiovisual media technologies, *KateModern* demonstrates the potential for online drama (and the internet more generally) to challenge the notion of media as space or time-biased. *KateModern* is both durable *and* temporary; it is both clay and papyrus. The implication of this dual capability, as demonstrated by the negotiation between anti- and hyper-ephemerality in *KateModern*, is the possibility of establishing a particular kind of audience engagement that is based not only on creating a broadcast event but also on building viewer agency and community. Unlike broadcast technology which shares this sense of ephemerality, the audience community for *KateModern* is both less 'imagined' and more in control of when and how they experience the series; viewers are explicitly encouraged to engage with each other *and* the text but they do not have to. Although the extent to which the audience is given true agency over the drama's narrative is limited (Kate would have presumably gone to Carnaby Street even if no one had identified it or shown up on 18 August 2007), the illusion of agency is crucial to the forms of engagement encouraged by the series. By heavily promoting such moments and giving them added value by recognising those who take this offered agency within the official narrative of the series, a clear message is sent to the viewers: you can be a very real part of the *KateModern* universe.

Notes

1. This is something that is exacerbated in terms of early television by the fact that many programmes literally cannot be recreated, as they were either deleted or never stored (see Jacobs, 2000).
2. With reference to television, this development of technologies that provide permanence is also, of course, central to the history of production technologies and the shift away from all-live broadcasting.
3. No audiovisual storage form has an unlimited shelf-life. Celluloid and videotape degrade, particularly after multiple viewings, digital forms can corrupt and discs can wear out. Equally, individuals can choose to wipe or destroy these forms. However, each continues to be an object and while the act of viewing them remains temporal, the content itself is taken out of the temporal stream in which it is positioned (an evening at the cinema or the broadcast flow). They are given a more permanent, captured existence for their viewers.
4. Commercial services in which viewers pay for content, such as iTunes, do allow the permanent downloading of programmes and films, and so they are transformed into permanent (albeit virtual) objects.
5. Videos were also made available via the main *KateModern* site.
6. The infamous party organised to mark the ban on drinking alcohol on the London Underground on 31 May 2008 is one example of the former (see Parker, 2008), resulting in a number of arrests. A year later, mobile phone operator T-Mobile developed the principle of the flash mob within an extended UK brand marketing campaign that saw numerous public stunts, ranging from spontaneous dance choreography in Liverpool

Street Station to a mass sing-a-long in Trafalgar Square (Grainge, forthcoming). See also
Rheingold (2002) for a detailed discussion of flash mobs.

Bibliography

Anderson, Benedict A. (1983) *Imagined Communities: Reflections on the Origin and Spread of
Nationalism* (London: Verso).

Bacon-Smith, Camille. (1992) *Enterprising Women: Television Fandom and the Creation of
Popular Myth* (Philadelphia: University of Pennsylvania Press).

Bolter, Jay David and Richard Grusin. (2000) *Remediation: Understanding New Media*
(Cambridge, MA: MIT Press).

Bregman, Alvan and Caroline Haythornthwaite. (2003) 'Radicals of Presentation: Visibility,
Relation, and Co-Presence in Persistent Conversation', *New Media and Society*, 5 (1),
pp. 117–40.

Burgess, Jean and Joshua Green. (2009) *YouTube: Online Video and Participatory Culture*
(Cambridge: Polity).

Carroll, Noel. (2003) *Engaging the Moving Image* (New Haven, CT: Yale University Press).

Chalke, Sheila. (2007) 'Early Home Cinema: The Origins of Alternative Spectatorship',
Convergence, 13 (3), pp. 223–30.

Dayan, Daniel and Elihu Katz. (1992) *Media Events: The Live Broadcasting of History*
(Cambridge, MA: Harvard University Press).

Ellis, John. (1992) *Visible Fictions: Cinema, Television, Radio* (London: Routledge).

EQAL. (2008) 'Bebo Soap to Air 12 Episodes in 12 Hours', 1 April, <www.eqal.com/
2008/04/01/bebo-soap-to-air-12-episodes-in-12-hours/> accessed 4 January 2010.

Evans, Elizabeth Jane. (2008) 'Character, Audience Agency and Transmedia Drama', *Media,
Culture & Society*, 30 (2), pp. 197–213.

Evans, Elizabeth. (2011) *Transmedia Television: Audiences, New Media and Daily Life* (London:
Routledge).

Gauntlett, David. (2004) *Web Studies*, 2nd edn. (London: Arnold).

Grainge, Paul. (forthcoming) 'A Song and Dance: Branded Entertainment and Mobile
Promotion', *International Journal of Cultural Studies*.

Gripsrud, Jostein. (1998) 'Television, Broadcasting, Flow: Key Metaphors in TV Theory', in
Christine Geraghty and David Lusted (eds), *The Television Studies Book* (London: Arnold),
pp. 17–32.

Hartley, John. (2003) 'Invisible Fictions: Television Audiences, Paedocracy, Pleasure', in Toby
Miller (ed.), *Television: Critical Concepts in Media and Cultural Studies* (London:
Routledge), pp. 54–71.

Hills, Matt. (2007) 'From the Box in the Corner to the Box Set on the Shelf: "TVIII" and the
Cultural/Textual Valorisations of DVD', *New Review of Film and Television Studies*, 5 (1),
pp. 41–60.

Innis, Harold A. (1972) *Empire and Communications* (Toronto: University of Toronto Press).

Jacobs, Jason. (2000) *The Intimate Screen: Early British Television Drama* (Oxford: Oxford University Press).

Levine, Elana. (2008) 'Distinguishing Television: The Changing Meanings of Television Liveness', *Media, Culture & Society*, 30 (3), pp. 393–409.

Lotz, Amanda D. (2007) *The Television Will Be Revolutionized* (New York: New York University Press).

Lury, Karen. (2005) *Interpreting Television* (London: Hodder Arnold).

Nelson, Robin. (1997) *TV Drama in Transition: Forms, Values and Cultural Change* (Basingstoke, Hants.: Palgrave Macmillan).

Newcomb, Horace and Paul M. Hirsch. (2000 [1976]) 'Television as Cultural Form', in Horace Newcomb (ed.), *Television: A Critical View* (Oxford: Oxford University Press).

Nicholson, Judith A. (2005) 'Flash Mobs in the Age of Mobile Connectivity', *Fibreculture*, 6, <http://journal.fibreculture.org/issue6/issue6_nicholson.html> accessed 29 January 2010.

Parker, Quin. (2008) 'Cocktail Party Plan to Mark the End of the Line for Tube Drinkers', *Guardian*, 16 May, <www.guardian.co.uk/society/2008/may/16/circle.line.cocktail.party> accessed 29 January 2010.

Patterson, Graeme. (1990) *History and Communications: Harold Innis, Marshall McLuhan, and the Interpretation of History* (Toronto: University of Toronto Press).

Rheingold, Harold. (2002) *Smart Mobs: The Next Social Revolution* (Cambridge, MA: Perseus).

Schneider, Steven M. and Kirsten A. Foot. (2004) 'The Web as an Object of Study', *New Media and Society*, 6 (1), pp. 114–23.

Silverstone, Roger. (1994) *Television and Everyday Life* (London: Routledge).

Uricchio, William. (2004) 'Storage, Simultaneity, and the Media Technologies of Modernity', in Jan Olsson and John Fullerton (eds), *Allegories of Communication: Intermedial Concerns from Cinema to the Digital* (Eastleigh, Hants.: John Libbey), pp. 123–38.

White, Mimi. (2004) 'The Attractions of Television: Reconsidering Liveness', in Nick Couldry and Anna McCarthy (eds), *Mediaspace: Place, Scale and Culture in a Media Age* (London: Routledge), pp. 75–91.

Williams, Raymond. (1974) *Television: Technology and Cultural Form* (London: Fontana).

Zielinski, Siegfried. (1999 [1989]) *Audiovisions: Cinema and Television as Entr'actes of History*. Translated by Gloria Custance (Amsterdam: Amsterdam University Press).

PART4 BELOW: WORKER- AND USER-GENERATED CONTENT

10 Corporate and Worker Ephemera: The Industrial Promotional Surround, Paratexts and Worker Blowback[1]

John T. Caldwell

Paratexts circulate well before and beyond the public world of the fan previews, DVD director's commentaries and the making-ofs viewed by consumers. In fact, they now serve integral functions within non-fan corporate media cultures and professional media worker communities alike (Caldwell, 2004, 2008), although scholars have paid scant attention to paratexts within these corporate and worker worlds. Lisa Kernan (2004) and Jonathan Gray (2010) have both productively adapted Gérard Genette's term 'paratext' (those elements that accompany a published work, such as a preface, introduction, illustration or appendix) to explain publicly circulated film and television media forms. Whereas Kernan's project examines trailers to discern which public and viewer the film industry *imagines* it is addressing, and Gray attempts to understand the textual 'DNA' of particular media franchises circulating in 'consumer culture', my research aims to understand the paratexts that circulate within professional 'production cultures'. I am particularly interested in the industrial logic driving the exchange of such paratexts 'off screen' among professionals, even as I recognise the tendency of many of these same texts to 'leak' publicly on screen. My focus on the increased production and circulation of (off-screen) worker and corporate paratexts in contemporary industrial culture helps clarify the kinds of socio-professional interactions and ephemeral textual exchange that surround or circulate in a different kind of public, below media's 'primary' texts.

Media industries do not simply produce popular culture; they are comprised of many local cultures in their own right. These industrial cultures habitually do all of the things that other cultures do to make sense of themselves, to seek legitimacy and to manage change (through self-expressions, self-narratives and collective rituals). To understand these industry cultural dynamics, I make a categorical distinction throughout this chapter between 'top-down' corporate paratexts and 'ground-up' worker paratexts. Examples of corporate paratexts and self-reflection include: branding promos, marketing tapes, making-ofs, electronic press kits, franchise cross-promotions, Q&As, DVD bonus tracks, authorised online sites, soundtracks, legal downloads, ancillary merchandise and box-set extras. In short, corporate paratexts include most of the things that fans view, use, collect and/or exchange, which are authorised for circulation by the conglomerate. The 'flipside' to this – of ground-up worker paratexts and self-reflections (my ultimate interest) – includes: demo tapes, comp reels, trade stories, how-to panels, technical retreats, collective craft rituals, mentoring rituals, union organising and events, trade columns to below-the-line workers, worker websites, unauthorised blogs, spoilers from crews, leaks from assistants and self-representations by technical, craft and professional associations and non-profits. Media paratexts and self-reflections like these play fundamental roles in maintaining the cultural identities, legitimacy and economic viability of the socio-professional communities that make film and television.

I hope in this chapter to chart the parameters of contemporary paratextual *exchange* within an integrated model of what I term the 'insider's industrial promotional surround' (hereafter, the IPS). Within this model, I intend to clarify how and why paratexts can be usefully understood not just in terms of their industry–audience or *extra-industry* relations within consumer culture, but in terms of their *intra-industry* functions in the worlds of professional media practitioners as well. My final aim is to articulate what I term the 'two warring flipsides' of the IPS. Specifically, this flipside model concerns the conflicted and contentious relations between 'top-down' corporate ephemera on the one hand (authorised by industry), and 'ground-up' worker ephemera (unauthorised productions by media workers) on the other. Since considerable scholarly attention has recently been directed to social networks and online 'user-generated content' (UGC), we would do well to consider online 'worker-generated content' (WGC) as a different kind of paratextual 'worker blowback'.

One side: top-down corporate reflexivity and paratexts

The insider's promotional surround is clogged with rhetoric about media distinctions, where new content can be posed as: a 'cinematic milestone', the 'television event of the season', the 'must-have digital app'. I begin by considering a three-part model of why these *constructions* of 'media specificity' are so important to many media corporations, and why multimedia conglomerates employ paratexts – which are distinction-making devices by definition – as essential parts of their business plans. Because many media *production distinctions* have now been levelled *technically* in the digital era, and because many *viewing distinctions* have been levelled *culturally* (when film, television and online media are all viewed on the very same screen), media marketers now have to work overtime to achieve their primary obligation: to inform and convince viewer-users that the screen experience they hype will in fact be distinctive (for example, 'cinematic' even though it may be cablecast, downloaded or streamed on the same flatscreen TV). Technical 'convergence' may be good for the multimedia conglomerates, the technology companies and their stockholders, but this cultural and technical levelling can be deadly for producers and their marketers, whose task of 'raising content above the clutter' is now more difficult than ever. This distinction-making imperative is why marketing can now be viewed as 'authoring' vast amounts of screen content, regardless of who the official screenwriters or producers are in the credits.

Industry's on-screen self-reflexive texts and paratexts can be usefully understood within a series of long-standing workaday practices and industrial strategies. Consider how my model comparing differing 'Comparative Media Business Models and Mythoi' among multiple media forms may complicate the function of paratexts (see Table 1). This comparative three-part model attempted to move beyond the now obsolete hard-line distinctions that once separated film, television and new media and to see them as part of integrated institutionalised systems. For some time, several supposedly 'essential' differences between film and television have blurred and then collapsed. For decades, most of film's revenues have come from television and electronic media rather than box office; primetime cable television has long eclipsed the US film studios as the site where the most stylistic innovation, cultural edginess and quality film production take place; most film production is now funded by television pre-sales and co-financing; film production and post-production are both now primarily electronic, just like television, from the start; film has now adopted the audience and market research posture that once defined television and advertising; just like television from the start, film now takes the in-home domestic screen as its target market; the film studios are now as frequently focused on repurposing, franchising and syndication as American television has been since the start; both film and television are inextricably woven together with digital and new-media platforms even as new media reiterates and hybridises film and television. And so forth. On the surface, this list may smack of a great and mighty congealing of several distinct media into one amalgam, perhaps instigated by contemporary transnational multimedia conglomerates. In many situations, there are few technical distinctions between film and television (film poses as television and television poses as film). But this levelling is true only in a limited sense.

Yes, Viacom, News Corp., NBC/Universal and Time-Warner/AOL produce all three of these ostensibly 'different' media (film, television, digital media) simultaneously as part of the integrated business plans and using roughly the same production firms and technologies. But while the technology distinctions between media continue to

Table 1 Comparative Media Business Models and Mythoi: *Media Specificity Habits from Marketing that Fuel Top-Down Paratext Production*

CINEMA	TELEVISION	CONGLOMERATE
→	→	*(Fiscal managerial pressures)*
Project-Specific	Series-Specific	Syndication-Focused
Extraordinary-Driven	Mediocracy-Driven	Predictability-Governed
Risk-Focused	Risk-Managed	Risk Aversion
Dynamic Adaptive Behaviour	Structured Adaptive Behaviour	Collateralised Adaptive Behaviour
Information Cascade Method	Programming/Scheduling Method	Cross-Promotion Method
Exceptionalist Creators/ Elites	Collective Creators/Teams	Outsourced Creation/ Externalised
Intuition-Based Decisions	Measurement-Based Decisions	Cost/Benefit Analysis-Based
Charismatic Management	Regulatory Management	Synergistic Management
Success via Blockbusters	Success via Longevity	Success via Market Diversification
Economic Scope via Stars	Economic Scope via Identity & Taste	Economic Scope via Sub-Brands
Economic Scale via Sequels	Economic Scale via Series Franchises	Economic Scale via Merchandising
Incremental Contracts	Seasonal Contracts	Cross-Ownership/Long-Term Equity
Box Office	Sponsorship/Subscription	Changes in Stock Value
Flow Uncertainty	Day-part Viewer Flow	Intra-Brand Viewer Flow
Appointment Viewing	Habitual Viewing	Affective Viewer Relation to Brand

(Marketing self-referencing pressures) ← ←

collapse, the cultural pretensions and industrial 'mythoi of specificity' are still extremely important within media production work worlds. Media creators, that is, have persisted in emulating the old distinctions between cinema and TV – but in largely symbolic and cultural terms. For example (as Table 1 indicates), cinema could once be credibly characterised as: project-specific (involving single-feature financing), extraordinary-driven (motion-picture 'event' seeking) and employing 'exceptionalist' creators (high-profile auteurs and moguls). Television, by contrast, was traditionally posed as: series-specific (dispersing risk over months of episodes), mediocracy-driven (least objectionable programming prone) and collectively created (using creative teams and lower-profile writers' rooms). In addition, the cultural activity of cinema production favoured and promoted: intuition-based decisions (execs who could spot

future winners 'in their gut'), charismatic management (leaders with a personal signature and visionary track record), deep economic scope (via stars and their long-term
fans) and wide economic scale (via high-concept genres and sequels). Television was
thought to have prospered by employing a set of contrasting strategies: measurement-
based decisions (ratings and market research), regulated management (locked to
internal corporate policies and heavy external government regulation), economic
scope (via narrowcasting identities and niche tastes) and economic scale (via series
franchises and blockbuster TV).

In the post-network, post-studio era, however, these binary oppositions are often
blurred: extraordinary authorship and charismatic management (once identified with
cinema) now entrenched in television; and mediocre programming and risk-averse
measurement-based content development and management now pervasive in film
studio majors. Production technologies per se no longer matter as much in guaran-
teeing media specificity and cultural distinction as they once did. Yet for the competing cinema-vs.-TV *cultures of production workers*, media specificities most certainly still
do matter, as their industrial critical practices and the incessant cultural posturing of
workers attest. These cross-cultural mythologies and differences between media unfold
even inside the same transmedia corporations. This workaday push to construct artifi-
cial media specificities is one of the reasons my research has focused on paratextual
forms of industrial self-disclosure and the cultural studies of production, rather than
some ostensibly self-evident media definitions, innate textual boundaries or macro-
scopic political-economic analysis of different mediums. Both the aesthetic and economic value of media's primary texts today are generated in part by industry's
distinction-making paratextual cultural practices. These cultural expressions of distinction, that is, are as likely to occur within marketing departments and the production
workforce as they are among critics and fans in culture at large. The dominance of the
multimedia conglomerate in the digital era adds a third set of powerful institutional
and economic pressures that push and impact production cultures beyond the traditional cinema-vs.-TV dyad. This conglomerate reach spurs industry's pursuit of the
distinction-making metatexts which are needed to constantly announce new screen
content and production to a distracted public.

Many individual paratexts have emerged out of one or more of the three broad institutional frameworks in this model. Marketing's focus on distinction-making and specificity lies at the heart of movement from one of these managerial states of mind to
another. We need to identify which industrial/marketing contexts generate the paratexts
we analyse, and to describe any paratexts we research as part of a grounded, economically driven, cultural system of exchange. Furthermore, paratexts and self-reflexive content matter, but in different ways to different sectors of the industry. I've begun this
chapter by considering the logic of paratexts from the top, from corporate perspectives.

As I have argued elsewhere (Caldwell, 2004), contemporary media corporations deploy complex forms of industrial self-reflexivity to pursue their goals of diversification, managerial flexibility, synergy, cross-promotion and branding. The tripartite table of industrial behaviours above can be viewed as a general road map that helps us better understand the metatextual strategies for different groups. First, paratexts and on-screen representations (of the production world made by the production world) guide the *viewer* as s/he deciphers and navigates the many channel/content options available in the multimedia environment. Successful modern media conglomerates no longer succeed by isolating and locking on to consumers within traditional or discrete media or 'channel' categories. Rather, media conglomerates today are effective only to the degree that they can manage flow and loosely guide user/viewers through two increasingly common situations: as they cycle and 'flow' sequentially from one multimedia platform to another – in what I have termed entertainment's 'second shift' (Caldwell, 2003) – and as they 'multitask' simultaneously across various media platforms.

For content providers, industrial self-referencing and self-commentary can also be viewed as symptoms of adaptive behaviours by corporations that are generated in response to intense market competition and structural uncertainties (Caldwell, 2008, pp. 274–315). For the large media conglomerates, that is, on-screen self-referencing content provides industry with resources for a specific kind of adaptive behaviour – what economist Arthur De Vany (2004, pp. 1–6) would call an 'information cascade' needed to concoct and assign 'extraordinary' status for the films or series being depicted. Hit films, by definition, need to be seen as rare and highly extraordinary to be deemed hits. Reflexive information cascades promise to reduce the great uncertainty and risk that defines the content development process. Many of the reflexive industrial artifacts and paratexts that make up information cascades in the IPS (like DVDs and video games spun off from films) also help the conglomerates dynamically follow or 'track' the transitory, unpredictable viewer or fan, whether for cinema or television.

The current amortised, cross-collateralised mediascape – in which content is repurposed and films/series are financed by dispersing production costs across numerous affiliated partners and distribution windows within the multimedia conglomerate – helps provide rationality to an otherwise diffused and unpredictable situation. Such a scheme, that is, allows corporations and their investors to more accurately appraise the cost and value of potential individual projects. Aggregating multiple platforms, in turn, allows the companies to be more systematic in selecting, capitalising and developing new projects. Newly networked affiliates linked within the conglomerates provide predictability in designing marketing plans and in projecting profits – both crucial tasks in the risk-defined, failure-prone world of content development. Succeeding at this now means producing and circulating *huge* amounts of paratextual material needed for multichannel and multiplatform cross-promotion. The genius of this scheme is that paratexts inevitably do 'double-duty'. Thus, in addition to their standard role as 'value-added' marketing materials, large swathes of any conglomerate's niches also now use paratexts as 'primary' forms of on-screen content as well. This in turn allows them to sell ads, place products or tap cable TV licensing fees to generate revenues – from paratexts – that go far beyond the economic value produced by mere promotion.

In some ways, this cross-collateralisation and repurposing strategy has created a schizophrenic identity for the conglomerates that pursue it. That is, it creates a disconnect and divergence between on-screen textual practices and inside managerial practices. For example, even as marketing departments intensify their distinction-making self-referencing in public (alternatively known as keeping the firm's titles 'above the multichannel clutter'), fiscal/managerial pressures within the very same conglomerate habitually push back to ensure clockwork-like bureaucratic predictability. Or, even as the large studio conglomerates concoct 'indie'-feature cutting edges and vanguard auteurs to snag niche audiences, festival buzz and critical acclaim, bottom-line business economics are pushing 'cinema' production further into the realm (and economic scheme) of television. Television, after all, first mastered the distribution of production costs and risks across affiliated partners (including the film studios in the 1950s) and systematically used audience/market research and analysis to produce less volatile business plans than film. Television's more conservative scheme was based on the predictability of alternatives to film box office: advertising sponsorship, merchandising and long-term licensing fees. Long ago, television mastered on-screen programming/scheduling as a strategic business strength. Long-term programming/scheduling (based on organised 'seasons' comprised of episodic series and continuing serials) was dynamic enough to adapt to market uncertainty, and predictable enough to build long-range plans around. Programming/scheduling departments in turn enabled TV to find and manage audience flow much more effectively than cinema.

For these reasons, I would characterise the economic logic and less dynamic managerial system of television – something the multimedia conglomerates now seem to favour on the inside – in an economist's terminology as a 'mediocracy'. TV stands, after all, in stark contrast to what De Vany describes as the far more 'dynamic behaviors' and outcome 'uncertainties' that have historically defined feature film's 'extraordinary' economy. Simultaneously, television corporations like HBO and Showtime have taken on the extraordinary mantle once owned by cinema. I have included a number of related distinctions and additional linkages in Table 1 that can be made between the economic and institutional behaviours of film/television/conglomerates. As feature film is gradually incorporated, disciplined and rationalised as but a single node within giant multimedia conglomerates (which are in turn dominated by television, digital and electronic media activities), film will increasingly emulate strategies of effective television programming to do what it needs to do to survive as film. Conglomerates will continue to pressure their film units to follow audiences more responsively in order to harvest their transient financial resources. Internally at least, the new conglomerates increasingly favour television's historic, research-based industrial rationality over film's historic, personality-driven, roll-of-the-dice fatalism. At the same time, multimedia companies operating far beyond the once elite confines of cinema cultivate cinematic exceptionalism by perpetually circulating distinction-making paratexts.

The flipside: ground-up worker-generated content and labour 'blowback'

In some ways, the account and rationale about the IPS I have just given is a prescriptive, top-down, boardroom fantasy. Yet the decades-old managerial marketing strategies just described still rotely guide corporate, programming and marketing executives as they struggle to keep all of their juggled multimedia balls visible up in the air. Two broad forces in the last decade, however, have forced these corporate multimedia jugglers to perform their acts on much more shaky ground: the rise of media producing fandoms and forceful online social networks on the one hand; and the increasingly unstable conditions of production labour on the other. Industry countered the first social media threat (within the consumer sphere) by shifting to viral marketing, fan-focused interactive narrative strategies and brand extensions. It counters the second threat (from rising labour instabilities and costs) through production outsourcing, de-unionisation, runaway production and transnational co-production. Reflexive texts and paratexts play central roles in *both* of these key industry counter-strategies, although academics seem to be mostly interested in the fan side.

Much has been written about the kinds of texts that have emerged in the world of viral fandoms, social networks and YouTube (Snickars and Vonderau, 2009). In some ways, this world of viral videos and 'user-generated content' offers yet another (initially unsanctioned) 'mythos' to add to the three top-down industrial tendencies outlined in the model above (Jenkins, 2006). One important lesson of the social media revolution is that the corporate conglomerates cannot profitably 'repurpose' all of their media properties across all of the many new platforms, since few of the new platforms come with predictable or viable revenue streams. Instead, they economically justify their many paratexts only as 'value-added' marketing, whose mission is to increase the value of the brand or franchise as a whole. Media companies cannot, in fact, now 'push' their viewers *anywhere*, certainly not on a revenue-generating basis. Producers have found that it is much more effective instead to fabricate huge narrative worlds as part of scripting and marketing initiatives; imaginary universes that will reward viewers who desire to navigate story arcs and characters across the conglomerates' many new multimedia platforms and brand extensions.

In the shadow of this new interactive love-fest between conglomerates and fans lies a striking complementary phenomenon. My own research has focused instead on this second recent complication – professional labour work worlds that operate in the shadow of both the multimedia conglomerates *and* the celebrated, ostensibly unruly, fans. Specifically, I have focused on 'worker-generated content' (WGC), 'producer-generated content' (PGC), the 'worker promotional surround' (WPS) and the 'corporate promotional surround (CPS) (see Table 2). In many cases, film and television production workers have the most to lose from the new conglomerates and their ever-affiliating fandoms. If convergence marketing and managerial pressures drive the production of paratexts within the corporate promotional surround, what forces and conditions cultivate and spur the anxious flipside: worker-generated content?

WGC and worker paratexts emerge in part from traditions that predate either the new multimedia conglomerates (and their top-down marketing fantasies) or the unruly new demands of fans and online social networks. I would argue that a long-standing tradition of 'industrial idea theft' in Hollywood now serves as a prototype and proving ground for worker-generated paratexts. Jenkins' influential 1992 book *Textual Poachers* proved a prescient primer and lexicon for the complex varieties of fan activities that were both creative and productive. Since that time, I've realised that these same forms of 'unauthorised' agency and cultural hijacking were fully at work inside the industry as well, as producers and workers poach, filk, mash up videos and circulate them off screen in social gatherings – as unauthorised individuals and as small craft groups and associations struggling to survive in the industry. In some ways my own work since that time has operated on what feels like the 'dark side' (industry's subterranean cultural activities) while Jenkins' work has operated on the implicitly 'sunny side' (the enabling public side) of the industry–audience interface. Marketing specialists now fully embrace the perspectives and terminology of *Textual Poachers* and its more broadly social and cultural sequel, *Convergence Culture*, in their own commercial discourses, trade conventions and business plans. The research framed by these two influential books has in fact provided an alternative road map for corporations as they struggle to rationalise the increasingly unruly *markets* of online fans and social networks. What I've spent considerable time trying to understand in my own research, however, is why industry and worker poaching, hacking, social networking, worker-fan-fic and spoiling have not received the same sort of attention by scholars *or* by the media corporations that employ these same 'unruly' craft and professional workers. From my experience, the marketing specialists and corporate executives that so ably pursue and attend to the needs and nuances of fan-consumer poaching and networked sociality have little interest in the *same* kinds of unauthorised activities by workers inside their corporate walls. With few exceptions (Gratton, 2007; Costykian, 2007), the media industries that now obsessively research external, morphing and unruly consumer markets show little interest in researching their internal, morphing and unruly labour markets.

I've begun to understand – through my fieldwork on aspiring writer 'pitch-fests', camera 'shoot-outs', editing 'bake-offs', effects 'reveals' and producer 'hook-ups' – that the poaching-social-networking revolution in *consumer* culture just discussed has a long pre-history fuelled by four sanctioned and well-oiled paratextual-producing *industry* practices and conventions: 1) idea-theft; 2) distributed creativity; 3) work-for-hire and 4) the vast oversupply of workers and aspiring workers. Unlike almost any other US business sector, the broad-based practice of serially 'pitching' story ideas to producers and executives through short, intense meetings arranged by agents means that ideas for new screen projects that circulate around Hollywood dwarf by thousands of times the relatively few feature films and TV shows actually produced. In practice, nobody really 'owns' the flood of pitched ideas until some studio, network or production company actually contracts and develops the rare, lucky project. This means that a huge number of hijackable ideas are in the air at any one time, ripe for picking, poaching, hybridising and reiteration by producers and executives when they inevitably borrow from this morass of other people's ideas. Of course, the fact that writers in Hollywood have been legally defined as 'work-for-hire' rather than 'authors' has helped decouple ideas from 'owners' in this pitch-driven free-for-all. But it doesn't stop there. Once producers poach ideas from the vast aspirant-hive, they 'distribute' the concepts to groups and socio-professional networks that then brainstorm them into scripts, films and series. The 'writers' room' is but one heavily rationalised example of this form of 'distributed-then-harvested creativity' (Henderson, 2009, pp. 224–30). A dozen writers, working sixteen-hour days, collectively generate, shoot down and hybridise the culled ideas into working form. Executive producers then dredge this story idea-pit for narrative and script elements from which episodes and series are produced. But the hiving and distribution doesn't stop there at production's 'front-end', since each script poached from the writers' room is then sent out and broken down by all of the area heads and distributed among their own production departments 'hives'. This distribution/harvesting continues until production's 'back-end', when the producing power structure artificially determines which executives will hijack 'creative' credit for features or series actually created by hundreds of other lower-level workers. Hijacking texts to recreate hybrid texts is a well-practised skill set in Hollywood.

To borrow a far more utopian and radical term from media outsiders, fans and activists, Hollywood's production worlds can also be thought of as an 'open-source movement'. This too helps stimulate the production of WGC. The examples of 'insider' textual poaching and paratextual production just described all unfold inside well-paid production sectors. Paratextual poaching gets even worse outside the signatory studios and networks, among the vast oversupply of underemployed and unemployed workers and aspirants. In these sectors, the hive is even more agitated, furious and prone to ephemeral textual production and poaching. This frequently unfolds in venues ostensibly hosted to 'teach' and 'help' the underemployed 'make it' in the industry. Theatrically staged 'pitch-fests' allow desperate ideas holders to give out their closely held pitches not just to celebrity agents on stage, but to hundreds of their registration-paying competitors out in the 'professional' audience as well. Sound editors screen segments for employed and unemployed craft colleagues, and reveal their secret recipes in 'bake-offs' (à la Pillsbury and Betty Crocker bake-offs). The visual effects society does the same through their annual 'reveals' (Malcolm, 2009, pp. 216–20). Equipment companies like Sony stage competitive 'camera shoot-outs' from which they poach the best spec scenes filmed by participants with new Sony equipment for use in Sony corporate demo tapes. Studios host competitive weekend 'shoot-outs' – manic, two-day short productions filmed by alienated below-the-line tenant workers on the lot – who want to be 'discovered' as above-the-line candidates through on-the-lot screenings that end the 'festival' weekend. Nobody pays for the profusion of new ideas that churn out of these dirt-cheap, industrial creative-ideas hives. Rote denials to the contrary, various iterations of the concepts freely circulated in these venues inevitably wind up in someone else's screen content.

This is why I frame Hollywood as an 'open-source movement'. This source-opening does not follow the collective DIY sharing ideology that circulates around software development. Hollywood now opens up more of its backstage world to the public than ever before (through making-ofs, showbiz programming, DVD bonus tracks, directors' blogs, etc.). At the same time, not coincidentally, it forces its desperate workers and aspirants (locked in a protracted battle against each other to get work) to freely 'open up' their own private intellectual capital to corporate employers. Sadly, this industrial strategy – stealing freely from workers to give freely to consumers – evokes the spectre of a new 'commercial commons'; a problematic free-for-all sanctioned by the therapeutic career discourses of 'mentoring', 'enabling' and 'making it'. These ubiquitous forms of self-disclosure and industry-critical reflection produce an endless stream of unauthorised worker metatextual and paratextual production that makes the material world of professional film/television workers as multimediated and cluttered as the world of their multimedia fans.

Table 2 The Two Warring Flipsides in the Industrial Promotional Surround

TOP-DOWN CORPORATE EPHEMERA (CE)
(Branding, Marketing, Making-Ofs, Metatexts, Franchises, DVD Extras, EPKs, etc.)

Corporate Logic

Industrial Levelling Strategies:
- To level hierarchies in market/distribution chain (fulfils the pre-digital notion of direct-to-consumer marketing).
- To level distinctions in production/labour chain (lower costs, eliminates union entitlements, creates inter-craft conflict).

Specific Film/TV Tactics:
- To create information cascades on multiplatforms (publicity, buzz about 'special' blockbuster properties).
- To cross-promote conglomerate properties (advertising unexceptional content in the clutter).

General Corporate Goals:
- To externalise risk (through co-productions, presales, outsourcing, merchandising).
- To cultivate flexibility (through outsourcing, contract labour, project-based incorporation).

Impact/Results

UNRULY WORK WORLD

CE stimulates volatile labour contestation while creating oversupply of content (and workers) at industry's 'input boundaries'. Economic anxiety fuels excessive 'spec' project creation. As costs and revenues decrease, and markets become more uncertain, theoretical justifications in ephemeral texts circulated by management to employees increase.

UNRULY TECHNOLOGIES

CE industrially rationalises new tech as 'user-friendly' to collapse existing, costlier workflows. CE disciplines new tech by theorising them within traditional aesthetic standards and conventional business practices (but apart from existing labour arrangements). The greater any new tech's disruptiveness, the more extreme the theorising in ephemeral texts needed to tame it.

UNRULY AUDIENCES

CE brands corporations emotionally by creating psychological relations with fans via viral marketing, multiple platforms and immersive, ancillary content. Fan loyalty is keyed to relative extent of corporate disclosure and organisational transparency as evidenced by corporate ephemeral texts circulating in viewer's promotional surround.

CE tries to intellectually manage and monetise instabilities through self-referencing as labour and consumption distinctions are levelled

WE resuscitates levelled distinctions through self-referencing to maintain professional communities, craft survival and career advantage

UNRULY WORK WORLD

WE constantly negotiates worker and craft identities for survival. The histories, socio-professional hierarchies and cultural symbolism of any craft represented in ephemeral texts increase in prominence as the oversupply of production of labour increases.

UNRULY TECHNOLOGIES

WE is used to legitimise one technical or craft group over another competing craft group, and to establish competence and exclusivity. Craft and worker theorising, self-referencing and cultural activities in and through ephemeral texts increase as the conveyer belt of technical obsolescence and uncertainty accelerate.

UNRULY AUDIENCES

Users and fans increasingly share production and aesthetic competencies with commercial film/TV workers. Thus, worker discourses of 'professionalism–vs.–amateurism' in ephemera become acute and more exclusionary in the era of prosumer social media and amateur user-generated content (UGC).

Labour's Cultural Practice

Craft Strategies:

- Make craft, union or guild self-perpetuating through medieval system of protracted mentoring.
- Maximise and codify degree to which production is distributed across department area and crew.

Cultural Tactics/Contradictions:

- Cultivate ideal of unified industry with management to protect incomes after contracts are signed.
- Convert work into cultural capital, via socio-professional rituals, ancestry and meritocracy.
- Buffer underemployment by displaying and leveraging cultural capital via credits, craft awards and demo reels.

General Work Goals:

- Network to survive morphing, nomadic system of short-term production start-ups/shut-downs in 'gift economy'
- Maintain high costs of entry and exclusivity. Preach collectivity in trade fora and texts, but bar aspirants from entry.

Labour Logic

GROUND-UP WORKER EPHEMERA (WE)

(Mentoring, How-to Panels, Trade Stories, Technical Retreats, Comp Reels, Craft Meritocracy)

The two warring, interrelated sides of industrial self-disclosure: top-down 'corporate reflexivity' versus ground-up 'worker reflexivity'

It would be a mistake, however, to write off all of the WGC described above as sequestered expressions made by cut-off professional communities. These professional workers are themselves very much influenced by the new and unruly fan and online social networking forces; and are in many cases media fans themselves. More importantly, they now increasingly produce WGC as a direct counter-response to texts and economic pressures from the marketing and corporate spheres described above. I have indicated the relationships between these two spheres in Table 2 'The Two Warring Flipsides in the Industrial Promotional Surround', which shows how closely bound together – and contested – the production of top-down corporate paratexts are to ground-up worker paratexts thrown out as part of what I term labour's textual blowback.

Both the general aims and practical strategies of media corporations and production labour differ in significant ways, as recent labour strife in LA has dramatised. Much of this battle – between production companies and production labour – is waged in and through secondary textual practices; other parts play out in the work worlds of physical production proper. The top half of the IPS table details the logic of reflexivity, self-disclosure and paratextual production from the corporate perspective. This corporate/public sphere includes most of the things that fans view, use, collect and/or exchange, which are authorised for circulation by the conglomerate. The 'flipside' of ground-up worker paratexts and reflexivity – beyond the demo tapes, comp reels and trade stories described earlier – include how-to panels, technical retreats, collective craft rituals, mentoring rituals, union organising and events, trade columns to below-the-line workers, worker websites, unauthorised blogs, spoilers from crews, leaks from assistants and self-representations by technical, craft and professional associations and non-profits. Some of this free-form, unauthorised stuff 'from the bottom' finally makes its way to the top, and does gain broader visibility in the public mediascape trafficked by the studio, the network and the fan. Other more ephemeral worker texts have a more tangential relationship to the public mediascape, but do, nevertheless, generally inflect and influence the primary textual production of workers.

The general logic and strategies of the two sides locked in this 'face-off' could not be more different. In many ways, the industry constantly seeks to level hierarchies in the market/distribution chain, in order to fulfil the pre-digital notion of the more efficient and cost-effective direct-to-consumer marketing now possible in the digital age. At the same time, it persistently works to level costly 'old media' hierarchies and distinctions in the production/labour chain in order to lower costs, eliminate union entitlements and create inter-craft conflict. This is the environment in which the media companies pursue the specific film/TV tactics outlined above: to create information cascades on multiplatforms (publicity, buzz about 'special' blockbuster properties); and to cross-promote conglomerate properties (advertising unexceptional content in the clutter). This inverse dynamic – corporations maximise 'content-distinction' via transmedia marketing even as they erase labour distinctions in hiring practices – reinforces some resilient general corporate goals: to externalise risk (through co-productions, presales, outsourcing, merchandising); and to pursue and cultivate flexibility (through outsourcing, contract labour, project-based incorporation).

Labour's general orientation could not be more antithetical to these corporate tendencies, with cultural and craft strategies thrown up like flak to counter the corporate top-down levelling impulses just described. Recent economic and new technology instabilities in Hollywood, for example, have pushed labour to make craft, union or guild distinctions and hierarchies self-perpetuating through a medieval system of protracted mentoring. Unions, in turn, maximise and codify the degree to which production tasks must be divided and distributed across department area and crew. But alongside these long-standing but threatened work traditions, labour now mounts a series of increasingly acute discourses and 'cultural' activities. These include: the cultivation of the myth of a unified industry with management in order to protect incomes after contracts are signed; the conversion of actual work into cultural capital, via socio-professional rituals, and paratexts that prove craft ancestry and meritocracy. This last tactic helps buffer increasingly widespread underemployment by allowing anxious workers to display and leverage cultural capital via credits, craft awards and attention-seeking demo reels. Standing back from this new churn of cultural expressions by craft workers reveals some more general and contradictory forces at work that have altered the goals of many workers. First, most below-the-line workers must now incessantly 'network' to survive the new morphing, nomadic system of short-term start-ups/shut-downs that now characterise production's 'gift economy'. WGC, paratexts and craft cultural rituals help them do this. Second, old-guard craft and labour groups continue to maintain high 'costs of entry' for newcomers. This means that worker blowback is not necessarily the heroic 'inside industry resistance' it might at first appear to be from the model outlined above. Many labour and craft groups preach collectivity in trade forums and texts, for example, but in reality bar new aspirants from entry. The labour market is overcrowded, which makes craft distinctions and hierarchies more crucial than ever for those on the inside.

In an odd way, this desperate contestation and launching of worker and craft paratexts just described can also be seen as the parallel to the 'attention economy' that now defines the media markets that consumers face. That is, corporate paratextual campaigns struggle to draw the *viewer's* attention to their proprietary content floating in the multichannel morass. At the same time, worker paratexts and self-reflections frequently clash against the paratexts and self-reflections of other workers in what are zero-sum games. In this setting, one worker or craft group churns out demos and spec projects to gain the attention of clients, producers and *professionals*, in order to get contracts that (implicitly) discredit competitors. This parallel attention economy in the world of workers is recognisably Darwinian.

The adversarial textual culture I am describing here can be usefully understood by looking at three increasingly contested industrial/cultural sites: production's unruly work worlds, unruly technologies and unruly audiences. It is important to note that both the industry and its production workers have been destabilised by changes in work, technology and audiences. These three sites of volatility/conflict have helped spur the increased production of worker *and* corporate paratexts that now flood the industrial promotional surround. One intensifying requirement of this work world is that the industry needs to generate an oversupply of content (and workers) at industry's 'input boundaries' in order to profit, given the necessarily high degree of ratings and box-office failure. Increased economic anxiety over this high content failure ratio (and the script/project/pilot overcrowding that goes with it) fuels excessive 'spec' project, script and pilot creation among producers. As costs and revenues decrease, and markets become more uncertain, theoretical justifications in ephemeral texts circulated by management and producers to both trades and audiences increase. Faced with the same unruly work world, however, labour amps up reflexive marketing of a different sort. Since it must constantly negotiate worker and craft identities for survival, the histories, socio-professional hierarchies and cultural symbolism of any craft represented in ephemeral texts tend to increase in prominence as the oversupply of production of labour increases.

New technologies are also unruly instigators of competing paratexts in the IPS, but in ways that resonate beyond the disruptive reorganisation of unruly work worlds just described. Media corporations embrace new technologies as 'user-friendly' despite steep learning curves and start-up costs given their potential to collapse existing, costlier production workflows. This means that lots of 'competing' paratexts circulate in an attempt to 'discipline' the arrival of any new digital technology. For example, paratexts directed at craftworkers by equipment manufacturers typically theorise new technologies to corral them within traditional aesthetic schemes and production standards. Users and craftworkers need this reassurance, and tend to reward it with purchase orders. Corporate paratexts to affiliates, partners and stakeholders, by contrast, tend to underscore how new technologies will fulfil underlying business objectives more efficiently by circumventing conventional labour arrangements. Finally, 'ground-up' WGC can get as partisan and more local. This final class of paratext frequently works to legitimise one technical or craft group over another competing craft group, in attempts to establish competence and exclusivity. Craft and worker theorising, self-referencing and the cultural traffic of unauthorised paratexts increase as the conveyer belt of technical obsolescence and uncertainty accelerates. One recurring characteristic of tech-driven paratexts – whether created by manufacturers, production corporations or craftworkers – is that the greater any new tech's disruptiveness, the more extreme the paratexts work to theorise and 'tame' it. How new technologies are ultimately tamed, disciplined and normalised, and whose interests will be best served by their adoption, lies at the heart of this paratextual conflict.

Unruly new audience and fan activities have created a third, strategic industrial arena. The cultural volatility and industrial instability in this sector has fuelled a flood of new paratextual practices. This mediaspace has been ably mined and mapped by Henry Jenkins (2006), Derek Johnson (2009, pp. 170–279) and Michael Clarke (2010). These authors tend to frame the new paratexts in this space as the result of fan agency and social networks, and have paid less attention to the unabashed corporate logic of fan and UGC. That is, corporations brand themselves by creating psychological relations with fans via viral marketing, multiple platforms, ancillary content and fan-produced media. Fan loyalty is keyed to the relative effectiveness of corporate disclosure and organisational transparency as evidenced by corporate ephemeral texts circulating in viewer's promotional surround. In some ways, this third space (unruly audiences) entails one of the most direct and conscious paratextual 'dialogues', since media corporations now obsessively cultivate, solicit and welcome *fan* paratextual production. The aims of corporate branding are very much aligned with the aims of fan communities (at least according to studio executives and producers). But again, a recurring faction rears its ugly paratextual head in the fan space – production workers. They demonstrate much less euphoria about the affective and subjective gratifications of the brand or franchise than the studio or fan community. The fact that workers throw water on the studio–fan love-fest may seem odd, since users and fans increasingly share production and aesthetic competencies with commercial TV workers in the digital age. What in fact happens, however, is that the new gift economy of fans+studios flies smack in the face of the wage aspirations and underemployment characteristic of the worker+studio dyad. The result is that worker discourses of 'professionalism (us)–vs.–amateurism (fans)' in *worker* media ephemera become acute and more exclusionary in the era of 'prosumer' social media and amateur user-generated fan content. For craft workers, peer production, fan creations and UGC are merely the latest disruptive 'outsiders' – another kind of 'scab' workforce – lining up to feed at the long-standing studio/network trough. These new, younger players are particularly threatening to paid workers, since many of them will now work for free. Thus worker and craft rituals, contests, demos, professional meetings and below-the-line trade columns regularly cultivate and laud highly technical competencies, a gambit that helps 'separate the men from the boys' and the fan-boy wannabes lined up behind them.

Many top-down corporate paratexts attempt to intellectually manage and mon-etise workflow, new technologies and audience instabilities through ubiquitous para-textual self-referencing and cross-promotion. At the very same time, a flood of insider paratexts and unauthorised worker blowback push to resuscitate levelled distinctions through earnest self-referencing. The goal: to maintain professional communities, craft survival and career advantage.

Conclusion

Worker blowback in the insider's promotional surround underscores several unsettling issues, and betrays some acute economic and cultural stresses. Part of the genius of the Hollywood system – one reason many other US industries aspire to mimic Hollywood's corporate structure – is that it has profitably exploited industry's out-sourcing and textual poaching practices together with labour's 'spec' culture and gift economy for several decades. This produces a 'dues-paying culture' of the worst kind (Hill, 2009, pp. 220–4), in which the pain of unpaid work now is justified as a ticket to upward mobility later. Hollywood production's gift economy is based on mutuality, quid pro quo exchanges, social networking and a great deal of free work and ephemeral textual production provided on a 'spec' basis. These industrial habits might at first evoke the new participatory social networks revolutionising consumer culture. Yet they also cultivate a formidable pairing: the long-standing capitalist principle of (endlessly) 'deferred gratification' among workers, together with the 'flexibility' and 'mass amateurism' that theorists hail in the new 'knowledge economy'. Chris Anderson praises the prospect: 'This is the world of "peer production", the extraordinary Internet-enabled phenomenon of mass volunteerism and amateurism' (Anderson, 2006, p. 73). Workers who make their living in film and television, how-ever, are far less enamoured.

If the focus of our studies is actually culture, then we necessarily have to engage with and account for the insider's promotional surround alongside the fan and con-sumer's promotional surround. Don't believe all of what you've heard about the listing of the big industrial media ship under the threatening weight of vast new forms of user-generated content, uploading, social media, and the cultural activities and cre-ativity of fandoms. Media-makers also generate excessive amounts of *unauthorised* tex-tual content, upload, network socially and try to 'talk back' to and influence the media corporations that underemploy them. Much of the symbolic 'listing' is of the corporate industry's own desperate making. Yet we seldom consider how this unruly, contested world of the worker and 'insider' impacts the media and culture that we experience, consume and throw back into the surround on a daily basis. Even a cursory look at the ostensibly ephemeral stuff churning in the worker blowback shows just how high, and non-ephemeral, the stakes have become.

Notes

1. Three paragraphs in the 'flipside' section of this chapter have been excerpted and adapted from my essay 'Hive-Sourcing Is the New Out-Sourcing', in *Cinema Journal* (Caldwell, 2009). I thank the University of Texas Press for allowing me to significantly revise the essay for inclusion in this chapter. The flipside model that also appears in this section is significantly adapted and developed from the table 'Corporate Reflexivity vs. Worker Reflexivity', first published in *Production Culture* (Caldwell, 2008, pp. 370–2).

Bibliography

Anderson, Chris. (2006) *The Long Tail: Why the Future of Business Is Selling Less of More* (New York: Hyperion).

Caldwell, John T. (2003) 'Second Shift Aesthetics', in Anna Everett and John T. Caldwell (eds), *New Media: Theories and Practices of Digitextuality* (Routledge: New York), pp. 127–44.

Caldwell, John T. (2004) 'Convergence Television', in Lynn Spigel and Jan Olsson (eds), *Television after TV: Essays on a Medium in Transition* (Durham, NC: Duke University Press), pp. 41–74.

Caldwell, John T. (2008) 'Industrial Reflexivity as Viral Marketing', in *Production Culture: Industrial Reflexivity and Critical Practice in Film and Television* (Durham, NC: Duke University Press), pp. 274–315.

Caldwell, John T. (2009) 'Hive-Sourcing Is the New Out-Sourcing', *Cinema Journal*, 49 (1), pp. 160–7.

Clarke, M. J. (2010) *Tentpole TV: Action Franchises, Reflexive Conglomerization, and the Business Culture of Contemporary Network Television*, PhD Dissertation, University of California, Los Angeles.

Costykian, G. (2007) *Scratchware Manifesto*, <http://209.120.136.195/scratch.php> accessed 15 June 2009.

De Vany, Arthur. (2004) *Hollywood Economics: How Extreme Uncertainty Shapes the Film Industry* (London: Routledge).

Gratton, Lynda. (2007) *Hot Spots* (London: Berrett-Koehler).

Gray, Jonathan. (2010) *Show Sold Separately: Promos, Spoilers, and Other Media Paratexts* (New York: New York University Press).

Henderson, Felicia D. (2009) 'The Writers' Room', in Vicki Mayer, Miranda Banks and John T. Caldwell (eds), *Production Studies* (New York: Routledge), pp. 224–30.

Hill, Erin. (2009) 'Hollywood Assistanting', in Vicki Mayer, Miranda Banks and John T. Caldwell (eds), *Production Studies* (New York: Routledge), pp. 220–4.

Jenkins, Henry. (1992) *Textual Poachers: Television Fans and Participatory Culture* (New York: Routledge).

Jenkins, Henry. (2006) *Convergence Culture: Where Old and New Media Collide* (New York: New York University Press).

Johnson, Derek. (2009) 'Intelligent Design or Godless Universe? The Creative Challenges of World Building and Franchise Development', in *Franchising Media Worlds: Content Networks and the Collaborative Production of Culture*, PhD Dissertation, University of Wisconsin-Madison.

Kernan, Lisa. (2004) *Coming Attractions: Reading American Movie Trailers* (Austin: University of Texas Press).

Malcolm, Paul. (2009) 'The Craft Society', in Vicki Mayer, Miranda Banks and John T. Caldwell (eds), *Production Studies* (New York: Routledge), pp. 216–20.

Snickars, Pelle and Patrick Vonderau (eds). (2009) *The YouTube Reader* (Stockholm: National Library of Sweden).

11 Re-enactment: Fans Performing Movie Scenes from the Stage to YouTube

Barbara Klinger

Every week at a New York City club called The Den of Cin, bar attendees perform their favourite movie scenes in front of an audience, courtesy of an attraction named 'Movieoke'. Referred to as 'karaoke for movie lovers', Movieoke was developed in 2003 by independent film-maker Anastasia Fite, a Den employee who herself participates in this festivity ('Movieoke Questions', 2004). Here, amateur thespians, presumably full of beer, choose a film scene that they would like to act out. They stand in front of a large screen onto which the scene is projected with muted sound and activated DVD subtitles that serve to guide them in their performance (Reuters, 2004). Matthew Dujnic, a computer programmer who participates frequently in Movieoke, has re-enacted Anthony Hopkins' fava beans and Chianti scene from *Silence of the Lambs* (1991) and Jack Nicholson's 'You can't handle the truth' scene from *A Few Good Men* (1992), along with moments from films such as *The Breakfast Club* (1985), *Evil Dead II* (1987) and *Fight Club* (1999). Dujnic's comments about his desire to perform at the Den, 'This is what I do in my living room anyway', suggest that Movieoke is a public extension of private fan practices ('Anastasia's Movieoke', 2010; Kennedy, 2004; Allwood, 2006). Indeed, audience research I have conducted on a related subject – viewers' quotation of movie lines – revealed that, after re-watching favourite films at home, some would re-enact a scene 'for fun' (Klinger, 2006, p. 182). The relatively new home technology, yoostar (<www.yoostar.com>), may encourage more of this kind of interaction, as it deploys a camera and green-screen technology that allow viewers to virtually take the place of characters in a scene.

As we shall see, film re-enactments by fans far exceed the provinces of the Den of Cin and yoostar. Such performances materialise by virtue of multiple showcases, from the dramatic theatre's stage to the web's viral milieu. Yet, despite diverse platforms, fan re-enactments have an uncertain status in the mediascape. They may be performed live only sporadically, disappear due to matters of copyright or materialise in recorded forms that compete with millions of other internet uploads. They are thus fragile creations that can easily fly under the radar. Their means of distribution, coupled with their amateur status, also make them seem like transient bits in an American media culture strongly characterised by high-profile Hollywood films and by the constant churn or turnover of media texts on screens both large and small. The fact that fan re-enactments by amateur and aspiring thespians may be regarded as silly and instantly forgettable enhances the sense that they occupy an unstable, even meaningless, place in visual culture.

They thus invite us to explore the phenomenon of ephemera within the heavily trafficked networks of intertextuality that define cinema's contemporary existence. It is precisely because subgenres of fan activity such as re-enactment and digital forums teeming with textual life such as YouTube are apparently so uncertain in their relationship to anything enduring that they become fertile territories for investigating ephemera's relation to the canon. What is the nature and impact of the association between such fan-produced ephemera (transitory media with little public visibility and low aesthetic and cultural status owing to their derivativeness and link to amateur enthusiasm) and the canonical (the Hollywood films often celebrated in this manner that have, by comparison, lasting public recognition)? I will contend that these two different modes of media production and circulation do not exist in separate spheres; they are significantly and intricately interrelated. Movie re-enactments demonstrate the strategic importance of ephemera's tangled relationship with its apparent opposite – the iconic and canonical. 'Re-enactors', while engaged in performances that are fleeting, are subtly involved in maintaining the source text's cultural circulation and continuity. Since all re-enactments are necessarily commemorative, fan-produced works serve an interesting vernacular archival function as well. As literal 're-doings', re-enactments help to preserve a film's place in cultural memory. Insofar as the means of distribution and exhibition – often websites like YouTube – act as repositories, showcases and 'circulatory systems' for fan performances, the archival status of these sites also becomes noteworthy.

While I am not uninterested in the aesthetics of quasi-professional and amateur productions (for more on this, see Jenkins, 2006, pp. 131–68; Jones, 2002, pp. 169–79; Klinger, 2006, pp. 191–238) or the daily micro-managing of identity signified by movie embodiment (Klinger, 2008), I wish to reflect more squarely here on how re-enactments contribute to our understanding of contemporary film circulation, consumption and popular preservation. Given the heterogeneous means of distribution and exhibition by which films appear in public, such iterative performances matter for grasping the relationship between commercial films and steadily increasing numbers of amateur productions in a multiply screened and otherwise highly mediatised culture.

As will be obvious throughout the chapter, although cinema itself is not typically defined as an interactive medium, fan-driven movie re-enactments suggest that it is indeed situated within this world. Films furnish more than foundations for video games or theme-park rides – recognised forms of immersive reciprocity. They themselves elicit types of interactive, performance-based audience behaviour that is not so different from that of other media that inspire mimicry formally and informally. Music's effects in this respect, for example, range from *Guitar Hero* video games, karaoke bars and tribute bands to singing along with a tune on one's iPod.

Before further theorising the place of fan film re-enactments in media's circulatory system, these iterations should be situated, at least briefly, within broader and related contexts of cinematic intertextuality. We need also to have a more concrete sense of the presence and variety of these DIY productions across forums. 'Acting out' is more of an everyday occurrence than we might expect.

Cinema redux

To re-enact, of course, means to perform again, to repeat actions and events that have already occurred. Re-enactment often involves role-playing – an acting out of some prior event by individuals who momentarily take on the identity and often the appearance and actions of persons, either real or fictional, in the context of an originating occurrence. That which is repeated in this manner is of necessity also changed. Because re-enactments are time-displaced derivative performances, they can never exactly replicate the source event; transformations of every conceivable kind are possible in the process. In the realm of actuality, perhaps the most familiar and prolific instance of this phenomenon is the historical re-enactment of significant military battles or other nation-defining events, globally popular ceremonies that date back at least to the Roman Empire.

With respect to cinema, the term *re-enactment* could be conceived to signify almost any form of intertextual allusion. The intertextual reference, a bedrock of cinema, appears countless times in a variety of guises in commercial feature films alone. Stanley Kubrick's infamous reimagining of the *Singin' in the Rain* (1952) sequence, where Gene Kelly joyously performs the titular song, as a tune Malcolm McDowell's character in *A Clockwork Orange* (1971) invokes as he brutalises and rapes a woman, provides a graphic case of citation via a mode of re-enactment. Such self-conscious acts of parody or deconstruction are joined by equally self-conscious moments of homage or pastiche – for example, *Body Heat*'s (1981) and other films' reanimation of facets of 1940s noir (see, for example, Dyer, 2007). At a more systemic level, diverse types of re-enactment continue to abound, among them adaptations, remakes, reboots and sequels. As we know, whether overt or subtle and diffuse, revisitations of the past are the norm in contemporary media, with films often patchwork quilts of what came before. No matter the motive or impact, though, the re-enactment is always a form of commemoration – a call to remembrance that brings the original to mind and into the present.

Aside from the pervasive intertextuality that defines cinema itself as a mode of 'performing again', a small body of narrative feature films exists that focuses more literally on movie re-enactment as subject matter.[1] For example, *Son of Rambow* (2007) features an English schoolboy who falls in love with *First Blood* (1982), the inaugural film in the Sylvester Stallone/*Rambo* series, and sets out to remake it with a friend and his video camera. After an accident erases the contents of the VHS tapes in their local video store, the characters in *Be Kind Rewind* (2008) produce and star in DIY versions of films as diverse as *Ghostbusters* (1984) and *Driving Miss Daisy* (1989) in order to restock their shelves and save the business. Feature films also sometimes include standalone sequences that portray a more limited version of this thematic – Vincent Gallo's performance of *North by Northwest*'s (1959) crop-dusting sequence for a small-town talent contest in Emir Kusturica's *Arizona Dream* (1993) comes to mind in this context. Other media too fix their sights on reliving famous scenes: for instance, *Vanity Fair* magazine faithfully restaged shots from several Alfred Hitchcock films with contemporary actors and actresses standing in for their earlier counterparts (i.e. Marion Cotillard as Janet Leigh's Marion Crane in the shower murder sequence from *Psycho*, 1960) ('The 2008 Hollywood Portfolio', 2008).

As this synopsis suggests, recreations of movies and their moments are common in the professional world of images. However, as both Movieoke and *Son of Rambow* begin to indicate, they have a special place in fan activities worth inspecting. Like narrative cinema's *mise en abyme* of self-referentiality, fan re-enactments signal cinema's function as an epicentre for intertextual production within a media culture deeply defined today by iteration. As cases of fan-driven movie re-enactments will show, such performances are intimately tied to the reissue, that is, the post-premiere reappearance of films on VHS, cable TV, DVD, the internet, and other technologies and media. At the same time, re-enactments are tethered to dynamics of viewing spurred by the ability to repeatedly re-watch films through these technologies. Within this iterative world, prolific forms of consumer-grade devices (e.g. the flipcam, webcam, mobile phone camera and digital video camera), producing what some in the trade refer to as 'casual digital video' (Lee, 2008), allow individuals to easily register their dedication to or desire to play with films and their scenes.

Repeated contact with a film is essential to the mastery required for amateur or aspiring thespians to clone it through their bodies and voices and to, with various attitudes toward authenticity and with differing degrees of ambition, reconstruct its *mise en scène* and soundtrack. In this sense, 'replayability' in its multiple manifestations helps to define contemporary cinema as a narrative and affective medium. Replay enables memorisation of a film's narrative and style, just as it heightens the potential for fragmentation, as certain scenes may be selected time and again for re-performance. Meanwhile, replay enhances the possibility of falling in love with a film or eliciting other emotions that focus a fan's labour and amusement on the act of physical replication.

Fan film re-enactments: a selective chronicle

Since 2002, Canadian actor Charles Ross has been touring dozens of cities and theatrical districts, from Off-Broadway venues in New York to London's West End, with his show 'One Man *Star Wars*'. Ross has written a condensed version of the original trilogy, which he performs in sixty minutes. Dressed in ordinary clothes, he voices multiple characters, gesturing in ways that conjure up character (e.g. hands cupped over his ears to represent Princess Leia and her famous 'cinnamon bun' hairstyle) and story, while also humming soundtrack themes and supplying sound effects. (Samples of his work are available on <http://www.onemanstarwars.com/index2.html/go> and YouTube). Ross has since appeared in his 'One Man *Lord of the Rings*' play, using similar principles of condensation and impersonation for this trilogy.

'Rambo Solo' (2009) provides another example of such stagecraft. In New York, Zachary Oberzan, a member of the experimental theatre troupe Nature Theater of Oklahoma, has performed a one-man re-enactment of David Morrell's 1972 novel, *First Blood* – the novel upon which the 1982 Sylvester Stallone film of the same name is based. Oberzan's monologue has a multimedia dimension, as it is accompanied by three videos he produced in his studio apartment that are 'projected onto white rumpled sheets hanging from a clothesline' behind him (Isherwood, 2009). These videos showcase the multi-character impersonation he relies upon to convey the narrative's protagonists and antagonists, while his on-stage persona loosely describes the novel. In the spirit of these videos, Oberzan has also shot, edited and acted in a cheaply made DIY feature-film version of the novel entitled *Flooding with Love for the Kid*. The action is set in his apartment, where once again he plays all of the characters involved, including Rambo, the sheriff who hunts him, Colonel Sam Trautman (Rambo's saviour of sorts) and the waitress at a local diner. The woods in which Rambo tries to escape from the police are simulated in Oberzan's cramped quarters by Christmas tree branches. Meanwhile, through the same aesthetic of bricolage, a toaster and its plug stand in for a short-wave radio and its microphone, and box fans perched on chairs and accompanied by sound effects represent a helicopter. Hungry and alone in the 'forest',

Rambo shoots an owl (read: a small teddy bear) and then roasts it over an open fire. (A trailer for Oberzan's show and clips from *Flooding with Love* are also available on YouTube.)

On less professional fronts, some amateur film-makers have also attempted to reproduce entire films. Such is the case with *Raiders of the Lost Ark: The Adaptation*, a remake of Steven Spielberg's 1981 film using a VHS camcorder. Two pre-teen boys, Chris Strompolis and Eric Zala, initiated this project in 1982, completing it over the next seven years. Producing a shot-by-shot, line-by-line, gesture-by-gesture remake of the film required some ingenuity in the days when quick video re-release was less common than it is today. After the film's premiere, Strompolis read the *Raiders* comic books to maintain conversancy with the film's world. During *Raiders'* theatrical reissue in 1982, Zala captured the dialogue and soundtrack with an audio cassette recorder. This, in turn, enabled the boys and others who became involved in the remake to memorise the actors' lines and delivery. Between the theatrical re-release and the film's 1983 reissue on home video, the two were also able to transcribe hundreds of shots and make sketches of the *mise en scène*. Their attempts at authenticity were challenged by a meagre budget and the ensuing makeshift appearance of props (including the creation of the large boulder in the film's opening sequences out of a cable drum and cardboard), suburban locations that had to represent heterogeneous *Raiders'* locales, changes in the characters' appearance as they aged, and video's poor quality as a recording and archival medium. This project could have stayed in the home movie vault as a labour of fan-boy love, but it came to public light in 2003 when horror film director Eli Roth of *Hostel* (2006) fame obtained a copy. Along with 'Ain't It Cool News' web impresario Harry Knowles, they convinced the owner of the Alamo Drafthouse Cinema in Austin, Texas, to screen it. This was the first in a number of US and UK travelling screenings (Windolf, 2004; 'Articles and Reviews', 2003–9).

Strompolis, Zala, Ross and Oberzan are clearly diehard fans of their respective materials, a devotion born out of a childhood encounter with what they experienced as life-changing texts. In Oberzan's origin story, he initially encountered Sylvester Stallone's *First Blood* when he was ten years old 'one magical weekend' when his household had free HBO ('Rambo Solo', 2009). Affected more powerfully by the novel, he describes his act as providing a means to create a better version of it than the Hollywood film. Ross' origin story involves a family move from Prince George, British Columbia, to an isolated farm in the province, with little access to broadcast or cable TV. As he tells it, when he was eight years of age, to relieve the boredom, he popped 'in a video of "Star Wars"' taped earlier off the TV. Before he or his parents knew it, he 'had watched the movie more than 400 times'. He later re-watched the two remaining films in the original trilogy, *The Empire Strikes Back* (1980) and *The Return of the Jedi* (1983), on dozens of occasions. Thus, *Star Wars* (1977) was 'soldered into [his] brain at [an] impressionable age', eventually inspiring him to conceive of his condensed stage version (Simonson, 2005). Strompolis and Zala were similarly thunderstruck by their first encounter with Spielberg's *Raiders*.

Although techniques of bricolage differ (i.e. Ross' minimalist *mise en scène* accompanied by intricate physical and vocal mimicry, Oberzan's avant-garde embrace of low-budget simulations and deadpan characterisations, and Zala and Strompolis' dedicated efforts at authenticity that necessarily fall short), they each portray the significance of at least white male childhood fantasies in forming powerful attachments to narratives that then lead to desires to personalise the sources via embodiment. These attachments depend on various mechanisms of replay, from cable TV to video camcorders, to render a private experience into a materially transformed public one that demonstrates the performer's particular kind of ownership of a beloved text. As a result, the source's genre (whether science fiction, proxy war film or action adventure) undergoes change, defaulting to comedy, a major genre in amateur remakes. The re-enactors affectionately caricature the originals, at the very least through the DIY film's low-tech aesthetic, by having one man play multiple, cross-identity roles and/or through the extensive condensing of a large body of work.

Few restagings are as ambitious as these and not all are inspired by fervent fandom or love.[2] Re-enactments of film scenes or moments are commonly more heterogeneously motivated. If we remain on the subject of theatrical restagings for a moment, we can see that film-related street theatre – loosely defined here as a public exhibition of embodied movie re-enactment from avant-garde impersonations to fan events – has been host to some of these performances. In the 1950s and 1960s, for example, movie fragments sometimes formed the bases of 'Happenings'. Happenings were a mode of spontaneous performance meant to fly in the face of established notions of art, while insisting on their own artistic validity. This kind of 'Living Theater' railed against the 'institutions (the museum, the concert hall, the theatre) that had kept art a prisoner locked away from society'. Instead, it offered 'street Happenings, found-objects, and pedestrian behavior [that] could … unite people and operate on the terrain of daily experience … [engaging] the broader community in a critical appraisal of its own relation to art and creativity' (Martin, 1990, p. 149).

Thus, during this time, Dorothy Podber and Ray Johnson, a member of Fluxus, an art movement that was heir to Dadaism (and whose name indicates the unpredictable flow and temporal uncertainty at the root of ephemera), would stage impromptu events in Manhattan. In a relevant example, Podber and Johnson would 'persuade people they had just met to allow them into their apartments' and, among other things, 'reenact the shower murder scene from *Psycho*'. They re-enacted this scene on the streets as well when the spirit struck (Kennedy, 2008; for more on Fluxus and Happenings, see, for example, Higgins, 2002). These particular hijinks had a disruptive aim – to perforate the rituals of everyday life with unexpected and out-of-context actions, based, in this case, on a film sequence that accomplishes exactly the same thing.

Other modes of street theatre based on movies, whether spontaneous or more carefully planned, arise from inspirational infrastructures that have far less of an art-based 'shock' agenda. In an interesting parallel to Happenings that indicates this difference, in Philadelphia, the setting for Sylvester Stallone's *Rocky* (1976), tourists routinely theatricalise institutional space by re-enacting and celebrating the title character's triumphant training run up the stairs of the city's Museum of Art. If the number of YouTube videos of the 'Rocky steps' uploaded from phone cams and digicams is any indication, this is a photo opportunity that may depart from the institutional etiquette of the museum, but only through the conventions of another powerful institution – tourism.

On another front entirely, holidays can also serve as occasions for fan re-enactments. As one instance among many, at Hallowe'en in Toronto one year, a blogger describes a moment of 'pure transcendental strangeness when the rain started and [people dressed up as] Alex and his Droogs went skipping down Church Street, recreating the moment in the film *A Clockwork Orange* when Malcolm McDowell as Alex improvised to "Singin' in the Rain" '. In this performance, the song is no longer a cinematic paean to falling in love or a twisted lyric accompanying an act of predation; in accord with the exhibitionism characteristic of Hallowe'en, it is a holiday-enlivened, weather-related chance to be, for a moment, playful bad boys.[3]

As we would expect, fan conventions serve as major sites for re-enactment. At the annual Lebowski Fest, for example, attendees indulge in cosplay (or costume role-play) to act out scenes from the Coen brothers' *The Big Lebowski* (1998) while the film is being screened or shortly thereafter ('Second Annual Lebowski Fest', 2003). Meanwhile, during the annual Blobfest held in Phoenixville, PA, in honour of *The Blob*, a 1958 sci-fi/horror film originally shot in the area, viewers at screenings of the film re-enact what they refer to as the 'Running Out' scene. When the titular creature from outer space invades the Colonial Movie Theater in the film, panic-stricken teenagers attempt to escape. During the Blobfest, fans simulate this moment, fleeing en masse screaming and laughing from the still-standing theatre, fuelled by the spirit of 'B' movie camp ('Blobfest', 2007–10). There are many other types of planned live movie re-enactments: university teams (from Princeton, Vassar and other East Coast schools) recently played a Quidditch World Cup, 'a real-life version of the soccer-like contact sport featured in the [Harry Potter] books and films' (Browne, 2009, E1).

This sampling of proto-professional and amateur film re-enactments suggests that these phenomena have a steady public presence. It also indicates the slipperiness of distinctions between live and recorded re-enactments. In each case, fans' performances are already clearly 'penetrated' by their source(s), to which they cannot help but pay tribute. At the same time, as we have begun to see, the broader visibility of the performance in question often depends on being recorded and uploaded to the internet. This symbiosis confirms Philip Auslander's contentions about live performance: that it 'exists within the economy of repetition largely … to promote mass-cultural objects [and] to serve as raw material for mediatization' (2008, p. 28). This is particularly true in the era of 'casual digital video', as it potentially makes all the world an uploadable stage.

Unquestionably, the most plentiful and accessible place for fan re-enactments is in recorded form on the internet. Numerous websites stream amateur films, many of which feature parodic remakes of Hollywood fare. These films sometimes involve personal re-enactments and are otherwise part of the broader media culture's penchant for self-referentiality. There are also numerous sites dedicated specifically to film re-enactments where 'ordinary' people attempt to re-do films or film scenes using their own bodies, voices and materials. One such site is the previously mentioned yoostar.com where web surfers can watch individuals assume the place of characters in *Casablanca* (1942), *Gone with the Wind* (1939), *The Godfather* (1972), *The Blues Brothers* (1980) and more. Although 'sweding', inspired by a term used in *Be Kind Rewind* to describe low-tech, imaginative movie remakes, can be found across the internet, swededcinema.com proclaims itself as seriously invested in 'the sweded film movement'. It invites 'sweding' of 'the best and worst movies to come out of Hollywood in the past 30 years' through 'the genius and ingenuity of their greatest fans' (<http://swededcinema.com/>). Along with the fact that sweded films must be based on already produced and fairly recent films, shorts have to emphasise 'comedy and a commitment to low-cost production [that represents] the very pinnacle of fresh-faced film-making' (<http://www.swededfilms.com>). Accordingly, amateurs post their bricolages of films such as *Star Wars*, *Jurassic Park* (1993) and *Forrest Gump* (1994), attempting to gain the site's imprimatur of 'genius'.

YouTube, although lacking such an overt manifesto, otherwise dominates as both a repository and destination for these productions. It contains clips of almost all of the re-enactments I have already discussed, plus countless other home-made videos by amateurs or aspiring actors and actresses who simulate movies, again, through a variety of motives. These include fulfilling the terms of a classroom assignment, trying to capture the industry's eye, expressing love for a film or simply goofing off. Similarly, there are differing commitments to accuracy. In keeping with the aesthetics possible via the phone cam and inexpensive digicams, most YouTube performances and the *mise en scène*, photography and sound are of low quality. By contrast, movie scenes are often drawn from pictures associated in some way with quality, popularity and/or critical esteem: contemporary blockbusters such as *The Matrix*

(1999), *The Lord of the Rings* trilogy (2001, 2002, 2003) and the *Twilight* saga (2008, 2009, 2010); older blockbusters such as *Jaws* (1975) and *Star Wars*; cult fare such as *Monty Python and the Holy Grail* (1975) and *The Big Lebowski*; classic films such as *Gone with the Wind* and *Psycho*; and art films, including *Schindler's List* (1993) and *Pan's Labyrinth* (2006).

Thus, for a class project, a young man and woman enact a scene from *Casablanca*, playing the roles of Laszlo (Paul Henreid) and Ilsa (Ingrid Bergman) in a manner that tries to capture, via low-key lighting, décor, music and other devices, a sense of the original's atmosphere ('Casablanca', 2007). Meanwhile, to express their fandom, two young women from an all-girl's school take on *Twilight*'s 'forest confession scene' (wherein Edward [Robert Pattinson] tells Bella [Kristin Stewart] that he's a vampire in love with her), playing the two main roles in a low-budget and gender-bending affair. While these are clearly fledgling 'one-off' performances, others, like Brandon Hardesty, have made YouTube a main stage and hopeful launching pad to the professional acting leagues. Hardesty has cultivated a reputation and a following on YouTube by doing dozens of scene re-enactments in the low-tech, one-man, multiple-character show style. Re-enacting a scene from *The Big Lebowski*, for example, against a relatively barren interior, he expertly voices Donny (Steve Buscemi), Walter (John Goodman), the Dude (Jeff Bridges) and others ('Reenactment #14: *The Big Lebowski*', 2006). Hardesty's popularity has grown to such an extent that he takes requests from users for which scenes to perform next, a dynamic that recalls live rock band performances and radio call-in shows.

With this abbreviated view of the expanse of the phenomenon of re-enactment, it remains now to explore some of its implications for cinema and media culture.

Recycling, ephemera and the popular digital archive

The film scene has traditionally been regarded as a building block of narrative – a mini-Aristotelian unit, marked off from others by a unified space, time and action, while being securely embedded in a narrative totality. Whether in Aristotelian formulations or Christian Metz's *la grande syntagmatique*, the scene has appeared to be an organic, constituent part of a text's formal logic and internal discursive composition. Yet, more than ever in a contemporary milieu, the film scene also provides a vivid example of the modularity and volatility of film narrative. There is a propensity for film elements, including those much smaller than the formal scene, to be spun off into spheres of recirculation and, hence, to be resituated in new contexts by a variety of players, from self-promoting media industries to camera-happy viewers. Scene re-enactments, from the *Vanity Fair* Hitchcock shoot to Hardesty's dead-on *Lebowski* impressions, represent a mode of media recycling. This recycling, in turn, occurs within a much larger media environment characterised by iteration and replay.

Most movie re-enactments could not take place without iteration in interconnected industrial and consumer manifestations. Just as one must have access to a poem to memorise its lines, viewers must be able to re-watch a title repeatedly to be able to conduct their experiments of vocalisation and embodiment, their reconstructions of *mise en scène* and other aspects of a film. As I have noted in Ross' and others' origin stories, their performances would be impossible without studio distribution practices focused on reissue. Ross' initial taping of *Star Wars* from a television broadcast later enabled him to screen it hundreds of times on his VCR, while pre-recorded VHS versions of the trilogy also provided access that would later ground his restaging of the Lucas films.

The immersive and encompassing force of iteration in its multiple facets is especially clear in the case of *Raiders of the Lost Ark: The Adaptation*. Strompolis and Zala's painstaking efforts to memorise Spielberg's film were initially dependent on the 1982 theatrical re-release, as well as on consumer-grade audio and video recording technologies. The reissue afforded Zala the opportunity to use an audio cassette to capture the film's dialogue and soundtrack and proceed with the adaptation's early stages. We should presume that the original film's record-breaking re-release on video cassette during the 1983 holiday season, as one of Paramount Pictures' successful initial attempts to conquer the sell-through market by lowering the prices of its titles for home purchase, figured even more centrally in the recreation (Prince, 2000, p. 104).[4] In the dynamically reciprocal world of replay, the industry's repurposing of Spielberg's film in theatrical and home reissues provided the conditions for its repetitive re-watching and re-doing by amateurs armed with user-friendly technologies. Since its discovery by media honchos, the adaptation itself, shown in select locales, takes a place – though far less visible – among *Raiders*' other iterations, including sequels, DVD sets, video games and paraphernalia. If rumours that Hollywood may make Strompolis and Zala's video valentine into a feature-length film are true, then the logic of replay culture comes full circle, with the industry remaking the story of an amateur re-enactment of a blockbuster.

Of course, because movie scenes and moments migrate through time across multiple media platforms for heterogeneous reasons, wholesale immersion in a film is not necessary for replay's realisation. We may never actually see a film that we otherwise encounter in what Victor Burgin calls 'image scraps' (2004, p. 9), such as movie posters. We may similarly experience audio scraps – soundtrack lyrics or melodies – from an unseen film. The movie moment (*The Blob*'s 'Running Out' scene or *Psycho*'s shower murder or *North by Northwest*'s crop-dusting sequence) can act as its most representative set piece, even becoming a synecdoche for the entire film. Among its

other functions, then, replay furnishes a kind of shorthand in the realm of film circulation – the errant bit of a film that becomes a repetitive part of a title's identity
through numerous reanimations.

The fragments involved in a film's replay circuit unavoidably enhance the presence
of ephemera. In the case of movie re-enactments, ephemera are short fan or amateur
creations characterised by no, little or fleeting circulation, access and extended visibility, by a sense of relative unimportance in the larger context of media culture and by
their scant attention in academe. As live, unrecorded performances, Dorothy Podber
and Ray Johnson's shower scene antics have vanished, except as a mentionable in her
obituary. Snippets of Charles Ross' and Strompolis and Zala's re-enactments are available on YouTube and elsewhere, but, because of copyright issues, among other things,
neither performance is fully available in recorded form on legitimate websites
(although copies of *Raiders of the Lost Ark: The Adaptation* exist on unauthorised
sites). The only way to see these texts legally and in their entirety is by inviting their
creators to your town. While Hardesty's work thrives, the two-women restaging of
Twilight's forest scene has been taken down, not because of any form of censure, but
owing to the vagaries of YouTube's turnover. Transient, with a potentially small window
of time to make their impressions – impressions that may never become popular or
may be otherwise forgotten by history – many of these performances can appear to
have an ontological fragility that leaves them little place in cultural transactions overall. However, whether or not re-enactments achieve lasting access and visibility, as part
of the intensive intertextualities characterising contemporary media, they have an indis-
pensable role in this terrain.

In his study of the function of iteration in oral traditions of storytelling, Richard
Bauman contends that the 'linked processes of decontextualizing and recontextualiz-
ing discourse – of extracting ready-made discourse from one context and fitting it to
another – are ubiquitous in social life, essential mechanisms of social and cultural continuity' (2004, p. 8). If we consider his remarks in relation to ephemera involved in
replay, we can see that iterative media forms too act as 'essential mechanisms of social
and cultural continuity' in their operation as life-support systems for canonical texts
and iconic moments. As part of the swirl of intertextuality that not only surrounds a
text, but that literally restages and recontextualises it, re-enactments have mnemonic
and value-laden effects. Their very presence attempts to guarantee that texts and their
moments will not be forgotten, will be sustained in some sector of the public eye, will
be canonised (like the 'Rocky steps') or bolstered in their existing canonic status (like
The Blob's well-established 'B' movie fame). As the case of re-enactment suggests,
ephemera are a key means by which the source, in proxy form, circulates.

At times, ephemeral occurrences directly enhance the status of an existing text.
Podber was most famous for entering Andy Warhol's studio, pulling out a pistol and

shooting a number of his silk screens of Marilyn Monroe stacked against a wall. This Happening ultimately improved these works' value. *Shot Red Marilyn*, as one of the pictures came to be known, alone sold for $4 million, the highest price ever paid for a Warhol work in the 1980s ('Dorothy Podber', 2008). However, the more common impact of the ephemeral is suggested by Podber and Johnson's restaging of *Psycho's* shower murder sequence in Manhattan locales. While this is an avant-garde appropriation lost to us, their activities suggest just how pervasive movie moments can be, just how available such moments are as raw material for *retournage*. Fleeting media, even those with a micro-presence, are part of an ensemble of referents responsible for maintaining the public profile of a work and/or its creative personnel. In this case, personal re-enactments hint at the many ways, beyond his much discussed film-maker-imitators and reissued titles, that Hitchcock's reputation has been sustained in popular culture.

To reflect upon this dimension of ephemera more closely, consider again Ross' 'One Man *Star Wars*'. His performance is part of one of the largest media life-support systems in existence – that surrounding the *Star Wars* franchise. Ross' condensing of the original trilogy into a sixty-minute theatrical venture plays off and transforms the source texts. Yet, even as he alters them, he testifies to their cultural status as cinematic touchstones capable of inspiring millions. Ross' performance is not integral, of course, to the success of George Lucas' franchise; take his show out of the cultural mix and little would be lost. What is important is its existence as part of an extensive series of intertextual networks that maintain the franchise's salience – one of the 'little guys' that participates and extends this network's provinces. Within these networks, texts are vitally 'rekeyed … reported, rehearsed, translated, relayed, quoted, summarized, or parodied' into different 'interpretive frames' (Bauman, 2004, p. 10). While one re-enactment might not matter, remove all of the various forms of rekeying and the franchise would lose a substantial part of its aura of omnipresence. As they help to build a legend around the film or one of its component parts, then, short-form ephemera are a vital means of forming and sustaining popular canons. Their selection too of elements to be deified helps to perpetuate such fragments as iconic cinematic moments. While not recreating the Battle of Gettysburg or of Hastings, movie scene re-enactments attempt to establish or to contribute to the memorability of certain moments. At the same time, the relative absence of ephemera can presage the invisibility and 'death' of the source text during particular periods of its circulation. Without such ephemera, the work of cultural continuity in the context of contemporary media would be radically transformed, even unimaginable.

Thus far I have argued, via the example of movie scene re-enactment, the impact that iteration has, first, on disassembling cinema into recycled parts and, second, on underwriting the production of ephemeral fan intertexts that heighten the pervasiveness and authority of source texts. The digital era has certainly accentuated both of these features of the mediascape, not only because of its impact on the circulation of media and media 'bits', but because of the archival function that some websites have assumed.

YouTube, a diverse and bountiful distribution and exhibition venue, is a shining example of an unofficial archive. It is not only a register of the 'passing parade' of short-form media texts, but an archive extraordinaire of ephemera. YouTube is one of the premier 'go-to' sites for uploading and finding image and audio scraps of popular mainstream fare (e.g. trailers for upcoming films), rare or almost completely forgotten mass cultural morsels (e.g. a 1968 BBC version of The Yardbirds performing 'Dazed and Confused') and what commentators refer to as a 'jumble of amateur videos' (Stelter and Helft, 2009).

Assessing this state of affairs, Jean Burgess and Joshua Green refer to YouTube as an 'accidental archive' that not only serves commercial interests, but the 'collective activities of thousands of users, each with their individual enthusiasms and eclectic interests'. By representing a 'living archive of contemporary culture from a large and diverse range of sources', YouTube has the potential to be a forum for the 'widespread popular co-creation of cultural heritage, supplementing the more specifically purposeful and highly specialized practices of state-based cultural archiving institutions like public libraries and museums; or media companies and broadcasters' (Burgess and Green, 2009, p. 88; see also on this subject, Hildebrand, 2009). However, YouTube's vernacular status and virtues of heterogeneity are also linked to its deficits as an archive – its lack of a mandate to store, preserve, organise and filter its catalogue (Burgess and Green, 2009, p. 89). Although Burgess and Green acknowledge that some filtering occurs, they contend that users are mainly responsible for it. That is, whatever keyword(s) a user types into the YouTube search window will reveal a 'family' of related videos. Yet, if we explore YouTube's archival function beyond Burgess and Green's brief comments, we will find not only that the situation is more complex, but that it leads us rather quickly back to the relationship between the ephemeral and the iconic.

Like other results for re-enactment searches on YouTube, the webpage that appears is often festooned with banner ads for related Hollywood fare or lists of streamable trailers or news stories. Once streaming of the re-enactment begins, the user may also be greeted first by promotions for upcoming films or television programmes, demonstrating again the pervasiveness of commercial interests in this space. More particularly, a search for the 'Rocky steps' on YouTube produces more than twenty pages of videos. Granting that some contain repeated titles, each page offers links for approximately twenty-five videos. This one search, then, elicits a significant showing of short films devoted to re-enactments of a cinematic moment. Many of these shorts have titles that are variations of 'me (or us) running up the Rocky steps'.

Others depict sports luminaries paying a visit ('Manchester United stars climb the steps'), while still others repurpose the steps for other activities, such as sledding or biking. Of course, clips from *Rocky* itself, featuring Stallone, populate the ranks of videos under this subject heading. A recent visit to this family of videos (and to the much smaller series of clips produced from a 'Rambo Solo' search) prominently offers a link to trailers for Stallone's newest venture, *The Expendables*, which arrived on US screens in mid-August 2010. Further, this video trailer has received hundreds of thousands of more hits than any single re-enactment, suggesting a canny commercial play that positions the DIY productions as modes of advertisement for a new film, while the new film legitimates and elevates their presence. The ephemera that flood YouTube's space preserve in cultural visibility and memory certain feature films, while these films, in turn, offer the chance for ephemera to survive, at least for a time, as riffs on their cachet. However re-enactments choose to rework the source, they help to create or sustain its legendary status, just as they may benefit, in terms of exposure, by association with a 'celebrity' text and its constellation of intertexts.

Hence, this digital archive is not somehow accidentally or haphazardly organised. It operates according to a logic of family resemblances that mixes DIY videos and Hollywood products for mutual promotion. It not so subtly places amateur and professional films into constant conversation, a conversation that has the bottom line as at least one of its motivations. In this way, YouTube benefits Hollywood enterprise (if the 'Rocky steps' or *Twilight* fan simulations are any indication) by attracting users to a DIY category that captures eyeballs for a studio production.

With these dynamic interactions in mind, amateur re-enactments on YouTube clearly do not simply coexist with major motion pictures or television programmes. But the reciprocity characteristic of the internet archive in this case raises questions about the uneven nature of these interactions. The disappearance of an individual DIY video on YouTube is not as important as the survival of the class of short films they represent (the all-female re-enactment of *Twilight*'s forest scene may be difficult to find, but other performances of the film's scenes surely are not). Thus, as long as there is constancy of some kind of the subcategory of DIY productions, fluctuation in the particulars is insignificant. Moreover, the effect of the archival filtering that does take place, as it groups similar re-enactments together, is not only to continue to deploy ephemera as a means of breathing new life into and showing the relevance of feature films, but to promote other films and filmic elements that join the 'family' in some way. In the example above, Stallone as iconic star is the tie that binds the 'Rocky steps' and 'Rambo Solo' clips with *The Expendables*. The type of ephemera I have discussed is thus both dispensable in terms of individual productions and vital as a larger enterprise insofar as it creates a phylum of videos that testify to the significance of a particular film and act as a ground of promotion.

Lest I overly minimise the significance of individual re-enactments, it is important to note that each is not without effects. For DIY re-enactments and other productions, digital circulation enables access, potential longevity and life as a text. On the issue of the sustainability and impact of ephemeral art, Sven Lutticken suggests that the value of the 1960s Happening is not to be found, as it had been for many critics, in its transitory uniqueness. Rather, he proposes that

> The essence of a performance or event lies in the reproductions that give it an afterlife – photos, films, and video descriptions. Is it not here that ephemeral art becomes truly alive, in its afterlife, giving rise to ever new interpretations – and fantasies? (Lutticken, 2005, p. 24)

This reminds us that, once ephemeral productions are given exposure through mediatisation, their status as texts with some endurance amplifies their capacity to signify. As these productions generate meaning within their lifespans, they enter into the interpretive fray that surrounds them. In the case of re-enactments, this has consequences for source texts during moments of mutual circulation. Source texts can be turned by re-enactments not only into bases for iconic moments, but, as we have seen, for comedy, camp and other generic play that may affect how the source is seen and regarded (e.g. after having watched 'Rambo Solo', can *First Blood* be experienced apart from the former's comedic pastiche?). Hence, re-enactments are not simply supports, but texts in their own right capable of 'massaging' the meaning and affect of sources in unexpected ways.

At the same time, this form of ephemera raises issues of performance, embodiment and the amateur aesthetic outside of the moral condemnation that often accompanies public awareness of violent 'copycat' enactments of movies. Further study of re-enactment could also lead to a more intensive exploration of cinema's relationship to other public forms of interactivity and embodiment, the connections between childhood, fantasy, nostalgia and amateur film-making, and the significance this expressive performance of a mediatised self has for understanding articulations of identity. For now, we can weigh the role played by even the most ephemeral of user-generated forms in the ebb and flow of today's media culture.

Notes

1. My essay focuses on the mimicry of Hollywood feature films, but documentary and avant-garde films are also associated with the term *re-enactment* (e.g. *The Thin Blue Line* by Errol Morris, 1988) and, more specifically, with redeploying Hollywood films clips. The avant-garde, for example, has long used feature films as a kind of 'found footage' that is re-performed to different ends. Some recent instances include Douglas Gordon's

24 Hour Psycho (1993) and Matthias Müller and Christoph Girardet's *The Phoenix Tapes* (2000), another resurrection of Hitchcock's work. For more on this topic, see Michele Pierson (2009).

2. *StarWarsUncut* is an important addition to ambitious, full-scale film reconstructions. It resulted from a collective endeavour in which devotees of *Star Wars Episode IV: A New Hope* reconstructed fifteen seconds of the film at a time through various methods (e.g. animation with action figures from different fictional worlds and live performance). The film won a 2010 Emmy for Outstanding Creative Achievement in Interactive Media. While not all of its parts have origins in live performance, it makes an interesting entry here. Beyond representing the re-enactment of an entire film, it demonstrates how such a feat can gain a place in movie history and critical acclaim, thereby passing from ephemera to durable good.

3. The link for this blog no longer exists.

4. According to Stephen Prince (2000), Spielberg's *Raiders of the Lost Ark* sold at less than $40.00, a low price in the video market at the time. It was the first video to sell, initially, half a million copies. It had sold more than a million by 1987 – an impressive figure for its relatively short life on the shelves by then.

Bibliography

'The 2008 Hollywood Portfolio: Hitchcock Classics'. (2008) *Vanity Fair*, March, <http://www.vanityfair.com/culture/features/2008/03/hitchcock_stills200803> accessed 6 June 2009.

Allwood, Mark. (2006) 'Film Fans Embrace Movieoke', <http://iscms.irn.columbia.edu/cns/2006-04-04/allwood-moviekaraoke> accessed 15 January 2008.

'Anastasia's Movieoke'. (2010) <http://www.movieoke.net/faq.htm> accessed 15 January 2008.

'Articles and Reviews'. (2003–9) <http://www.theraider.net/films/raiders_adaptation/articles.php> accessed 22 June 2009.

Auslander, Philip. (2008 [1999]) *Liveness: Performance in a Mediatized Culture* (New York: Routledge).

Bauman, Richard. (2004) *A World of Others' Words: Cross-Cultural Perspectives on Intertextuality* (Oxford: Blackwell Publishing).

'Blobfest'. (2007–10) <http://www.thecolonialtheatre.com/about-the-colonial/blobfest/> accessed 6 June 2009.

Browne, David. (2009) 'Harry Potter Is Their Peter Pan', *New York Times*, 23 July, <http://www.nytimes.com/2009/07/23/fashion/23nostalgia.html> accessed 1 January 2010.

Burgess, Jean and Joshua Green. (2009) *YouTube: Online Video and Participatory Culture* (Cambridge: Polity Press).

Burgin, Victor. (2004) *The Remembered Film* (London: Reaktion Books).

'Casablanca: AmuseMeProductions'. (2007) <http://www.youtube.com/watch?v=
    UVakjzEyeC8&feature=geosearch> accessed 12 March 2008.

'Dorothy Podber'. (2008) Obituary, *The Telegraph*, 22 February, <http://www.telegraph.co.uk/
    news/obituaries/1579445/Dorothy-Podber.html> accessed 20 October 2008.

Dyer, Richard. (2007) *Pastiche* (London: Routledge).

Higgins, Hannah. (2002) *Fluxus Experience* (Berkeley: University of California Press).

Hildebrand, Lucas. (2009) *Inherent Vice: Bootleg Histories of Videotape and Copyright*
    (Durham, NC: Duke University Press).

Isherwood, Charles. (2009) ' "First Blood" Obsession: No Man, No Law, No War Can Stop It',
    New York Times, 23 March, <http://theater2.nytimes.com/2009/03/23/theater/
    reviews/23rambo.html> accessed 23 March 2009.

Jenkins, Henry. (2006) *Convergence Culture: Where Old and New Media Collide* (New York:
    New York University Press).

Jones, Sara Gwenllian. (2002) 'Phantom Menace: Killer Fans, Consumer Activism and Digital
    Filmmakers', in Xavier Mendik and Steven Jay Schneider (eds), *Underground USA:
    Filmmaking Beyond the Hollywood Canon* (London: Wallflower Press), pp. 169–79.

Kennedy, Randy. (2004) 'Amateur Celebrities Pick a Movie and Join In', *New York Times*,
    10 March, <http://www.nytimes.com/2004/03/10/movies> accessed 15 January 2008.

Kennedy, Randy. (2008) 'Dorothy Podber, 75, Artist and Trickster, Is Dead', *New York Times*,
    19 February, <http://www.nytimes.com/2008/02/19/arts/19podber.html> accessed
    20 October 2008.

Klinger, Barbara. (2006) *Beyond the Multiplex: Cinema, New Technologies, and the Home*
    (Berkeley: University of California Press).

Klinger, Barbara. (2008) 'Say It Again, Sam: Movie Quotation, Performance, and Masculinity',
    Participations: Journal of Audience and Reception Studies, 5 (2), <http://www.
    participations.org/Volume%205/Issue%202/5_02_klinger.htm> accessed 18 July 2011.

Lee, Jennifer. (2008) 'City Room: Ephemeral Video Moves to the Arts', *New York Times*,
    5 November, sec. 1, p. 27.

Lutticken, Sven (ed.). (2005) *Life, Once More: Forms of Reenactment in Contemporary Art*
    (Rotterdam: Center for Contemporary Art).

Martin, Randy. (1990) *Performance as Political Act: The Embodied Self* (New York: Bergin &
    Garvey Publishers).

'Movieoke Questions'. (2004) *Palimpsest*, 4 March, <http://palimpsest.stanford.edu> accessed
    15 January 2008.

Pierson, Michele. (2009) 'Avant-Garde Re-Enactment: *World Mirror Cinema*, *Decasia*, and *The
    Heart of the World*', *Cinema Journal*, 49 (1), pp. 1–19.

Prince, Stephen. (2000) *A New Pot of Gold: Hollywood under the Electronic Rainbow,
    1980–1989* (Berkeley: University of California Press).

'Rambo Solo'. (2009) <http://www.theateronline.com/pb.xzc?PK=20306)--stage> accessed
    12 December 2009.

'Reenactment #14: *The Big Lebowski*'. (2006) <http://www.youtube.com/watch?v=ml-
    PxIRWhRo> accessed 16 July 2008.

Reuters. (2004) 'Karaoke's Offspring, Movieoke, Hits NYC', 12 February, <http://www.msnbc.
    msn.com/id/4252908> accessed 15 January 2008.

'Second Annual Lebowski Fest'. (2003) <http://www.lebowskifest.com/PastFests/Louisville/
    2ndAnnualLebowskiFest/tabid/105/Default.aspx> accessed 2 October 2007.

Simonson, Robert. (2005) 'Geeks, Get Out Your Light Sabers! Imposter Alert', *New York Times*,
    31 July, <http://www.nytimes.com/2005/07/31/theater/newsandfeatures/31simo.html>
    accessed 5 February 2008.

Stelter, Brian and Miguel Helft. (2009) 'Deal Brings TV Shows and Movies to YouTube', *New
    York Times*, 17 April, sec. B, pp. 1 and 2.

Windolf, Jim. (2004) 'Raiders of the Lost Backyard', *Vanity Fair*, March, pp. 254–72.

12 Digital Intimacies: Aesthetic and Affective Strategies in the Production and Use of Online Video

Rosamund Davies

In 2007, I made an online hypermedia narrative, *Index of Love* (Davies, 2007), which used video to signify fragments of experience that are both lost, in that they have been lived through in time, and yet found, in that they continue to be endlessly replayed in the space of the archive. *Index of Love* investigates the aesthetic of the database as a structuring form of narrative and memory by presenting the reader/user with an archive of past experience in the form of different menus that catalogue a database of video clips.

These can be accessed by clicking on a word or phrase in the index. The story then becomes the narrative journey taken through the archive, as the reader/user picks over the remains of a love affair in the form of video clips of domestic spaces and scenes, which have the feel of moments from home videos. Fleeting glimpses of domestic interiors and exteriors and everyday objects combine with text and audio clips to suggest connections and possible stories.

However, the narrative fragments within the archive refuse finally to resolve themselves into a unified whole, into a coherent love story with a definite ending, be it happy or sad. The contents of the archive thus assert the material immediacy of their individual presence, but remain resistant to its attempt to systematise them in any definitive form. If there is a sense of meaning and narrative satisfaction to be found within the work, it comes not from a linear closure of narrative but from a spatial closure: a sense of having explored and exhausted the possible connections,

Index of Love (Davies, 2007), <www.indexoflove.net>

having travelled all pathways. *Index of Love* thus enacts something similar to the Freudian concepts of both 'deferred action', where the present continually recomposes the past, and the 'psychical working out', where, through the process of repetition, memories lose their investment of affect and trauma dissipates. The original question of 'what happened?' remains, however, unanswered, and indeed unanswerable.

I was trying in this work to use the particular time/space properties of video and the internet to enact an affective experience of time that was both ephemeral and eternal. I was also attempting to achieve something that I found was often lacking from web-based media, namely a sense of emotional intensity and intimacy. As a result of this work, I became interested in the extent to which my own creative use of, and engagement with, online video was related to affective and aesthetic strategies in online video more generally.

There is a discernible tendency within online video towards an expression of experience as ephemeral. This experience is mediated through values of immediacy and everydayness, through a low-fi aesthetic and through the propensity of online video to consist of clips of very short duration. I will argue in this chapter that the expressive tendency of online video can be seen as an emergence of a particular form of realism which seems to assert the subjectivity of the ordinary person, caught up in the messy materiality of the moment, as more 'real' than the professional mediation of experience. I would also contend, however, that the ephemeral, contiguous nature of this reality, lived through in linear time, is simultaneously offset by its performance within the eternal, time-looped space of the internet.

Internet research takes the researcher into a bewildering, vast realm of enquiry, posing the problem of where to start and how to narrow down the field (Markham and Baym, 2009). Having begun from what might be termed an auto-ethnographic starting point, my own approach was to go to the opposite end of the spectrum of research data in search of industry statistics. According to the trade magazine *eMarketer* (2009a), 82 per cent of internet users worldwide watched online video in 2008. Of this content, 71 per cent was 'ugc/video posted by people like me'. As reported in the same magazine (2009b), email was the preferred sharing route for video clips in the late 2000s (50 per cent), followed by social networks (23 per cent). In each case, people paid the most attention to video clips shared by a friend. It is not clear from these statistics how much of the 'video posted by people like me' is actually 'video originated by people like me' and how much of it is professional media that is not originated but only 'redistributed by people like me'. However, in order to focus on the particular properties of video online, I chose to concentrate on so-called user-generated content (UGC), for which the internet is the chief distribution mechanism, rather than on professional media intended originally for other distribution platforms.

Much of this UGC consists of home video clips. As with the content broadcast on TV shows such as *You've Been Framed* (1990–present), which originally set out to exploit the explosion in the consumer video camera market at the end of the 1980s, these clips tend to focus on various combinations of the everyday and the bizarre. Events captured by ordinary people in their ordinary lives provoke an immediate emotional reaction; they register as cute, funny, horrific or amazing. Familiar settings become the stage for unusual happenings and the event is captured on camera with the idea that it is unique, and might never happen again. Many clips focus on the cute or otherwise bizarre exploits of animals and children. Animals in particular are rife on the internet, starring in hundreds of thousands of pet clips on video platforms like YouTube as well as online video sites dedicated to pet videos exclusively.

One particularly popular and controversial[1] example is a video clip of a pet slow loris (a small, nocturnal primate) being tickled. In this short clip, the loris is tickled under its arms by human hands, the owner of which remains outside the camera frame. The tickler engages in conversation behind the camera with the camera operator about the animal, which appears to be enjoying the experience, putting up its arms as soon as the tickling stops, as if to instigate more tickling. The expression on the animal's face is ambiguous, however; its apparent smile remains so fixed that it also appears comically deadpan and is ultimately hard to read.

The animal appears to be the pet of the people who have videoed and posted the clip, and the joy and fascination that they express in witnessing and displaying the inextricable cuteness and strangeness of their pet is similar to the attitude expressed by many posters and viewers of online pet-centred clips. Here, anthropomorphic weirdness is a familiar trope, from piano-playing cats to snowboarding ostriches, and it is epitomised in the title, *Weird Animal Getting Tickled*, which was given to the clip on the site where I first viewed it, *Today's Big Thing*.

As the name of the site makes clear, however, *Weird Animal Getting Tickled* is only today's big thing. Tomorrow it will disappear from view, replaced in the 'cute animals' section by a cat fighting a losing battle with a laser printer. I started with a reading of this particular clip, in comparison with my own video work, in order to see where it would lead me in terms of thinking about online video. There are certain similarities that can be identified immediately. Both works represent a domestic, everyday

Weird Animal Getting Tickled (2009), <www.todaysbigthing.com/2009/04/20>

space and feature low production values (e.g. low picture quality, everyday lighting, unedited footage). *Index of Love* features short video clips of a couple of minutes' duration like the loris video. At the same time, the ephemeral moment of these clips can also be repeated ad infinitum. The video on *Index of Love* runs on a continuous loop and *Today's Big Thing* allows you to replay *Weird Animal Being Tickled* as many times as you want from its archive.

However, the loris video clip also differs from my own work in several respects. Notably, it presents itself as funny and cute, and as an attraction, in a way that mine does not. It also exploits the audience's prurience, as the animal appears to be aroused by its tickling treatment. In a similar way to the proto-films of early cinema, this clip appeals to the audience's voyeurism and taste for novelty and spectacle. Like the home videos on *You've Been Framed*, it succeeds in offering a potent mix of the ordinary and the remarkable, the everyday and the one-off. Furthermore, and also like early cinema and home video clips, the loris video clip very clearly stages presence. It offers an event in progress – a unique episode that can never be repeated, but which has been captured and made repeatable by the camera.

Short duration is a recurring feature of UGC online video, from the daily video log entry to the lip-sync video, and is partly a product of the internet as distribution medium. Technical limitations, combined with fluid viewer attention spans, make long-play video forms less successful than short clips, privileging the moment over the narrative. This focus on the momentary event, which is a recurring feature of online video, offers a very particular construction of time. The momentary event is neither an image, which as Sean Cubitt (2002) notes stands outside time, nor a narrative with a beginning, middle and end. Instead, the video event projects the viewer into an immediate, perpetual 'nowness'. Whether the content of the event is remarkable or mundane, it is the immediacy of the moment, the fullness of presence, of witnessing something as it happens, apparently unmediated, that provides much of the satisfaction of the viewing experience. The loris video clip can thus be seen as continuing the aesthetic of immediacy, which, from Italian Renaissance painting onwards, has sought to erase the presence of the medium itself and to place the viewer directly 'in the same space as the objects viewed' (Bolter and Grusin, 1999, p. 11).[2]

In contrast, the video clips in *Index of Love* stage absence rather than presence. Rather than an animate being upon which to project emotions or desires, they present a montage of empty rooms: an unoccupied unmade bed, an empty hallway, an open window looking out onto an unpopulated landscape. Instead of the event itself, they present the empty stage after the event has happened. They offer not presence itself but a memory of presence, an entry into places that are haunted by a present, which has now become a past. However, if these clips refuse the spectacle of presence, they belong nevertheless to the same particular time/space as the loris video:

as if, after the tickling event was over, the camera had been left running. The loris video offers the fullness of the present moment in an eternal loop, while *Index of Love* employs the same aesthetic strategies to endlessly replay its loss.

My viewing of *Weird Animal Being Tickled*, however, involves more than the immediacy of being connected to an unfolding, apparently unmediated event, and to the people who are filming, via their first-person viewpoint of the shared experience. When I first view it, it also connects me to the person who sent it, allowing me to share an experience with him in his absence. In viewing what he has viewed and shared with me, I am able to share the same emotions that he felt when he viewed it. If I laugh, I think of him laughing. As I respond to the cuteness and bizarreness of what I am watching, I think of his response. Later I might then email him back and talk about the video. But, even if I don't, the video has still served as a mode of communication between us. Here, online video becomes part of a 'conversational universe' (larrythewineguy, 2009) consisting also of the face-to-face communication, telephone calls, emails and letters that are exchanged between people. It is above all phatic communication (Miller, 2008). What matters in this communication is the exchange and the emotional connection it achieves. Video is used here as a conversational mode, as much as a representational medium. The clip is presented on the *Today's Big Thing* site not only as an experience in itself, but as an impetus for further activity. The buttons below it encourage the viewer to 'share this video', by emailing it, as my friend did, or by posting the link, as others have done.

On online video sites such as YouTube or Vimeo (<http://www.vimeo.com>), video viewers also post comments, create tags within the video or upload their own video responses. On the video blogging site Seesmic (<http://seesmic.com/>), video becomes the sole mode of posting, creating multiple ongoing video dialogues between the bloggers around different conversation strands. Video online thus becomes a flexible form of communication that can be used alone or combined with other media as part of a dialogue. It is perhaps not surprising that, in their survey of YouTube content at the end of the 2000s, Burgess and Green (2009, p. 45) found video blogging to be the most discussed and responded to form of online video; video blogs made up the majority of all user-generated video clips rated 'most viewed' on YouTube and 70 per cent of all video clips, whether professional or amateur, that were rated 'most discussed' and 'most responded to'. Vlogging is video in its most obviously conversational form, initiating and inviting dialogue. That it is also the most viewed type of user-generated video on YouTube would seem to demonstrate both the importance of immediacy and intimacy as part of the online video viewing experience, and the appeal of its conversational potential. The affective power of the video blog lies in its capacity to elide the distinctions between experience, representation and conversation.

As a time-based medium, video is a situated practice which links time with space; it can enunciate a unity of here and now that text and images cannot. As a communication medium, it can therefore share certain characteristics with spoken language, which are most evident in the video blog, but which are present also in the other types of video. At the same time, however, the hypermediacy of the web means not only that video can be used to quite different ends in remixes and montages, but that the here and now of online video realism can be easily recontextualised as video clips circulate within the 'conversational universe'. Thus when I view the loris video clip again, this time posted by *Wired* on YouTube as *Tickling Slow Loris* (2009), I enter a very different conversation, one in which the circumstances and the ethics of the clip are hotly debated in comments on the site. Some rhapsodise over the animal's obvious delight at being tickled, others claim that the animal's behaviour is defensive and that it is in distress. Once I am part of this conversation, the clip's significance for me changes, as I try to decipher whether the cute moment I am viewing could also be an act of torture and realise that, if an answer can be found, it does not lie within the clip itself. The latter's performance of presence does not articulate any definitive meaning, a point I will return to below.[3]

In any consideration of online video as a communication medium and conversational mode, the distinction between amateur and professional becomes less relevant. I would draw the analogy here between the expansion of video and that of writing as a technology. Just as writing developed from being a trade practised by craftsmen to an everyday human practice, so has video moved from being a particular medium of representation, with associated professional skills and values, to an increasingly everyday medium of communication, which has no need to employ or adhere to such skills and values. This expansion of the role of video occurred in the 1980s with the advent of home video, an expansion that built on existing practices of home-movie-making on celluloid. Both the subject matter and aesthetics of home video were different to that of professional video production, but this does not mean that they did not refer to, overlap with or indeed aspire to its characteristics. TV series such as *You've Been Framed*, while establishing and promoting home video's unique aesthetic, also simultaneously highlighted those aspects it had in common with professional television production. The categories of the cute, the horrific and the comedic belong as much to professional drama and factual programming as they do to amateur video in this regard. The *longueurs* of the home video, which is usually unedited footage, were also avoided. Even if the material was not extensively re-edited, this could be achieved simply by isolating the relevant portion of the footage, showing only the 'newsworthy' moment. The creation of such clips was simple for the television company, but not so straightforward for the amateur creator.

At the same time, how-to books on video production in the 1980s, aimed at the amateur, constantly reinforced professional visual conventions of framing, editing and narrative construction, and video cameras were made to incorporate fades, dissolves and titles as a way of bringing a level of professionalism to amateur production. Much use of home video remained, however, outside of such contexts. Records of significant and insignificant occasions could be enjoyed without any particular concern for professional standards. Video also already functioned as a nexus and impetus for conversation, both in its most narrow sense as talk and in its wider sense of interaction with others. People could gather round to watch a video played back on the television, promoting remembrance, discussion, projection into the future. But it is of course with the advent of digital technologies (basic video editing software on every computer, the internet and mobile communication) that video obtains, along with a much wider reach, a qualitatively different level of immediacy, casualness and flexibility as a communication medium.

The affective experience that can be generated through online video, and its circulation as media, is not only one of immediacy, or indeed hypermediacy, but also one of *intimacy*. A pet video or a vlog provides not only the pleasure of an apparently unmediated experience but also, both through what it represents and how it connects me to other people, offers me a privileged access to private experience.

The relationship between intimacy and realism has a long history, equal to that between immediacy and realism. Early novels were often written in the first person, claiming to be diaries or letters by real people. The truth value of the personal document lent an aura of authenticity to these early experiments in a new media form. In the same way, the ubiquity and popularity of variations of the online video diary could be seen as fulfilling a similar function for both producers and audiences of online video content. As part of her research into video blogging, Patricia Lange recounts how her analysis of vlogs and interviews with vloggers reveals the extent to which intimacy is valued by both vloggers and their viewers, as a means of bringing the private into the public sphere and using it to question and refashion 'social boundaries and pre-existing assumptions' (Lange, 2007, p. 1).

The connection between the revelation of private experience and the project of realism is defined by Fredric Jameson in *Signatures of the Visible* as:

> the deconcealment – within the public sphere – of certain kinds of hitherto occluded group reality and experience … the moment in which a 'restricted' code manages to become elaborated or universal … when its private class experience is for a time that of the world itself. (Jameson, 1992, p. 166)

The opposition of the words 'private' and 'public' has several connotations here. The history of realism and the novel is partly the story of the intimate details of private everyday life becoming public entertainment as art. The shocking innovation of such intimate revelations lies not only in the emotional, psychological or sexual insights they might offer but also in their very mundanity. Prior to the publication of Flaubert's *Madame Bovary*, the editors required sixty-nine passages to be cut (Harrison, 1995, p. 50). It appears that not all of these passages concerned morally questionable material. Many of the editors' objections were in fact to the inclusion of 'pointless' ('inutile') mundane details, such as the particular preparation involved in a piece of meat that was eaten by one of the characters. This accumulation of such apparently redundant details, hitherto not considered worthy of representation, is a recurring trope of realism. It is partly through the ordinariness of such details that the audience encounters a representation of the 'ordinary person' and the reality of their experience that feels new and authentic in a way that has never been represented before. Realism needs constantly to create new vistas if its reality effects are to remain fresh. The video blog and other types of online video provide such new vistas, new windows into the casual intimacies and mundanities of everyday life.

However, Jameson's account of realism is concerned not so much with reality effects as with the way that a particular subjectivity can come to seem a universal one. He argues that 'the conquest of a kind of cultural, ideological and narrative literacy by a new class or group' (Jameson, 1992, p. 155) is expressed in different textual forms, the novel realising the experience of the middle classes, and cinema (such as neo-realism) realising that of the working classes. Following Jameson's definition, I would argue that online video can be seen as another new variant of realism, where the 'restricted' code that is becoming universal is linked, not to a particular class consciousness, but rather to the experience of the 'ordinary person' as defined against the 'professional'. Along with the thrill that comes from seeing hitherto unrepresented experience, apparently being communicated by those who are actually undergoing the experience, comes the assertion of a new hierarchy, which accords a truth value to the non-professional that is superior to that of the professional. If culture is undergoing a 'participatory turn' (Burgess and Green, 2009, p. 13), then the aesthetics of user-generated video are central to the reprogramming of subjectivity that this involves.

That this subjectivity is becoming a universal code is apparent in the way that professional video productions online tend to be coded as 'amateur', both in their aesthetic and in their mode of distribution. One established example of this is the various professional versions of the 'video diary' such as *Online Caroline* (2001) and *lonelygirl15* (2006–8). These professional productions help create both immediacy and intimacy through direct first-person address of the viewer, drawing them into the video blogger's personal space. In the case of *Online Caroline*, this was carefully customised for each user. Personal details entered by the viewer as part of the initial registration would be used to create an individualised greeting each time the viewer logged on subsequently to the site. My own work, *Index of Love*, uses a different interface but similarly blurs the distinction between professional and amateur, public and personal in the way that it positions itself in the space of the web.

Another established genre of professional 'amateur' production is the viral video. A campaign by Barclaycard on YouTube in the late 2000s called the *Waterslide Challenge* typifies the genre. The original Barclaycard *Waterslide* ad, first broadcast in 2008, was a standard television commercial. A professionally made spot distinguished by high production values, an elaborate *mise en scène* and complex camerawork, it featured a comic fantasy scenario in which an office worker made his way home from the office via the novel and exhilarating transport mode of waterslide. En route, the man is able to seamlessly make purchases with his Barclaycard at the supermarket and other locations without needing to interrupt or delay his onward trajectory.

However, Barclaycard further developed the campaign by creating the *Waterslide Challenge* in 2009, in which the original advertisement was posted on YouTube together with a 'response video' (a video response to a video post) which reimagined *Waterslide*'s fantasy universe as a real-life vérité scene. While posted by Barclaycard, both the form and content of the response video took the form of a non-professional video. It featured an attempt by two young men to create a functioning waterslide in order to send an action man carrying a loyalty card from the window of their apartment to the local grocery shop. As with the video clips discussed previously, the video captures the unfolding/recording of an unrepeatable event. Shot with a handheld camera, it emphasises both the 'real-time' and point-of-view aspects of the video coverage. But in fact, the overall immediacy and urgency that is conveyed by the video is produced above all through skilful 'professional' editing which juxtaposes two simultaneous points of view on the event, an aspect that is usually absent from much actual user-generated online video.

The *Waterslide* response video was posted to YouTube with an invitation to viewers to go one better and video their own waterslides. Viewers subsequently posted their clips on YouTube as part of an ongoing video conversation and were asked to vote on their favourites. The video with the most votes won the campaign. Although Barclaycard's involvement was signalled in the YouTube campaign, the *Waterslide Challenge* deliberately blurred the lines between Barclaycard's own advertising and the response of YouTube viewers. The initial response video was also circulated widely outside this specific conversation. The link was forwarded to me, for example, by someone who had no idea of its connection with Barclaycard, or indeed that it was anything but an amateur home video. The viral video clearly illustrates not only the extent to which the aesthetic of the non-professional has penetrated the professional but also the way that professional institutions are ready and able to exploit video's new conversational potential without fully being able to control it. Certainly, the intense professional interest generated by UGC and social networks is as much motivated by anxiety about the fugitive nature of the viewing and consuming public as it is by enthusiasm for new markets and financial opportunities (Cova and Dalli, 2009).

The valorisation of the 'ordinary person' as documenter, as well as subject, of experience can be interpreted in various ways. In one sense, the advent of the audience as producer, or the prosumer, is the obvious continuation of the trajectory of the aesthetic of unmediated experience as defined by Bolter and Grusin (1999). If the media professional appears to have been eliminated, then the sense of immediacy between audience and event is increased. Furthermore, the first-person address that emerges with the ordinary person as author as well as the subject of representation increases the sense of intimacy as well as immediacy.

The (apparent or actual) elimination of professional mediation from the recording of experience also defines experience as something that cannot be made sense of, that resists narrativisation. It puts emphasis on the event itself and its materiality as constituting the 'real', rather than on what it means.[4] In this respect, it takes ever further the drive of realism towards the reconfiguration of everyday experience as art. I can video what I see in the street, what I am doing right now and communicate it instantly to a friend or to a wider public. Every second of my life becomes a potential media event and subsequent media artifact. However, since online video is not only turning everyday life into media but also operating in the reverse direction by turning the medium of video into a form of conversation, it seems that online video brings not only increased immediacy and intimacy but also increased disposability of the media artifact. Digital photos and videos online become as prolific and as ephemeral as digital text, part of a conversational universe that is constantly renewing itself.

And yet, the digital clips, snapshots, emails and chats remain. They do not evaporate into thin air once we have finished with them. These fleeting phenomena of text, image, sound, movement are stockpiled in the, as yet, unlimited storage capacity of the communications companies over whose channels we distribute them, constituting a vast archive, the cultural, political and legal implications of which we have yet to get to grips with. The ephemerality of online video is thus a question of subjectivity and aesthetics rather than actual physical longevity. Digital ephemera, even more than previous ephemeral documents, seem likely in fact to endure in the archive.

It is worth elaborating, finally, on the way that the particular construction of time and space produced through the online videos discussed above comes not only from the content and mode of production of the video clips themselves but also from their situation in the space of the web. Digital video lacks both the materiality and accompanying fragility of analogue video, of which the capacity to degrade functions as a key signifier of both presence and loss. The online video clip's ability to engender a sense of presence as well as of the ephemeral is enabled differently. It is produced, in fact, partly through its situation within the timelessness of the web architecture that frames it, which in commercial websites can be rather impersonal and off-putting. The video clip punctures a hole in the spatial timelessness of the web to create a window into time. This is why businesses uniformly report on the higher level of user engagement they get through use of video on their websites.

At the same time, the sense of loss that comes with the replaying of the ephemeral, unrepeatable event is attenuated by its very spatialisation in the web where it can be databased and replayed, and by its participation in a wider conversational universe in which it may continue to be circulated and recontextualised. Even when *Today's Big Thing* becomes yesterday's news, I can still access it from the archive if I have the link url. It is not lost, as long as I know where to find it. The affective and aesthetic strategies of online video thus operate an exchange between the loss of the ephemeral in time and its recuperation in the space of memory as archive. The ephemeral moment is, in this sense, also eternal.

The particular configuration of space/time constructed through online media is a fragmented, discontinuous time, but one where all the fragments are so abundant as to be inexhaustible and where the fragments connect us into a network. The fact that everything becomes media-worthy, dissolving and reconfiguring established distinctions between private and public, contributes simultaneously to the sense of confusion and to the sense of abundance in what would appear to be a never-ending feedback loop.

I do think, then, that what we are seeing with online video, to quote Jameson again, is the construction of 'whole new subject-positions in a new kind of space; ... the production of new categories of the event and of experience, of temporality and of causality' (Jameson, 1992, p. 165). If now, more than ever, we have a sense that every facet of life is transitory, contingent, casualised and relative, that only the individual moment is real, then the video clip perfectly captures this subjectivity.

The ephemeral has a long history of representation. In art and literature, the fleeting phenomena of life have often been articulated against life's eternal cycles or eternal life itself. The ephemeral in representation, while serving as a reminder of mortality, thus has also often seemed to effect its transcendence. It has tended to have a certain magic, ineffable quality, signifying the free, the untamed, the unpossessable. The contemporary ephemeral, however, as discussed in this chapter, occupies the role of the real, rather than the magical. The ephemeral is no longer a particular facet of existence. It is existence. Video performs this ephemerality most poignantly, because, unlike a photograph, it fails to become an object that can disconnect from time and obtain a permanent existence in space. In a sense, not only the videos in my web work *Index of Love*, but all online video clips, constantly replay absence even as they assert presence.

The temporality of online video is thus the experience of intense but ephemeral events, in endless succession. It is an experience of 'now' that does not offer the narrative closure of a 'why' or a 'how'. Rather, the fragmented nature of this experience in time is recuperated through the timelessness of online space and the ceaseless exchange of our conversational universe. The fragments are not lost, but stored within an archive, an archive of experience that we share with others and that we can access at will. And even if we never return to these fragments, still we know that they are there.

Notes

1. Originally posted on Vimeo (Sergeyev, 2009), the clip was extensively reblogged and, by May 2011, had obtained over ten million views on YouTube. However, not all the attention was positive. Concerns were raised by the environmental science and conservation news site mongabay.com (Hance, 2009, 2011) that such video clips might encourage the illegal international trade in and cruel treatment of slow lorises (including practices such as pulling out their teeth without anaesthetic). *The Telegraph* and *The Independent* also ran similar stories in March 2011 (Sherwin, 2011), when International Animal Rescue, supported by primate conservation expert Dr Nekaris from Oxford Brookes University, launched a petition for the removal of such clips from YouTube.

2. Bolter and Grusin also suggest that the demand for immediacy in representation is countered by a parallel desire for hypermediacy. While the mediatisation of contemporary culture provokes a desire for immediacy, at the same time the awareness that 'the world comes to us through media' leads equally to an enjoyment of the experience of the medium itself as an experience of the real (Bolter and Grusin, 1999, p. 70).
   Such hypermediacy is exemplified by the way that the *Weird Animal* video clip is framed within the *Today's Big Thing* website and can be commented on, shared, linked to and embedded on other sites.

3. Henry Jenkins (2009) points out how the circulation and recontextualisation of video online can produce effects both productive and damaging. He cites the particular example of videos of human rights abuse, where, on the one hand, videos produced by abusers might (like the Abu Ghraib photos) serve to incriminate their creators, but, in another kind of recontextualisation, video meant to highlight the horrors of abuse might become a source of entertainment. The loris video, meanwhile, provides an example of how a video clip intended as a source of entertainment highlights for some the horrors of abuse.

4. The assertion of presence that I propose as a noticeable feature of online video can be interpreted nonetheless as indicative of a contemporary dematerialisation of culture. According to Hayles (1999), a logic of information rather than materiality mediates contemporary experience, constructing a reality in which both money and digital video, for example, exist as informational patterns, rather than as physical material. It is precisely the displacement of the presence/absence dialectic as a grounds for discourse, according to Hayles, which has seen it 'forced into visibility' (ibid., p. 44) as a subject of discourse.

Bibliography

Barclaycard Waterslide Challenge. (2009) <www.youtube.com/watch?v=-MZSun44KE8&
feature=related> accessed 10 June 2009.

Bolter, Jay David and Richard Grusin. (1999) *Remediation: Understanding New Media*
(Cambridge, MA: MIT Press).

Burgess, Jean and Joshua Green. (2009) *YouTube: Online Video and Participatory Culture*
(Cambridge: Polity Press).

Cova, Bernard and Daniele Dalli. (2009) 'Working Consumers: The Next Step in Marketing
Theory?', *Marketing Theory*, 9 (3), pp. 315–39.

Cubitt, Sean. (2002) 'Visual and Audiovisual: From Image to Moving Image', *Journal of Visual
Culture*, 1 (3), pp. 359–68.

Davies, Rosamund. (2007) *Index of Love*, <www.indexoflove.net>.

eMarketer. (2009a) 'Digital Entertainment Meets Social Media', 12 June,
<www.emarketer.com> accessed 12 June 2009.

eMarketer. (2009b) 'How People Share Online Video', 16 June, <www.emarketer.com>
accessed 16 June 2009.

Hance, J. (2009) 'YouTube Videos May Be Imperilling Cuddly Primate', 24 February 2009,
<http://news.mongabay.com/2009/0224-hance_slowloris.html> accessed 9 May 2011.

Hance, J. (2011) ' "Cute Umbrella" Video of Slow Loris Threatens Primate', 13 March 2011,
<http://news.mongabay.com/2011/0313-hance_umbrella_loris.html> accessed 9 May 2011.

Hayles, N. Katherine. (1999) *How We Became Posthuman: Virtual Bodies in Cybernetics,
Literature and Informatics* (Chicago: University of Chicago Press).

Harrison, Nicholas. (1995) *Circles of Censorship* (Oxford: Clarendon Press).

International Animal Rescue. (2011) 'IAR Launches Petition to Stop YouTube Showing "Cute"
Clips of Captive Slow Lorises', <http://www.internationalanimalrescue.org/news/2011/421/
IAR+launches+petition+to+stop+YouTube+showing+%5C%27cute%5C%27+clips+of+
captive+slow+lorises.html> accessed 9 May 2011.

Jameson, Fredric. (1992) *Signatures of the Visible* (London: Routledge).

Jenkins, Henry. (2009) 'What Happened before YouTube', in Burgess and Green (eds),
YouTube, pp. 109–25.

Lange, Patricia. (2007) 'The Vulnerable Video Blogger: Promoting Social Change through
Intimacy', *The Scholar & Feminist Online*, 5 (2), <www.barnard.edu/
sfonline/blogs/lange_01.htm> accessed 2 January 2009.

'larrythewineguy'. (2009) 'Why I Hate Social Media', *Advertising Age* (posted reply), 17 June,
<www.adage.com> accessed 17 June 2009.

lonelygirl15. (2006) <www.youtube.com/watch?v=-goXKtd6cPo> accessed 1 January 2009.

Markham, Annette and Nancy Baym. (2009) *Internet Inquiry* (London: Sage).

Miller, Vincent. (2008) 'New Media, Networking and Phatic Culture', *Convergence*, 14 (4),
pp. 387–400.

Online Caroline. (2001) <www.onlinecaroline.com/> accessed 30 January 2009.

Sergeyev, Dmitry. (2009) 'And Now … at Last – Sonya!!!! (Slow Loris)',
<http://www.vimeo.com/3057473> accessed 6 May 2011.

Sherwin, A. (2011) 'YouTube Sensation Fuelling Trade in an Endangered Species', *The Independent*, 22 March 2011, <http://www.independent.co.uk/environment/ nature/youtube-sensation-fuelling-trade-in-an-endangered-species-2248930.html> accessed 9 May 2011.

'Slow Loris YouTube Videos Fuel Endangered Species Trade', *The Telegraph*, 22 March 2011, <http://www.telegraph.co.uk/earth/wildlife/8397234/Slow-loris-YouTube-videos-fuel- endangered-species-trade.html> accessed 9 May 2011.

Tickling Slow Loris. (2009) <www.youtube.com//watch?v=g9f-6jygRJk> accessed 9 May 2011.

Weird Animal Getting Tickled. (2009) <www.todaysbigthing.com/2009/04/20> accessed 20 April 2009.

Index

Page numbers in **bold** indicate detailed analysis; *n* denotes endnote